THE DISAPPEARANCE OF EVE AND THE GENDER OF CHRIST

Praise for *The Disappearance of Eve and the Gender of Christ*

Carnahan's book fills a significant void in scholarship on theology and trans* identity. He engages a breadth of sources, including scriptural and patristic sources and gender theory, to join theologians past and present in searching for the universal accessibility of transformation through Christ. Carnahan addresses the soteriological problem by recognizing that sex and gender, while not the highest good, are intertwined with our identities and are part of the callings to which we respond. Ultimately, he makes the bold, inclusive claim that Christ incarnates gendered/sexed diversity, opening salvation to all who accept Christ. Carnahan's naming of Christ as trans* beautifully embraces the deep, abiding mystery of Christ bringing salvation to all of humanity. His book challenges theologians to pursue "the creative opportunities" of dialogue rooted in tradition.

—Elizabeth Sweeny Block, associate professor of Christian ethics, Saint Louis University

Carnahan offers a bold, brave, original, and provocative argument that Christ must be trans to save all genders. More widely, this is one of the best discussions I have seen of sex and gender as calling and responsibility—embodied, social, dynamic, yet not entirely open-ended. Agree or disagree, the reader will learn much from this engaging testament.

—Lisa Sowle Cahill, J. Donald Monan, SJ, Professor of Theology, Boston College

The Disappearance of Eve and the Gender of Christ delightfully exceeds categorization, drawing on and weaving together a wide range of biblical, historical, theological, and theoretical scholarship to offer a fresh contribution to the classic question: Who must Christ be to achieve what Christ did? Through this dialogical and constructive theology, Carnahan proposes, and makes a compelling argument for, a trans Christology as well as a liberative ethic rooted in responsibility and calling. This book is a welcome addition to the ongoing conversations in—and a helpful and important contribution to—feminist, queer, and trans theologies.

—Brandy Daniels, assistant professor of theology and codirector of gender, women, and sexuality studies, University of Portland

THE DISAPPEARANCE OF EVE AND THE GENDER OF CHRIST

WHY TRADITIONAL SOTERIOLOGY REQUIRES A TRANS* SAVIOR

KEVIN CARNAHAN

FORTRESS PRESS
Minneapolis

THE DISAPPEARANCE OF EVE AND THE GENDER OF CHRIST
Why Traditional Soteriology Requires a Trans* Savior

30 29 28 27 26 3 4 5 6 7 8 9 10

Library of Congress Cataloging-in-Publication Data

Names: Carnahan, Kevin, author.
Title: The disappearance of eve and the gender of Christ : why traditional soteriology requires a trans savior / Kevin Carnahan.
Description: Minneapolis : Fortress Press, [2025] | Includes bibliographical references and index.
Identifiers: LCCN 2024033748 (print) | LCCN 2024033749 (ebook) | ISBN 9798889833055 (print) | ISBN 9798889833062 (ebook)
Subjects: LCSH: Gender identity in the Bible. | Gender nonconformity. | Sex role--Biblical teaching. | Adam (Biblical figure) | Eve (Biblical figure)
Classification: LCC BS1199.G36 C375 2025 (print) | LCC BS1199.G36 (ebook) | DDC 220.8/3053--dc23/eng/20241021
LC record available at https://lccn.loc.gov/2024033748
LC ebook record available at https://lccn.loc.gov/2024033749

Cover design: L. Whitt

Print ISBN: 979-8-8898-3305-5
eBook ISBN: 979-8-8898-3306-2

CONTENTS

Preface vii
Introduction ix

Prologue
In the Beginning xxiii

1. Blaming Eve 1
2. Erasing Eve 23
3. The Mary Solution 57
4. Theological Reflections on Sex and Gender 97
5. Toward the Trans* Christ 139

Postscript
Fortuitous Convergence 177

Bibliography 183
Scripture Index 203
General Index 207

PREFACE

Two conversations with students prompted this book. One focused on an arrangement of Psalm 23 by Bobby McFarrin. In that setting, the shepherd is referred to with feminine pronouns. One student wondered if it was appropriate to refer to the shepherd, whom they associated with Jesus, in this way. The other came from one of the college Bible studies organized and overseen by Rev. Kayla Kelly, our Campus Minister. Looking at Romans 5:12, Britt Dush, one of our religion majors, asked where Eve had gone in the verse. As the 2022 school year wound down, I was finishing out the last of my work as co-editor of the *Journal of the Society of Christian Ethics*. With my newfound "free time," I sat with these questions. I thought proposing an answer might make for a good article. More than three years later, I have done my best to answer these questions in what has become this book.

My debts for the work presented here extend back much further. As I started writing, I thought I was doing something that was quite different from anything I had previously worked on. But as I developed my thought, I found myself again and again appealing to the traditions that I had learned from Joette Bassler, William Babcock, and Robin Lovin in graduate school. As I progressed, I was able to send portions of the text to each of these mentors for comments and recommendations. I am endlessly grateful for their contributions to my work.

Many others have served as conversation partners along the way. Travis Smith, J. Aaron Simmons, Nicholas Wyant, and especially Daryl Jefferies listened to my ramblings and contributed useful ideas. The staff at Central Methodist University's Smiley Library were essential in importing many of the resources for the project to Fayette, MO. My other colleagues in the humanities department, Kavita Hatwalkar, Travis Johnson, John Porter, Ryan Woldruff, Amanda Arp, Erika Gotfredson, and Eric (Cody) Smothers have created a supportive community that allows me to keep going day to day. The students in my Religion Sex and Gender class were gracious in going along with me as we reviewed basic literature in the area. I also owe a debt to two anonymous reviewers who read the entire manuscript and offered extremely helpful suggestions. The administration at Central Methodist University supported this project by granting a semester sabbatical as I wrapped the work up.

More than anyone else, my wife Jennifer had to listen to the manuscript worked out day after day on our walks. For this and for so much more, I am grateful to her. She and my children put up with me disappearing randomly to work on the book when a thought struck me, and being a generally flighty academic when I should have been paying attention to more practical things. Since the time that I last dedicated a book to my family, my son's name has changed. So, it is to him that I dedicate this work. For Lukas.

INTRODUCTION

> The [Adam/Christ] typology always inevitably fails to recognize, contain, or resolve coherently the full spectrum of human differences with respect to gendered embodiment. . . . The inevitable anthropological failures found in both the Pauline typology and the history of its uptake are ones that constructive theology ought to foreground and continue to explore.
>
> —Benjamin Dunning, *Christ without Adam*, 88.

As is often the case in examinations of Christian theology, we should start our inquiry with an odd thing Paul once wrote: "just as sin came into the world through one man, and death came through sin . . . death exercised dominion from Adam . . . who is a type of the one who was to come" (Rom 5:12). The one who was to come is, of course, Jesus Christ. Here we find a pattern that would influence a great swath of the Christian tradition that would grow from Paul's messianic Judaism. The first Adam brought sin. The last Adam brings salvation. The pattern is so well trod today that it might strike our ears as banal. But there is something in Paul's claim that "sin came into the world through one man" that should befuddle us.

It is a strange claim. It has no pre-Pauline, biblical precedent or justification. Certainly, no one who has read Genesis 3 with any care could draw this inference from the story. The primary actor in Genesis 3, indeed the only really active human agent in the story when originating sin occurs, is Eve, not Adam. If sin came through any one person, it was a woman (though it would be more accurate to say that sin came through a man and a woman). So, why did Paul write that sin came through a man alone?

Those who are familiar with various historical interpretations of Genesis 3 might take Paul's focus on "man" to be a refreshing alternative. The tendency prior to Paul's work was to lay blame on Eve and exonerate, or even glorify, Adam. Blaming Eve was one way to distort her place in the story of sin and salvation. But it was not the only way. Before we embrace Paul for failing to blame Eve, we should take a moment to wonder where Eve has gone in his formula, and why she has fallen out of the narrative.

When dealing with narratives, patriarchal society has myriad strategies to diminish the roles of women. Two of those strategies are blame and erasure.

Women can be cast as villains, as Cleopatra was painted as "seductress or sorceress."[1] Or women can be minimized or erased, as happened in the classical world to Theano of Crotone, Hypatia, and so many that we will never know.[2] In this context it is useful to look to James Charlesworth, who once surveyed the theme of culpability in early retellings of the Genesis narrative. He found four ways of approaching Adam and Eve: (1) Adam is absolved, (2) Eve is responsible, (3) responsibility is shared, but it was mostly Eve, and (4) only Adam is mentioned.[3] Either Eve was the main character and was blamed, or she was disappeared from the story. More interesting than this scheme in general is what sits at the hinge between the first three options and the last, where Eve is most effectively erased: Romans 5.

As a survey in the first chapter of this work will show, no extant text that comes from before Paul's letter to the Romans produces a formula that locates Adam alone as the origin point for sin. In these texts almost all eyes were on Eve when contemplating originating sin, and none were focused solely on Adam. After Romans, that "sin came through Adam" became a common trope—so much so that the formula raises few eyebrows even among most biblical scholars. But what is the cost of the erasure of Eve?

The crucial theological problem concerns location in the narrative of fall and redemption. If Eve is erased from the narrative of the fall, how does she fit into the narrative of redemption? If sin came through one man, and salvation came through one man, does the woman find herself on the outside of the story? This is especially problematic when the theme of blaming Eve returns. In the order of sin, the Genesis narrative is clear: Eve sinned first, followed by Adam. If salvation through Jesus treats sin from Adam through Christ, what happens to Eve's sin? Is it not redeemed? For women, do we need another route of salvation to be added to what has been achieved in Christ?

This line of questioning may seem highly hypothetical until one looks back at texts like 1 Timothy 2:15, which suggests that women must be saved through

---

1. Duane W. Roller, *Cleopatra: A Biography*, First issued as an Oxford Univ. paperback, Women in Antiquity (Oxford: Oxford University Press, 2011), 1–6.

2. For a starting point on this topic, see Lois Agnew, "The Classical Period," in *The Present State of Scholarship in the History of Rhetoric: A Twenty-First Century Guide*, ed. Lynée Lewis Gaillet and Winifred Bryan Horner (Columbia: University of Missouri Press, 2010), 12–14. Each chapter has a section on women in the era being treated. On this phenomena in early Christianity, see Anne Jensen, *God's Self-Confident Daughters: Early Christianity and the Liberation of Women* (Louisville, KY: Westminster John Knox Press, 1996), 30–58, and references to Anonyma throughout the book.

3. James H. Charlesworth, "A History of Pseudepigrapha Research: The Re-Emerging Importance of the Pseudepigrapha," in *Aufstieg Und Niedergang Der Römischen Welt*, ed. Wolfgang Haase and Hildegard Temporini, vol. 19, no. 1 (Boston: De Gruyter, 1979), 77–81.

childbirth. Still living out the punishment from Eden, women may be saved through their own suffering.[4] This was not the last time that such an idea would be put forward.

The situation was not much helped by early church theologians who attempted to sort out some of these problems. Perceiving, at least inchoately, the lack in Paul's formula, many early Christian writers attempted a patch. If Christ was the new Adam, Mary the mother of Jesus must be the new Eve. Though her role as the *Theotokos* (mother of God) and guarantor of the humanity of Jesus was key in the development of early Mariology, the parallel between Eve and Mary also played a significant role.

Unfortunately, as a theological "solution" this approach never freed itself from the original problem. The effort to draw parallels between the first couple and the later mother and son pair created a set of insoluble problems for the dual typology. But more significant was the enduring problem of soteriology. In the order of fall Eve comes before Adam. In the order of bringing redemption, could Mary come before Christ? Early Christian writers were thrust upon the horns of a dilemma: Did Mary offer salvation to Eve in the same way that Christ offered salvation to Adam? If so, then Mary must be a savior in the same sense as Christ himself. Did Mary offer only a second-rate soteriological lifeline to Eve? If so, then Eve's sin must still sit somehow outside the true salvation offered through Christ. Different theologians threw themselves on one or the other horn. No adequate solution was ever reached.

There is a solution to this problem that has bewitched so many theologians. But it requires going back to revise Paul's formula. To adequately locate Eve in the narrative of sin and salvation, we should augment the claim that Christ is the new Adam. Christ must be the new Adam *and the new Eve*. To fulfill this role, Christians should recognize Christ as assuming/incarnating both characters. As such, Christ must assume/incarnate gendered difference. Christ must be trans*.

Though the language for framing this doctrine is recently coined, the proposal is not novel. In his own context, Christ's sex and gender were deeply complicated. As a Jewish peasant, Jesus could not fit into the paradigm of the true Roman *Vir* (man), his teachings often require what appeared as effeminacy in the Roman context, and his death was inextricably linked to effemination. In the early church, even as some theologians were working unsuccessfully to unsnarl the problem of Eve's relation to Mary, other theologians were exploring images of Jesus as mother and source of the milk of salvation. Eventually theologians developed accounts of how Christ transcended sex and gender, or even presented Christ to Christians as wet nurse. These traditions, developed in the right way, offer a means to fill out the claim that Christ is trans* and thus provide a suitable

4. Jouette M. Bassler, *1 Timothy, 2 Timothy, Titus*, Abingdon New Testament Commentaries (Nashville, TN: Abingdon Press, 1996), 61.

development of the central argument here. Such is the basic argument of this book. The prologue offers a brief critical review of the early chapters of Genesis in their own context. Chapter 1 reviews the tradition of blaming Eve for sin as it exists in Second Temple literature. Chapter 2 is a close reading of Paul's Adam/Christ typology in Romans 5. It explores how and why Eve is removed from the narrative in Paul's scheme. Chapter 3 looks at the way that early church theologians attempted to find a place for Eve in the narrative via a new Eve/Mary typology. Given the failure of this kind of solution, at this point I posit the conclusion to which the argument is driving. To adequately locate Eve in the narrative of sin and salvation, we need Christ to be the new Adam *and the new Eve.* Chapter 4 interrupts the historical narrative to explore a theology of sex and gender that could underwrite the conclusion to which the argument is taking us. Chapter 5 moves on to fill out what it might mean to locate Christ as trans* with an exploration of the ways that recent theology has seen Christ as transcending gender, a look at the way that the Jesus of the Gospels transgressed against the prevailing gender constructs of Roman society, and a review of the ways in which Christ was seen as transitioning across gender boundaries in medieval mysticism.

This is where this work is going. Before beginning in earnest, however, it is worth pausing to locate this project and introduce some key terminology.

Theology and Dialogue

Christian theology is an ongoing conversation among people divided by time and culture but united by the conversation itself. In this conversation, the contemporary theologian receives from the past. But even if the theologian tried only to repeat what had come before, they would inevitably contribute something of themself. There is, doubtless, a kerygma without which the conversation would cease to be Christian theology; there are more and less stable themes, questions, and conclusions. The constructive theology in this book, for instance, presupposes Nicene orthodoxy. But there is also a liveliness and openness to novelty as the theologian attempts to make sense of the world through the conversation.

Scripture does not stand outside this conversation. Rather, it represents some of the first contributors to the dialogue. Today, these contributors are designated by their names, letters (J, E, P, and D) and pseudonyms (Matthew and Mark, Isaiah two and three). Many are lost to history. Each has placed their mark on the exchange, often leaving dialogical friction in their wake. Genesis 1 is in tension with Genesis 2 and 3. Chronicles rehearses and reinterprets Kings, at times quite liberally. In intra-biblical interpretation, the text did not simply dictate to the reader. The interpreter was an active participant in picking, choosing, contesting, correcting, and reinterpreting. They contributed meanings that, over generations, came to layer the text.

In this process, the most recent interlocutor was never free of the text. Earlier authors imposed some boundaries that could not be crossed. The final editors of the Pentateuch did not feel qualified to harmonize all the divergent versions of ancient stories, nor could they reconcile themselves with rejecting one or the other narrative, even if they were apparently contradictory. But they never merely maintained what had come before. Even in offering the most conservative restatement of ancient stories in new contexts, the interpreter became a new author of the text. Biblical theology has always been dialogical theology.

This has not always been recognized within Christianity. Following the Jewish tradition of the previous three hundred years, most early Christians posited a kind of univocality to scripture.[5] Origen, the early church theologian, taught that the scripture was uniformly authored by the Holy Spirit. This doctrine, however, did not stop Christians from continued participation in dialogue that drew upon, contributed to, and directed the growing tradition. It opened spaces in which the dialogue continued. "God's intended" meaning for the text could go beyond, and in quite different directions from, the meaning intended by historical authors. Through allegory, typology, and moral readings of the text, Christians continued to both receive from the tradition and to donate their own voices to the growing cacophony.

As Christianity perdured, the dialogue enlarged, branched out, and diverged. Even, or perhaps especially, when theologians thought of themselves as repeating earlier themes, they contributed innovative additions to the conversation. Where Paul claimed that "sin entered the world through one man . . . with the result that (ἐφ' ᾧ) all have sinned," (Rom 5:12), Augustine could extend the claim that it was Adam "in whom (*in quo*)" all have sinned.[6] Where Paul was concerned with "works of the law (ἔργων νόμου)" (Gal 2:16) (i.e., circumcision, dietary laws, and sabbath obedience), Martin Luther could read concern about "works righteousness" (i.e., a belief that one could achieve righteousness independent of God).[7] Much of the dialogical nature of this work remained hidden, certainly from the public, but also often from the interpreters themselves. Christianity maintained both connection across the tradition and dialogical flexibility to articulate doctrine in new and helpful, or even provocative, ways.

In the aftermath of the Reformation, this approach to the Bible became more difficult to uphold. The increased pressure on the text to sort out disagreements

---

5. James L. Kugel, *How to Read the Bible: A Guide to Scripture, Then and Now* (New York: Free Press, 2008).

6. Joseph A. Fitzmyer, "The Consecutive Meaning of ΕΦ' Ω in Romans 5.12," *New Testament Studies* 39 (July 1993): 321–339.

7. James D. G. Dunn, *The New Perspective on Paul*, rev. ed., Wissenschaftliche Untersuchungen Zum Neuen Testament 185 (Grand Rapids, MI: W. B. Eerdmans, 2008).

(a task once left primarily to the institutional church), the need for a meaning accessible to a more general public, and the development of modern hermeneutics, often influenced by scientific constructions of literalism, led to significant shifts in what was possible when approaching the text. More important than any other development, however, modernity (and even more postmodernity) brought an appreciation of historicism—the extent to which original authors and their intentions are necessarily culturally distanced from contemporary readers.

Today, it is impossible to read scripture in the same ways that pre-modern Christians did. But this hardly requires an end to theology as dialogue with the scripture and tradition. Indeed, it allows the dialogical nature of theology to be more self-conscious and explicit. It further requires that we recognize the biblical authors as some among the many partners that join us in the long tradition of Christian theology. Self-critical Christians must take seriously their own role as dialogue partners with the biblical text and the tradition that comes after the Bible. As Kathryn Tanner writes, when doing theology, one must accept that one is in "a constructive dialogue and intellectual contest with all those other Christians, past and present, who have been similarly concerned."[8] For present purposes, we can expand this statement to include those many Jewish contributors without whom the Christian tradition would never have come to be.

Locating the Current Project in the Dialogue

This work takes up this kind of self-consciously dialogical theology. The methodology within and ordering of the book reflect awareness of participation in a long historical tradition. As such, the argument moves generally from earlier to later sources, tracing out the evolution of the treatment of Adam and Eve, then Mary and Jesus. In the process, the argument is built on elements taken from each source. The creation narratives in Genesis provide the original dialogical space that shaped the possibilities for interpreting Adam and Eve in relation to themes of sin and, eventually, of salvation. For the current work, the sequence of creation (Adam and then Eve) and sin (Eve and then Adam) from that narrative will be of key importance. Paul contributes the wish to see salvation as inclusive of all of humanity, and the typological interpretation of Christ as an answer to the sins of Eden. With early Christian theologians, the argument wrestles with how to make sense of this inclusivity in the light of the problem of the Adam/Christ typology taken from Paul. Tracing out a long history of Christian reflection on the sex/gender ambiguity of Jesus, and contributing to contemporary theologies of sex/gender, this work ultimately offers a solution to the problem: locating Jesus as trans*.

8. Kathryn Tanner, *Jesus, Humanity and the Trinity: A Brief Systematic Theology* (Minneapolis, MN: Fortress Press, 2001), xvi.

In this dialogue, while all sources are treated with respect, none are treated as inerrant. And this work is certainly an active contribution to the dialogue. Second temple sources are wrong in blaming Eve for sin. Paul creates problems by positing the Adam/Christ typology and excluding Eve from the narrative in Romans 5. Early church theologians chased the possibility of an Eve/Mary typology down a theological cul-de-sac. And, the conclusion of the present argument, while not as novel in the history of Christianity as it may at first appear, goes beyond what has come before.

The kind of continuity maintained within the tradition throughout the argument is, however, theologically robust. This work is an effort to achieve goals that were embraced by theologians at every stage of Christian history. With Paul, this work seeks to articulate a soteriology that can embrace the whole of humanity. With early church theologians, I am trying to solve the problem of the Adam/Christ typology that Paul left to us.

In this sense, this project is in keeping with quite conservative accounts of the role of the theologian in the church. This role is expressed as follows by the Vatican's Congregation for the Doctrine of the Faith:

> The theologian has the duty to make known to the Magisterial authorities the problems raised by the teaching in itself, in the arguments proposed to justify it, or even in the manner in which it is presented. They should do this in an evangelical spirit and with a profound desire to resolve the difficulties. Their objections could then contribute to real progress and provide a stimulus to the Magisterium to propose the teaching of the Church in greater depth and with a clearer presentation of the arguments.[9]

Being more Protestant than Catholic, I must interpret "Magisterium" in the above quote as referring to the *ecclesia* writ large; the priesthood of all believers, as it were. Or at least the "wise" among that priesthood. But the basic task undertaken in this work fits within the above picture. The problems highlighted in the work of Paul and those in the early church are unresolved problems *for* Paul and the early church. None of those treated in this book wished to set Eve outside

---

9. Congregation for the Doctrine of the Faith, "Instruction on the Ecclesial Vocation of Theologian," sec. 32, accessed October 5, 2022, https://www.vatican.va/roman_curia/congregations/cfaith/documents/rc_con_cfaith_doc_19900524_theologian-vocation_en.html. I have corrected for gendered language in the original. This passage is quoted in Eugene F. Rogers, *Sexuality and the Christian Body: Their Way into the Triune God*, Challenges in Contemporary Theology (Malden, MA: Blackwell, 1999), 6. If it were academically acceptable, I would just lift the entire prolegomena from Roger's book and place it in the above text. Unfortunately for my reader, they will have to go look up the original.

the scope of salvation. Rather, they lacked an adequate formula to achieve their broader intentions. At times, this lack was shaped by the patriarchal cultures and theological traditions in which they worked. But none of them meant to endorse the problems this work points out in their theologies. As such, the current project is done in service to the tradition that they represented, even if it offers critiques of and new alternatives to their own theologies. Christian theology is an ongoing dialogue, and dialogues are open to creative opportunities.[10]

Strands of Theology

In many ways, the argument of this book is a classical theological argument, deeply influenced by the shape of patristic disputes. As did the Christological arguments of early Christianity, the argument of this work moves from soteriology to Christology. The central question is: "Who must Christ be to achieve what Christ did?" Of course, to answer this question several prior premises need to be filled in; premises that are bound to particular lines of development in the Christian tradition itself. What did Christ achieve? How did Christ achieve it? What is the shape of Christ's achievement? These questions take us into the realm of soteriology, which is itself a live topic in the broader dialogue of theology.

There is no one Christian way of answering such questions. As Kathryn Tanner writes:

> Christianity is simply too complex a phenomenon to be an easy and obvious whole: its symbols and sacred texts are too multivalent and diverse; its beliefs too tension filled (for example, monotheism combined with a claim for the divinity of Jesus); internal inconsistencies among its practice and beliefs as pronounced as in any way of life developing over time in the push and pull of real life struggles. Figuring out what Christianity is all about requires, therefore, intellectual effort, and intellectual effort of a primarily systematic sort. . . . This systematic effort requires one to select and highlight.[11]

The present work shall not proceed as systematically as does Tanner. Rather, premises will be filled in as the text develops, usually drawing from dialogue partners.

---

10. Kathryn Tanner, "Experiments in Early Christian Theology, Lecture 1" (Costan Lectures, Virginia Theological Seminary, March 1, 2022), https://www.youtube.com/watch?v=GZPkDxYFtSg.

11. Tanner, *Jesus, Humanity and the Trinity*, xiv–xv.

From Paul the work takes the goal of salvation offered to all, regardless of sex/gender or other distinguishing characteristics. But also from Paul is taken the significance of the existence of sexed/gendered difference. From the patristic development of Paul's thought, the work draws up the framework of salvation by recapitulation. From the medieval mystics, it takes images of Jesus as wet nurse and mother of church and believer.

The work also draws consistently upon Augustinian theology. For instance, in contrast to the more Greek, eastern tradition, I shall side with Tertullian and Augustine in holding that eschatological existence must be sexed/gendered in some way to embody individual distinctiveness.

Similarly, when the work comes to reflect on the theology of sex and gender, the argument will draw on Augustinian anthropological and sociological thought. The anthropology assumed is influenced by the tradition running from Augustine through Kierkegaard to the neo-Augustinian work of Reinhold Niebuhr. The sociology drawn upon emerges from the Augustinian tradition as represented in the works of figures like Emil Brunner and Dietrich Bonhoeffer. In each of these areas, the reader will find the work of Robin Lovin, who has produced a coherent social theology that draws from these traditions. It is from these sources that this work will develop an account of sex and gender as a "context of responsibility" in which individuals find their callings.

While some supporting arguments will be offered along the way for drawing on these strands of the Christian tradition as dialogue partners in the text, it must be acknowledged they are not the only alternatives in the broader tradition. Theology, as Tanner notes, requires that one "select and highlight." Working from different strands of theology might produce quite different arguments. In the end, the work cannot offer a complete apology for all its choices of dialogue partners. These choices emerge organically either from the shape of the dialogue itself or from the theologian's position in the dialogical process of doing theology. No one does theology from a God's eye point of view.

Is this Queer Theology?

Queerness is, by its own definition, an essentially unstable term. "Queer" writes David Halperin, "is by definition *whatever* is at odds with the normal, the legitimate, the dominant. *There is nothing in particular to which it necessarily refers.* It is an identity without an essence."[12] Such apophaticism, however, must be qualified in practice. Queer scholarship generally draws from a set of semi-canonical

12. David M. Halperin and Michel Foucault, *Saint Foucault: Towards a Gay Hagiography* (New York: Oxford University Press, 1997), 62.

sources, including Sigmund Freud and Michel Foucault.[13] Its methodology often draws upon a specific set of hermeneutic strategies.[14] And it frequently justifies its claims by the extent to which these claims destabilize what are seen as oppressive structures in society. Thus far, queer theology has primarily focused on the destabilization of sex, sexuality, and gender expectations, though it can be applied in other areas. As such, Marcella Althaus-Reid could write that the task of her "indecent" theology was to "deconstruct a moral order which is based on a heterosexual construction of reality, which organizes not only categories of approved social and divine interactions but of economic ones too."[15] And Linn Marie Tonstad can write that queer theology is fundamentally "about visions of sociopolitical transformation that alter practices of distinction harming gender and sexual minorities as well as many other minoritized populations."[16]

The current work is not a piece of queer theology in any of the above senses. I do, at points, engage queer theorists and theologians as dialogue partners. But they are only some of a myriad of dialogue partners throughout the work. And I do not draw directly from either Freud or Foucault (though every appreciation of historicism today is partially indebted to the latter). I do not draw upon queer hermeneutic strategies to advance my argument. While the upshot of the study may strike many as queer, the argument is not structured specially to produce a conclusion that challenges established institutions, and its claims are not justified by their effectiveness in bringing about such an end.

None of this is to say that I am opposed to queer theology. In the postscript to this volume, I shall return to this issue to explore the extent to which the conclusions of the argument of this work produce a serendipitous overlap with conclusions from queer and liberationist theology. I only note here that there is nothing in the argument, or in the dialogue partners I engage along the way, that make the work particularly queer itself. In many ways, as I have already suggested, the argument is quite classical, even patristic, in its shape. And it never strays from working out a goal that is perennial in Christian theology: namely, the universal accessibility of transformation through Christ's activity.

---

13. Brandy Daniels, "Queer Theory," in *Religion: Embodied Religion*, ed. Kent Brintnall, Macmillan Interdisciplinary Handbooks (Farmington Hills, MI: Macmillan Reference USA, a part of Gale, Cengage Learning, 2016), 289–308.

14. See, for instance, the strategies deployed in Linn Marie Tonstad, *God and Difference: The Trinity, Sexuality, and the Transformation of Finitude*, Gender, Theology and Spirituality 17 (New York: Routledge, 2017).

15. Marcella Althaus-Reid, *Indecent Theology: Theological Perversions in Sex, Gender and Politics* (New York: Routledge, 2010), 2.

16. Tonstad, *Queer Theology: Beyond Apologetics*, Cascade Companions 40 (Eugene, OR: Cascade Books, 2018), 2.

It may be that this starting point is sufficiently queer. As Gerard Laughlin has written:

> Theology is a queer thing. It has always been a queer thing. It is a very strange thing indeed, especially for anyone living in the modern West of the twenty-first century. For theology runs counter to a world given over to material consumption, that understands itself as "accidental," without any meaning other than that which it gives to itself, and so without any fundamental meaning at all. Against this, theology relativizes all earthly projects, insisting that to understand ourselves we must understand our orientation to the unknown from which all things come and to which they return, that which—as Christian theology ventures—is known and received in the life of Jesus.[17]

One of the upshots of the argument of this work is that an adequate theology will lead us to relativize the very human project of maintaining sex/gender distinctions. Not to eliminate it, but to relativize it. If this is sufficient to be included in the category of queer theology, I should not be disappointed at inclusion. Whether that is sufficient is a judgment I shall leave to others.

Sex, Gender, and Trans*

I do not want to belabor here the articulation of key terms in gender studies. There will be much more to say about them in Chapter 4. But some introduction is needed, especially for terms that are often contested or may be unfamiliar to the reader.

It has been common in the recent past for sex and gender to be distinguished, where sex refers to one's "biological" status and gender refers to one's socially constructed, performed, or projected identity. This distinction reflects assumptions about the relative stability and objectivity of the former and contingency and subjectivity of the latter. More recent work has undermined the objective/subjective binary in this distinction, and thus has thrown into question the function of the sex/gender distinction itself.

Both sex and gender are related to one's biology, and both are in some sense socially constructed. How one determines "biological" sex depends on what one includes in the relevant criteria for such determination. Is sex about genes? Chromosomes? Gonads? Gametes? Hormones? Genitalia? A doctor's pronouncement at birth? Brain chemistry? Body morphology? All of these are biological

17. Gerard Loughlin and Gerard Loughlin, eds., "Introduction: The End of Sex," in *Queer Theology: Rethinking the Western Body* (Malden, MA: Blackwell Pub, 2007), 7.

traits, but as different cases of intersex conditions show, there are instances in which they do not line up in clear patterns of "male" or "female." And at times the chromosomes, gonads, hormones, genitalia, and so on are ambiguous if viewed through the lens of binary sexuality. How one "sexes" a person depends on what one includes or excludes in making the judgment. Such choices about inclusion and exclusion are not in themselves determined by "objective" observation. They are cultural products that reflect particular values, political stances, communal standards, and so on.[18]

On the other side, one's public status as "masculine," "feminine," "butch," "fem," or whatever has never been, and cannot be, purely subjective. Identities are always negotiated in a social context. These contexts limit and make possible certain ways of being, presenting oneself, and being perceived. And such contexts do not necessarily make any clear distinction between, say, body morphology and gendered performance. This is one of the reasons that sex-affirming medical services, such as hormone replacement and surgery, remain crucial elements in some individuals' gender presentation. We should also not think that choices about gender presentation are somehow entirely separable from issues of relatively "sexed" brain chemistry, hormones, genes, etc. We do not understand all the connections among these varied factors, but they are certainly often related.

Another concern that is relevant to the present study is that the sex/gender distinction does not have a deep history. While one can often find differences between what it means to be a man, and what it means to be a *real* man, or a *manly* man, or some such, different societies have drawn these distinctions in diverse ways. It is unhelpful, and at times obscurantist, to project the modern distinction on historical cultures.

For reasons like these, this work generally avoids making the sex/gender distinction. Rather, it tends to refer to sex/gender as a category that takes up both biological and social factors in determinations of identity related to maleness, femaleness, and other alternatives. This hopefully allows the exploration of multiple different contexts across various eras without doing too much damage to the logics intrinsic to those contexts. And it allows this investigation to honor the inherent overlap between what we often categorize separately under the terms *sex* and *gender*.

The other term which merits some treatment here is the term *trans**. As with sex/gender, this term is useful as much for what it does not say as for what it does. Labels for people who have transgressed and/or transitioned across gender and sex boundaries have proliferated in recent years as significant distinctions have been recognized between, for instance, transgender, transsexual,

18. Katrina Karkazis, "The Misuses of 'Biological Sex,'" *The Lancet* 394, no. 10212 (November 2019): 1898–1899.

and cross-dressing persons. The term trans* has been put forward as an umbrella term covering all different forms of transgressing and or transitioning across these lines. The asterisk functions, as it does in computer searches, as a fill space, capable of capturing all possible endings to the term.

Such a term is theologically useful in the current work because it functions to unseat established patterns of thinking about gender and sex categories without replacing them with a new clear taxonomical system. In this way, it can function much like *ousia* and *hypostasis* in classical Christology. The doctrine of the Trinity holds that God is one *ousia* (substance) in three *hypostases* (persons) while maintaining that the exact meaning of these terms is mysterious. Trans* can function similarly when describing Christ's sex/gender. In the first sense it is apophatic, reminding us of what we cannot say about Christ—that Christ fits within the sex/gender categories of our own social context. But it must also do more work than this. In Chapter 5, drawing on contemporary theology, Roman conceptions of sex/gender, and medieval mystical experiences, I shall explore how Christ has been said to transcend, transgress, and transition across sex/gender boundaries within the Christian tradition.

My argument will give new significance to these traditions as it locates them in relation to Christ as the new Adam and new Eve in the narrative of sin and salvation. But I am not innovating in recognizing Christ as moving across these boundaries. In this regard, the most novel element of my proposal is naming this phenomenon with the language of trans*. At key points in the history of Christology, the church has found that the language of its own time, in terms like *ousia* and *hypostasis*, presents a better framework for thought about God than what had existed previously. In a comparable way, the development of trans* identity presents the church with an opportunity to express more adequately the mystery of Christ's being in bringing salvation to the whole of humanity. Naming this mystery reminds us of an already existing tradition and offers an encapsulation of the proposed solution to the central problem of the present work.

A Work of Constructive Theology

What follows covers a wide territory, both in terms of history and discipline: the study of pseudepigrapha, Pauline studies, patristics, gender theory, and theology. No one person could be a specialist in all the fields and periods that must be traversed to make the argument. The work is thus dependent on many specialists in these fields. Without their expertise the argument would have been impossible to produce.

While the argument engages (with occasional creativity) with these many specialties, it is not a work in any of these areas. It is a work of constructive theology that inevitably must trespass upon the fields of others to participate in the ongoing dialogue of which it consists. This is said not to insulate the present work from criticism from these disciplines. This work is put forward as a respectful contribution in the dialogical tradition of theology. Respectful dialogue depends on generously listening to one's partners along the way. But it should be remembered that, at the end of the day, this is not a work about any one of those dialogue partners, or their specific contexts. It is a work that aims to advance the dialogue itself.

PROLOGUE

In the Beginning

> And when they tasted of the tree, their nakedness was exposed to them, and they began to sew together the leaves of the Garden to cover themselves. And their Lord called out to them, "Did I not forbid you from that tree and tell you that Satan is a manifest enemy unto you?"
>
> —Quran, al-Aʿrāf 7:22–23

Before examining how Eve's role in the narrative of sin and salvation was treated later, we must say something about her original performance. This is not because we need a thorough interpretation of Genesis to get started. Mostly here I shall try to avoid offering much interpretation. I shall leave the text in the full glory of its ambiguousness. Still, it is helpful to have a sense of the text that provides a backdrop (even if not always a primary source) for the interpretation of Eve's relation to Adam, sin, and eventually Christ. It is useful to look at the text to gain clarity on a particular set of claims.

Here are the points that we need to highlight: (1) Genesis 1 is the only chapter in which the image of God is explicitly discussed. In this chapter, both male and female are created in this image. (2) In Genesis 2, Adam is located as coming first, and being in some sense the source of all humanity in the order of creation. Eve comes from Adam, and shares in his nature. (3) In Genesis 3, Eve is the primary, active human agent in the story of "originating" sin.[1] She is tempted with the offer of Godlike status. She engages in thought about her actions. Inasmuch as her sin is identified as eating from the fruit of the forbidden tree, her sin comes first (before Adam's) in the order of sin. Yet, (4) Genesis does not place disproportionate blame upon Eve for her part in the narrative. Both Eve's and Adam's sin follow the same basic pattern, each receives the suggestion to eat from another being. Each eventually takes and eats. The text leaves open the possibility (and perhaps even suggests) that Adam was present through the entire series of events, thus observing and failing to act as Eve engages with the serpent and eats the fruit. Interpreters can find reasons in the story to differentiate the two acts of sin, but none of these seem to be of great interest in the Genesis

---

1. I borrow this phrase from Terrence Fretheim, "Genesis," in *New Interpreter's Bible*, Vol. 1, ed. Leander Keck (Nashville, TN: Abingdon Press, 1994), 367.

narrative as it stands. One can draw reasonable inferences from the text about the seriousness of Adam's sin and Eve's sin from the story of their punishment, but none of these require attributing distinct levels of responsibility to Adam or Eve.

Each one of these points will become significant at different moments in the following chapters. Paul (and many others) will make a hash out of the claim that both males and females are created in the image of God. Theologians will wrestle with the problem of coordinating the differing orders of sin and creation in developing their soteriologies. Eve will be disproportionately blamed for what happened in the garden. Adam will be given an alibi that places him away from Eve during her temptation and sin. Then, in later retellings, Eve will strangely disappear from the narrative, often with at least parts of her role (especially her engagement with the serpent/Satan) being explicitly taken over by Adam.

When developing a theology of sex and gender, I eventually will return to Genesis to offer a more developed interpretation of the sex and gender difference created by God in these chapters. As we shall see by the end of the book, there are multiple ways to parse this issue, and my theological proposal for conceiving of Jesus as trans* will incline me toward a particular way of sorting out some of the ambiguity. For the present, let us turn our focus toward Genesis without trying to sort all of it out, but rather look at it as a starting point for the wild ride on which Eve and Adam will go in later interpretation.

A Selective Retelling

Genesis 1 and 2 relate two different tales of creation, though they are now woven together into a single narrative. In the first God creates אָדָם (*adam*) in God's image (1:26). Careful readers of the text have understood *adam* here to refer to "humankind," though the term itself is ambiguous.[2] It can mean "humankind," "man," or function as the proper name "Adam." In context, the most general term fits at this early stage. Otherwise, it would be hard to make sense of the immediate note that "male and female God created them" (1:27) and the divine command to "Be fruitful and multiply" (1:28). As such, when it says that *adam* was created in the image of God, this includes both men and women.

This is all straightforward enough when read in isolation. However, later interpreters will struggle with how to make sense of Genesis 1 in relation to the parallel story of creation in Genesis 2. As we shall see, parts of the two could be combined to produce a kind of Frankenstein creation narrative, they could be read as referring to separate acts of creation (say, one spiritual, the other physical),

2. It hardly helps that, as a function of the gendered grammar, the Hebrew text goes on to state that "in the image of God he created him (אֹתוֹ); male and female he created them (אֹתָם:)" (Gen 1:27).

or they could be read as alternative visions of creation (as is common in contemporary biblical scholarship). Each of these approaches could produce various upshots, leaving extreme differences in perceptions about the proper message to be taken from the text.

To return to more immediate textual issues, both Genesis 1 and 2 concern the creation of *adam*. It is not entirely clear when in the text the translation of *adam* should shift from referring to "humankind" to referring to "the man" and then becoming a proper name.[3] As such, I will keep using the italicized, lower-case "*adam*" for the second creation narrative. In Genesis 2, God forms *adam* from the dust of the earth (הָֽאֲדָמָ֔ה/adamah). God creates the garden, including the Tree of Life and the Tree of the Knowledge of Good and Evil. Placing *adam* in the garden, God gives *adam* (alone) a command: "You may freely eat of every tree of the garden; but of the tree of the knowledge of good and evil you shall not eat, for in the day that you eat of it you shall die" (2:16–17). After trying to solve the problem of *adam*'s aloneness with the creation of other animals, God fashions from *adam*'s rib a woman (לְאִשָּׁה/ishshah). From this point, *adam*, now clearly a sexed/gendered man, recedes in the narrative.

The crafty serpent (no relation to Satan in the original)[4] asks the woman if God's command placed a prohibition on eating from all trees. The woman responds that God said: "You shall not eat of the fruit of the tree that is in the middle of the garden, nor shall you touch it, or you shall die" (3:3). Notably, this differs from the earlier recorded command. It adds the prohibition on touching, and it omits that death will come on the day one eats from the tree. We are provided no account of from where the woman learned this command. The serpent tells the woman that she will not die if she eats from the tree, but she will come to be like God. The woman then "saw that the tree was good for food, and that it was a delight to the eyes, and that the tree was to be desired to make one wise," and so she took the fruit and ate. Adam now makes an (almost entirely passive) appearance in the text: "she also gave some to her husband, who was with her, and he ate" (3:6). Notably, the text provides no reason to think that she

3. Tamara Eskenazi argues that context supports using "the man" from 2:23–3:22, but not necessarily before. "Genesis," in *The Torah: A Women's Commentary*, ed. Tamara Eskenazi and Andrea Weiss (Women of Reform Judaism, Federation of Temple Sisterhood: URJ Press, 2008), 7–12. Nahum Sarna argues for 2:20 and on being the proper name Adam, *The JPS Torah Commentary: Genesis*. (New York: The Jewish Publication Society, 1989), 18–19. The NRSV and NIV begin using "man" in 2:7. Terence Fretheim notes that Genesis 4:25 is the first unequivocal usage of the term without the definite article. Fretheim, "Genesis," 353.

4. Edwin M. Good, *Genesis 1–11: Tales of the Earliest World* (Palo Alto: Stanford University Press, 2011), 36; Terence E. Fretheim, "Genesis," 359–360, 363. For a full discussion of the identity of the serpent, see Claus Westerman, *Genesis 1–11: A Commentary*, trans. John Scullion (Minneapolis, MN: Augsburg Publishing House, 1984), 237–239.

"seduced" Adam or did anything to "tempt" him other than handing him the fruit. Where has Adam, Eve's "silent partner,"[5] been throughout this exchange up to this point? Does "who was with her" in 3:6 suggest that he was listlessly watching on the entire time? We are not explicitly told.

After the two humans deal with the new (or newly noticed?) problem of their nudity by making leaf skirts, God interrogates them. The man blames the woman, noting that she gave him the fruit, and implicates God for giving the woman to him. The woman blames the serpent, claiming that it tricked her. God then metes out punishment. The serpent will wallow on the ground eating dust, and enmity will exist not only between the woman and the serpent, but between their descendants. The woman will suffer in childbirth yet will desire for her husband while he rules over her. The man shall have to work to produce food from a ground that is now cursed. To the man, God says that this punishment will last "until you return to the ground, for out of it you were taken; you are dust, and to dust you shall return" (3:19). No one is killed that day, and death is not explicitly treated as a part of the punishment. Adam will have to work the ground until he returns to the ground. His returning to the ground is not a punishment; it is the natural endpoint of his endurance of punishment. Only at this point does Adam name his wife "Eve (חַוָּה/ḥawwāh) because she will be the mother of all living (חָי:/ḥāy)" (3:20). After God provides the two with new clothes of skins, God confirms the serpent's claim: the man and woman have become "like one of us" (3:22). For this reason, God sends the man and woman from Eden so that they cannot (or can no longer?) eat of the fruit of the Tree of Life.

There is more information missing than provided. How should the sex/gender of *adam* be interpreted prior to the creation of woman?[6] Why does God prohibit eating from the Tree of the Knowledge of Good and Evil?[7] Why did the

5. Fretheim, "Genesis," 360, 361. Fretheim suggests that Adam has been with Eve throughout the entire exchange.

6. Phyllis Trible suggests that prior to the creation of woman, "adam" should be considered not to have sexual identity: Trible, Phyllis, *God and the Rhetoric of Sexuality* (Philadelphia: Fortress Press, 1978), 79–80. Tamara Eskenazi is open to this suggestion: Eskenazi, "Genesis," 13. Terence E. Fretheim rejects Trible's thesis: Fretheim, "Genesis," 359. The explicit term "man" (אִישׁ) is first used in Genesis 2.23 when "woman" (אִשָּׁה) is named as such by *adam*.

7. Edwin Good outlines three possible meanings of "knowledge of good and evil": (1) moral knowledge; (2) knowledge that is good to have and knowledge that is bad to have; (3) "good and bad" as a metaphor for "covering everything." Good, *Genesis 1–11*, 24–25. To this we should add that it has often been interpreted as connoting sexual knowledge. Eskenazi, "Genesis," 11. On further possible interpretations of the "knowledge of good and evil," see Clause Westerman, *Genesis 1–11: A Commentary*, trans. John Scullion (Minneapolis, MN: Augsburg Publishing House, 1984), 242–245 and Sarna, *The JPS Torah Commentary: Genesis*, 19.

serpent choose Eve to talk to?[8] Was Adam with Eve through the whole narrative?[9] Did the serpent ever lie to or deceive Eve?[10] If the serpent's "craftiness" does have a negative edge, how did it come to be a part of God's "good" creation?[11] Did God lie when saying that Adam would die the day he ate of the tree?[12] Why does Eve relate a variant version of the command to the serpent?[13] Was Eve

---

8. Edwin Good suggests that the reasons are sexist, assuming "that the woman is perhaps more vulnerable." *Genesis 1–11: Tales of the Earliest World* (Palo Alto, CA: Stanford University Press, 2011), 17. Terrence Fretheim suggests that it may be because the woman was not there to hear the command from God firsthand. Fretheim, "Genesis," 360.

9. Gary Anderson reads the story to indicate that Eve is alone when the serpent approaches her. *The Genesis of Perfection: Adam and Eve in Jewish and Christian Imagination* (Louisville, KY: Westminster John Knox, 2001), 215. Tamara Eskenazi reads the text to suggest that "the man was with the woman all along": Eskenazi, "Genesis," 15. Terrence Fretheim concurs with Eskenazi: Fretheim, "Genesis," 361.

10. Eve claims that she was deceived, but is this just self-justification? Henry Kelly appears to question whether the serpent ever lied. See his "Adam Citings before the Intrusion of Satan: Recontextualizing Paul's Theology of Sin and Death," *Biblical Theology Bulletin* 44, no. 1 (2014): 15. Fretheim claims that, in telling Eve that she would not die from eating the fruit, the serpent functions as a "truth teller": Fretheim, "Genesis," 361. There is no doubt that some of the things the serpent says end up being true. However, there is also a tension between the serpent's original (feigned?) ignorance about the command and the serpent's apparent inside knowledge about the nature of the tree that raises significant questions about whether the serpent is being deceitful. To resolve this, one also need to interpret "death" in the death warning to Adam.

11. Some have suggested that the serpent is a demythologized, and thus downgraded, version of the serpent as venerated by non-Jewish traditions as a deity or mystically powerful creature. See Eskenazi, "Genesis," 14.

12. "Death" in the threat has been interpreted variously, some of which allow for the threat to be true. Henry Kelly summarizes some of the options: instant death, violent or painful death, premature death (shortened life), loss of immortality, allegorical death (vicious life, painful life), death of the soul (annihilation), punishment of the soul after death (another kind of allegorical death): Kelly, "Adam Citings before the Intrusion of Satan," 14. On the idea that Adam and Eve lost immortality, see the note below attached to that question.

13. Fretheim, finding that either Adam relayed the command to Eve or that she received it directly from God, simply concludes that "*either* the man or the woman misstated it": Fretheim, "Genesis," 360. Tamara Eskenazi suggests that we might see here Eve participating in the Rabbinic practice of creating a "fence around the Torah" to avoid coming near to breaking commandments: Eskenazi, "Genesis," 14. Later Rabbinic commentary would posit that Adam related the command to Eve but that he condescendingly added the command not to touch. This then contributed to Eve's temptation to take the fruit. Later Christian interpreters following a mistranslation in the Septuagint would claim that both Adam and Eve were present at the time of the original command from God. See Anderson, *The Genesis of Perfection*, 77–84 and James L. Kugel. *Traditions of the Bible: A Guide to the Bible as It Was at the Start of the Common Era* (Cambridge, MA: Harvard University Press, 1998), 102–103.

wrong in thinking that wisdom gained from the tree is good?[14] Was loss of the chance at immortality part of Adam and Eve's punishment?[15] Why does God reclothe the couple before expelling them?[16] Why is "being like God" a reason for expulsion from the garden?[17] The text teems with gaps and opportunities for diverse interpretations.

We will plug none of these gaps at present. To anticipate the central concerns of the next two chapters, we need only emphasize two of the points noted above among my list of important implications of the narrative. First, Eve is the pivotal figure in the story of originating sin. Second, Eve does not bear unique blame for sin in the story.

In the text provided in Genesis 3, Eve is the "protagonist."[18] She "plays the lead role in the transgression."[19] Though the serpent chooses to approach her, Eve chooses to engage the serpent in dialogue. The serpent "engages in no coercion here, no arm twisting, no enticement through presentation of fruit from the tree."[20] Eve "was the one who had talked with the snake and been persuaded by him, she had done the thinking about the matter in so far as any thinking was done at all, she had taken the forbidden fruit, and she was the one who had given

---

14. Fretheim suggests that the issue in view is "the way in which wisdom is gained": Fretheim, "Genesis," 361.

15. It is generally accepted today that 3:19 does not refer to a punishment of death. It only indicates that Adam will have to toil against the cursed ground *until* he dies. But there is the further issue of whether humans (originally created mortal) are cut off from eternal life by being cut off from the Tree of Life, and thus de facto lose immortality as a part of their punishment. See Fretheim, "Genesis," 360 and Sarna, *The JPS Torah Commentary: Genesis*, 18–19, 21.

16. Fretheim suggests it may be related to salvation, and it stands for a re-establishment of relationship after sin. Fretheim, "Genesis," 364.

17. Westerman sees the verse giving this as the reason for expulsion as an addition to the original text because it seems to conflict with the idea that the two were removed from the garden for disobedience. *Genesis 1–11: A Commentary*, trans. John Scullion (Minneapolis, MN: Augsburg Publishing House, 1984), 271. He posits that the ejection from the garden is the "real punishment" of Adam and Eve's transgression: *Genesis: A Practical Commentary*, trans. David Green (Grand Rapids, MI: Eerdmans, 1987), 27.

18. Susan Niditch, "Genesis," in *Women's Bible Commentary*, expanded edition, ed. Carol Newsom and Sharon Ringe (Louisville, KY: Westminster John Knox Press, 1998), 16.

19. Fretheim, "Genesis," 359.

20. Fretheim, "Genesis," 361, 365–366. Clause Westerman writes that "the serpent is nothing more than the narrative symbol of this power of temptation, which mysteriously speaks through the mouth of one of God's creatures." *Genesis: A Practical Commentary*. Elsewhere he concludes that "the woman acts independently in transgressing the command and so is fully responsible." Clause Westerman, *Genesis 1–11: A Commentary*, trans. John Scullion (Minneapolis, MN: Augsburg Publishing House, 1984), 236, 248.

it to her husband."[21] If we locate the eating of the fruit as the originating sin, it is Eve who committed this sin.

Yet, Adam and Eve are both culpable. Eve is no temptress. She does not deceive Adam or coerce him.[22] If Eve is condemned for her activity, Adam is equally responsible for his inactivity.[23] This is especially true if one reads the story to say that Adam was present with Eve through the entire exchange.[24] It is *adam* alone who we saw receive the prohibition against eating. God appears to reference this fact in 3:17. As God punishes Adam, God explicitly calls Adam out for having "eaten of the tree about which I commanded you. 'You shall not eat of it.'" The "you" in this verse is singular.[25] Adam is condemned for having "listened to the voice of your wife," but one must keep the context in mind here. First, in the story, Eve is not recorded as saying anything to Adam. She simply offered him the fruit, and he took it. Second, the point here is not about Eve. It is that Adam had a choice about who to listen to, and he did not listen to God. Who the other voice was is functionally irrelevant. Finally, Adam's punishment is the longest and most detailed of those given out, indicating the weight of his transgression.[26]

One can make arguments for the greater guilt of either Adam or Eve. But in the end their sins are parallel. The serpent suggests that Eve eat. Eve suggests that Adam eat. Neither is coerced. Both fall to temptation. Eve is the more active. Adam the more passive. But both share the weight of the transgression.

It is against this backdrop that we should take up the later interpretations of this narrative, which go in two different directions. Prior to Paul, Second Temple treatments of Adam and Eve lay special blame upon Eve. When we reach Paul in Romans 5, Eve, the primary human agent in the story, is omitted. The next two chapters will take these developments in turn.

---

21. James Barr, *The Garden of Eden and the Hope of Immortality* (Minneapolis MN: Fortress Press, 1993), 9.

22. Fretheim, "Genesis," 361; Sarna, *The JPS Torah Commentary: Genesis*, 25; and Clause Westerman, *Genesis 1–11: A Commentary*, trans. John Scullion (Minneapolis, MN: Augsburg Publishing House, 1984), 250.

23. Edwin Zulu notes that in a patriarchal society, the guilt would fall on Adam for failing to do his duty to protect his family: "Sin, Gender, and Responsibility: A Contextual Interpretation of Genesis 3" in *Genesis*, ed. Athalia Brenner, Archie Lee, and Gail Yee (Minneapolis, MN: Fortress, 2010), 60. We will have the opportunity to revisit this note in our treatment of Paul.

24. See the note above on this question.

25. See Eskenazi, "Genesis," 17.

26. "The longest address is reserved for the man, for his is the greatest share of culpability since it was he who received the prohibition directly from God." Sarna, *The JPS Torah Commentary: Genesis*, 28. See also Clause Westerman, *Genesis 1–11: A Commentary*, trans. John Scullion (Minneapolis, MN: Augsburg Publishing House, 1984), 263 and Fretheim, "Genesis," 363.

CHAPTER ONE

Blaming Eve

> Why did the serpent not attack the man, rather than the woman? You say he went after her because she was the weaker of the two. On the contrary. In the transgression of the commandment, she showed herself to be the stronger, truly the man's 'assistance'. For she alone stood up to the serpent. She ate from the tree, but with resistance and dissent, and after being dealt with perfidiously. But Adam partook of the fruit given by the woman, without even beginning to make a fight, without a word of contradiction—a perfect demonstration of consummate weakness and a cowardly soul.
>
> —Pseudo-Irenaeus

THE FIRST THREE chapters of Genesis were clearly written by authors located within patriarchal cultures. Yet, in retrospect, what might be most notable about these chapters is the relative egalitarianism in their treatment of sex and gender. Both male and female are created in the image of God. Adam is created first, but the term describing Eve as Adam's "helper" (עֵזֶר) (Gen 2:18) does not imply inferiority. God could similarly "help" humanity (e.g., Exod 18:4, Ps 146:5). Indeed, as we have seen, what Adam was primarily in need of was sociality, and Eve is appropriate to fulfill this need exactly because of her similarity to Adam (she is flesh of his flesh). Misogyny is clearly in play when part of Eve's punishment consists of being ruled by her husband. But even here we should note that this is not posited as the original or ideal relation between the two. Humans are not, to borrow Aristotle's term, "political animals" in that they are naturally made for hierarchical relationships. As such, there is room in later Judaism and Christianity for ideals of return to original equality: for example, in Christ there is no male and female (Gal 3:28).

Most relevant for our purposes, however, is the lack of explicit distinction in responsibility for sin. Just as Adam existed first, and yet we find no inequality between the two, Eve sins first and yet we find the two to be equal in their responsibility for sinning. Sin came into the world through a man *and* a woman (and a snake!). Perhaps equality in failure is not the most desirable of equalities, but it is none the less a form of equality. Unfortunately, it was not an equality that was to go unmolested in later generations.

The stories of Adam and Eve do not appear to have played a significant role through most of the period during which the Hebrew Scriptures were written. References to Adam and Eve in pre–Second Temple literature are rare, and those that exist fail to address the themes with which we are interested. The Second Temple period witnessed a revitalization of interest in the narrative of Adam and Eve. And here we find the role of Eve corrupted. Quite far from Paul's eventual claim that sin came into the world through a man, blame in almost all extant texts before Paul falls disproportionately on Eve. "In this late pre-Christian Jewish literature there is . . . the tendency to exalt Adam. . . . But whereas Adam is thus extolled, sin, death, and evil are traced to Eve."[1]

In what follows I will provide a survey of documents associated with Second Temple Judaism. This survey establishes the pattern of blaming Eve. It also reveals the strangeness of Paul's formula. We do not find, prior to Paul, formulas that claim that sin came into the world through Adam. Nor do we find the character of Adam used as a synecdoche for the broader Genesis narrative or the activities of (the serpent and) Adam and Eve. Nor do we find Adam treated as a type or symbol for all of humanity in the act of sin. As I shall note in the next chapter, there is some evidence from documents after Paul that there was possibly a tradition of identifying sin with Adam that was developing in Paul's era. But we do not find that tradition represented in any documents that might have existed prior to Paul.

The texts in my survey are selected because they likely fit into the relevant period that preceded Paul's writing and because they include substantive references to Adam, Eve, and sin. The window of time we are interested in starts with texts written after 200 BCE and ends with texts that were possibly written before 70 CE. The 70 CE date is useful because it provides an oft-referenced point in dating first century documents: the destruction of the Second Temple.[2]

My primary purpose in the chapter is to document the misplacement of Eve via blame. My secondary purpose is to highlight the strangeness of Paul's formula, which is articulated near the end of the Second Temple period. Since my secondary claim is negative (i.e., no text prior to Paul offers a formula where sin is attributed exclusively to Adam) it strengthens my argument if I am more rather than less inclusive regarding selection of texts for review. As such, so long

1. Joseph A. Fitzmyer, *Paul and His Theology: A Brief Sketch*, 2nd ed. (Englewood Cliffs, NJ: Prentice Hall, 1989), 73. See also Kugel, *Traditions of the Bible*, 100–103; Gérard-Henry Baudry, "La Responsabilité d'Eve Dans La Chute. Analyse d'une Tradition," *Mélanges de Science Religieuse* 53, no. 3 (1996): 293–320.

2. See John R. Levison, "Portraits of Adam in Early Judaism: From Sirach to 2 Baruch," *Journal for the Study of the Pseudepigrapha*, Supplement Series 1 (Sheffield: Sheffield Academic Press, 1988): 29–31. My criteria for inclusion are similar to those deployed by Levison. However because my interest is in traditions that may have come before Paul, I end my window of interest at 70 CE rather than 135 CE. In my effort to be inclusive, I treat the Sibylline Oracles, the Book of Similitudes, and 2 Enoch where Levison did not. I am sensitive to Levison's argument that Second Temple Jewish documents deserve to be interpreted independent of their relevance to Christian concerns, but I also see value in studying them in the light of Christian concerns for delimited purposes. This is how I would locate this study.

as there is a notable coterie of scholars that places the text within my window, I include it here. If any reader estimates that texts that are included fall outside my date window or are too marred by later interpolation to be trustworthy, they are free to disregard those sections.

In terms of order, I generally proceed from earlier to later texts with the qualification that, on many, the possible date ranges for original production are so wide that the ordering does not make any difference. In an exception to my general rule, I reserve the treatment of The Wisdom of Solomon and *Liber Antiquitatum Biblicarum* for last because they are the texts that most rigorously test my claim about the uniqueness of Paul's formula.

The Wisdom of Jesus son of Sirach (Ben Sira)

James Dunn labels Ben Sira as "the most important of the deuterocanonical Jewish writings."[3] Unlike most of the other works noted in this survey, for this source we have a reliable account of its author (Ben Sira) and its date of origination (c. 180 BCE). It would have been available in Hebrew and Greek languages by 116 BCE.[4]

Ben Sira shows an interest in the Genesis narrative, though he was anything but a slave to the original text. He deviates so far from Genesis that he claims that after God creates humans, "With wisdom and knowledge he fills them; good and evil he shows them" (17.7).[5] This appears to be both a reference to and a rejection of the tradition in Genesis that Adam and Eve were denied access to the Tree of the Knowledge of Good and Evil. Sira's concern here is primarily to establish that human beings (even the first human beings) are morally responsible for their actions.[6] Knowledge of the law is, Sira believes, a precondition of responsibility, as is freedom.[7] "It was he [God], from the first, when he created humankind, who made them subject to their own free choice" (15.14).

---

3. James D.G. Dunn, *The Theology of Paul the Apostle* (Grand Rapids, MI: Eerdmans, 2008), 84.

4. Chris W. Lee, *Death Warning in the Garden of Eden: The Early Reception History of Genesis 2:17*, Forschungen Zum Alten Testament. 2. Reihe 115 (Tübingen: Mohr Siebeck, 2020), 117.

5. Alexander Di Lella calls v7b "a clear allusion to Gen 2: 17 and 3:5, 22." This quote and all translations for Ben Sira are taken from Patrick William Skehan and Alexander A. Di Lella, eds., *The Wisdom of Ben Sira: A New Translation with Notes*, The Anchor Bible 39 (New Haven, CT: Yale University Press, 2007), 282. See also Levison, *Portraits of Adam in Early Judaism*, 37.

6. See Shane Berg, "Ben Sira, the Genesis Creation Accounts, and the Knowledge of God's Will," *Journal of Biblical Literature* 132.1 (2013): 139–157; also Levison, *Portraits of Adam in Early Judaism*, 34–35.

7. On whether or not Ben Sira wis a compatibilist concerning free will and divine predestination, see Skehan and Di Lella, *The Wisdom of Ben Sira*, 81–83 and Xi Li, "Ben Sira on the Free

Sira's emphasis on responsibility begins in Eden, but it was targeted at contemporary Jews whom he wanted to claim also had the freedom and knowledge to do right if they wished. As such, we are here quite far from any doctrine of original sin. Yet, some verses appear to refer to the ongoing punishment meted out in Genesis: "A great anxiety has God allotted, and a heavy yoke, to the children of Adam: From the day a person leaves his mother's womb to the day he returns to the mother of all the living" (40.1).[8] One verse may even reference the punishment of death: "All flesh grows old, like a garment; the age-old law is: all must die" (14.17), though interpretation of the verse is contested.[9]

So, who, if anyone, is responsible for sin? One verse has led some scholars to conclude that Sira is "the earliest extant witness to the view that Eve was responsible for the introduction of sin and death."[10] In the middle of a section on the dangers of life with an "evil wife" Sira writes: "In a woman was sin's beginning: on her account we all die" (25.24).

There has been significant debate concerning whether the author intended to refer to Eve in this verse, or more generally to an abstracted evil wife.[11] There is no doubt that the verse reflects more of Sira's misogyny

---

Will Problem: A Comparison with Chrysippus," *Harvard Theological Review* 114, no. 3 (July 2021): 328–345.

8. Compare to Gen 3:17–20. "And to the man he said, 'Because you have listened to the voice of your wife, and have eaten of the tree about which I commanded you, "You shall not eat of it", cursed is the ground because of you; in toil you shall eat of it all the days of your life; thorns and thistles it shall bring forth for you; and you shall eat the plants of the field. By the sweat of your face you shall eat bread until you return to the ground, for out of it you were taken; you are dust, and to dust you shall return.' The man named his wife Eve, because she was the mother of all who live." Clause Westerman connects the two verses. Claus Westermann, *Genesis 1–11: A Continental Commentary* (Minneapolis, MN: Fortress Press, 1994), 268. Though whether this is a reference to Eve is debated.

9. Compare to Gen 2:16–17 "And the Lord God commanded the man, 'You may freely eat of every tree of the garden; but of the tree of the knowledge of good and evil you shall not eat, for in the day that you eat of it you shall die.'" Ben Sira has been widely read as viewing death as a natural part of creation. See John R. Levison, "Is Eve to Blame? A Contextual Analysis of Sirach 25:24," *The Catholic Biblical Quarterly* 47, no. 4 (October 1985): 617–623; Levison, *Portraits of Adam in Early Judaism*, 33–48; and John J. Collins, "Before The Fall: The Earliest Interpretations of Adam and Eve," in *The Idea of Biblical Interpretation: Essays in Honor of James L. Kugel*, ed. Hindy Najman and Judith Newman, vol. 83, Supplements to the Journal for the Study of Judaism (Leiden: Brill, 2004), 296–301. For a subtle treatment of the whole issue, see Lee, *Death Warning in the Garden of Eden*, 115–136.

10. John J. Collins, *Jewish Wisdom in the Hellenistic Age*, The Old Testament Library (Louisville, KY: Westminster John Knox Press, 1997), 67.

11. For challenges to the claim that the verse refers to Eve, see Theresa Ann Ellis, "Is Eve the 'Woman' in Sirach 25:24," *The Catholic Biblical Quarterly* 73.4 (October 2011): 723–42, and

than a careful exegesis of Genesis.[12] And if this verse and verse 14.17 refer to some kind of death as a punishment for the human race, this would be a very early statement of this tradition.[13] As such, there are serious questions about whether the text should be read in this way. Even with these qualifications noted, by the late first century BCE, once a more robust tradition had developed around blaming Eve, it would have been reasonable for the verse to be read as indicting Eve, even if that was not the original intent. This is especially clear concerning the Greek translation of the verse.[14] For our purposes, it is sufficient to say that either Sira has nothing to say on our topic, or that Sira directly or indirectly lays blame on Eve. There is clearly nothing close to a parallel to Paul's formula.

The Book of Jubilees

Generally accepted to date from the second century BCE, The Book of Jubilees is a window into Second Temple Judaism under the pressures of Hellenism.[15] Retelling the stories of the Bible, including the story of creation, the text ties the narrative to Levitical legal tradition by making it a repository of examples of particular laws.[16] This often requires restatement of, or significant additions to, the biblical text. For instance, in the Jubilees narrative, Adam and Eve begin outside of the garden of Eden and are only brought in when they have passed standards of purity that were later required for temple admittance (3.9–14).

The story of Adam and Eve is retold in a way that minimizes the lasting impact of their sin. The book posits what Todd Hanneken has called "realized

---

Levison, "Is Eve to Blame?" 617–623. Levison argues that the 'woman" is simply the "evil wife" who (hyperbolically) brings death to her husband. Without providing an argument, Di Lella notes his disagreement with Levison's interpretation. Skehan and Di Lella, *The Wisdom of Ben Sira*, 349. Ellis proposes that the text may refer to Pandora of Greek myth.

12. Collins, "Before the Fall," 289; Skehan and Di Lella, *The Wisdom of Ben Sira*, 90–92; Pamela Eisenbaum, "Sirach," in Newsom and Ringe, eds., *Women's Bible Commentary*, Expanded ed (Louisville, KY: Westminster John Knox Press, 1998), 289–304.

13. Kelly, "Adam Citings before the Intrusion of Satan," 13–28.

14. On the differences between the Hebrew and Greek versions of the verse, see Ellis, "Is Eve the 'Woman' in Sirach 25:24," 723–742.

15. Michael Segal, *The Book of Jubilees: Rewritten Bible, Redaction, Ideology and Theology*, Supplements to the Journal for the Study of Judaism 117 (Boston: Brill, 2007), 35–41.

16. Segal, 47–58; James L. Kugel, *A Walk through Jubilees: Studies in the Book of Jubilees and the World of Its Creation*, Supplements to the Journal for the Study of Judaism 156 (Boston: Brill, 2012), 37–43.

justice."[17] Moral failing is punished relatively quickly and effectively, thus removing the potential for any doctrine of original sin. The author even holds that God enforced the threatened penalty of death upon Adam and did so in an appropriately timely manner. In Genesis, God had threatened that if Adam and Eve ate from the tree, they would die on that day (Gen 2:17). Drawing on Psalm 90:4, the author of Jubilees takes a "day" to equal a thousand years. Since Adam is said to have lived 930 years, his death made the cut (Jub. 4.30).[18]

Thus, we certainly do not find original sin in Jubilees. What we do find once we sort out the justification of Levitical law is a retelling of the Genesis narrative that presents Adam in the best light possible. Genesis 3:8–1, where Adam and Eve are found naked, is excluded from Jubilees, possibly because these verses "present Adam as cowardly and guilty" in contrast to the author's wish to present him as an honorable patriarch.[19] And in Jubilees 3.26–32, after being sent out from Eden, the story of Adam is augmented to include a vignette where Adam offers a sacrifice to God, thus locating Adam as a patriarch and the first priest in a tradition that continues through to Israel.[20]

As concerns Eve, there are fewer changes to the text. After eating the fruit, Eve dresses herself in leaves before going to Adam. This slight change is probably intended to advocate modesty (3.21, see also 3.31). The text faithfully records from Genesis that Eve ate the fruit first, she then offered it to her husband. The most significant addition to the scene of punishment is the authors note that God "was angry with the woman" for her part in the narrative (3.23). No similar note is added concerning Adam.

The Sibylline Oracles

Originally attributed to a legendary, aged prophetess (Sybil), the Sibylline Oracles proliferated across the ancient world. Eventually "the Sybil" came to be used as a title for a series of seers. As the authority of the Sybils spread, different Oracles were associated with various locations (the Persian Sybil, Libyan Sybil, Delphic Sybil, and so on). In the process, the oracles and the identity of the Sybil could be shaped to fit regional predilections. The Jewish Sybil was said to be Noah's daughter-in-law, though she was still recognized to be a pagan. This gave her ostensible culturally independent authority, which was useful for apologetic purposes.

17. Todd Russell Hanneken, *The Subversion of the Apocalypses in the Book of Jubilees*, Early Judaism and Its Literature 34 (Atlanta, GA: Society of Biblical Literature, 2012), 31–38.

18. For text with translation and commentary, see James C Vanderkam, trans., *Book of Jubilees: A Critical Text.*, Corpus Scriptorum Christianorum Orientalium 511 (Lovanii: Peeters, 2001).

19. Levison, *Portraits of Adam in Early Judaism*, 92.

20. Kugel, *A Walk through Jubilees*, 42–44; Levison, *Portraits of Adam in Early Judaism*, 93–95.

The first two books of the Jewish/Christian Sybil are a unit that includes an earlier Jewish collection heavily interpolated by later Christian authors. While dating of the distinct parts of the two books is by no means certain, John J. Collins provides arguments that the first part of Book 1, with which we are interested, was written between 30 BCE and 70 CE, with the most likely dating at the turn of the era.[21]

Given the ostensibly female source for the Sibylline Oracles, it may be surprising that the treatment of the Genesis narrative comes across with as much androcentrism as it does. God created "lovely Eve, a wedded wife, whom he bestowed on him to live in Eden" (1.29–30).[22] For a while the couple lived happily, but "an evil snake deceived them into entering Death's domain and learning knowledge of both good and ill. But she, the woman, first betrayed the man; she gave, and tempted the unknowing man to sin. Coaxed by the woman's words, he quite forgot his immortal Maker, broke his clear commands" (1.39–45).

The next verse goes on to specify that in God's punishment, "ill, not good, they got, for what they did" (1.46). Thus, their guilt is certainly shared. As throughout the era, we lack a theory of original sin. But there can be no doubt that it was Eve who committed the first sin by eating the fruit, and even the second by betraying her husband. As J. B. Lightfoot notes, "Since the Sibyl omits the colloquy with the serpent, no rationale is or can be offered for the woman's treachery."[23] In contrast, Adam is partially exonerated by his "unknowing."

The Book of Similitudes (1 Enoch 37–71)

The Book of Similitudes is one of a set of manuscripts that came eventually to form the composite work 1 Enoch. While thematically related, the composite pieces were likely written at separate times and in different social contexts. Ephraim Isaac suggests that Similitudes was added to the Book of Enoch by the end of the first century CE.[24] James Davila notes a consensus that it was written in the first century BCE or CE, but himself favors a date early in the first century CE.[25]

---

21. See Collins's introduction to Books 1 and 2 in James H. Charlesworth, ed., *The Old Testament Pseudepigrapha. Vol. 1* (Garden City, NY: Doubleday, 1983), 331.

22. Translation taken from J. L. Lightfoot, ed., *The Sibylline Oracles: With Introduction, Translation, and Commentary on the First and Second Books* (New York: Oxford University Press, 2007). I have removed poetic line breaks and capitalization.

23. Lightfoot, 345.

24. See his introduction to the text in Charlesworth, *The Old Testament Pseudepigrapha. Vol. 1*, 7. All translations for 1 Enoch are taken from this source.

25. J. R. Davila, "The Similitudes of Enoch" (Lecture, University of St. Andrews, March 2, 2007), https://otp.wp.st-andrews.ac.uk/abstracts-lectures/the-similitudes-of-enoch/ Accessed July 2, 2022.

Following the overall pattern of 1 Enoch, Similitudes does not lay the blame for sin or death primarily on humanity. The Book of the Watchers, a section of 1 Enoch written before the Book of Similitudes, notes a version of the Genesis story very briefly, including Adam and Eve being "driven from the garden" (32.6). But it provides no explanation for the cause of their exile and appears unaware of any wider significance to the tale.[26] Rather, The Book of the Watchers focuses its account of evil in the world on the actions of a group of fallen angels who start a domino effect that corrupts the whole of creation.[27]

The Book of Similitudes follows a similar pattern and would be of little interest to the present argument except for one verse. While discussing the "chiefs" of the fallen angels, it relates the following brief note:

> The third was named Gader'el; this one is he who showed the children of the people all the blows of death, who misled Eve, who showed the children of the people (how to make) the instruments of death (such as) the shield, the breastplate, and the sword for warfare, and all (the other) instruments of death to the children of the people. Through their agency (death) proceeds against the people who dwell upon the earth, from that day forevermore (69.6–8).

The text here clearly represents a unique tradition concerning Eden, one where the fallen angel involved is identified differently than in later lore. And it locates the fallen angels as more responsible than the humans in bringing about evil and death in the world. Still, it is notable that even with all the variations to the Genesis narrative, it is Eve who is remembered as misled.

The Apocalypse of Moses

The Apocalypse of Moses was likely written in the first century CE.[28] The text relates the story of Adam and Eve from their own perspectives. In it, the story

---

26. Collins, "Before the Fall," 305.

27. On the various accounts of evil in 1 Enoch, see Michael Stone, "The Axis of History at Qumran," in *Pseudepigraphic Perspectives: The Apocrypha and Pseudepigrapha in Light of the Dead Sea Scrolls*, ed. Esther G. Chazon, Michael Stone, and Avital Pinnick, Studies on the Texts of the Desert of Judah 31 (Leiden: Brill, 1999), 133–149.

28. M. D. Johnson states that "the most natural span for the original composition would be between 100 B.C. and A.D. 200, more probably toward the end of the first Christian century." See his introduction to the text in James H. Charlesworth, ed., *The Old Testament Pseudepigrapha, Vol. 2* (Garden City, NY: Doubleday, 1985), 252. Translations of the text of The Apocalypse of Moses are taken from this source. James Dunn writes that "an original cannot be

of originating sin foregrounds Eve's role.[29] Seth comes to Adam, who is suffering from sickness and pain, and inquires as to how this state came to be. Adam responds: "When God made us, me and your mother, through whom I am dying, he gave us every plant in Paradise, but concerning one he commanded us not to eat of it, (for) we would die by it" (7.1). In addition to the explicit blaming of Eve, it is notable that Adam claims here that both he and Eve were given the command not to eat, a point never stated in Genesis. Adam then continues to explain that the devil waited until he and the angels protecting Eve were gone before approaching her (7.2–3). Unlike Genesis, this explicitly removes Adam from the scene when the serpent arrives, thus eliminating any question about his culpability for silence in the scene.

While sitting at Adam's deathbed, Eve claims responsibility: "This has happened to you through me; because of me you suffer troubles and pain" (9.1). Adam then sends Eve on a quest to gain oil from paradise to anoint him. On the way, Eve's son Seth is set upon by a wild beast. Eve weeps, saying, "Woe is me! For when I come to the day of resurrection, all who have sinned will curse me, saying that Eve did not keep the command of God" (10.2–3). The beast, gifted with speech, agrees: "O Eve, neither your greed nor your weeping are due to us, but to you, since the rule of the beasts has happened because of you. How is it that your mouth was opened to eat from the tree concerning which God commanded you not to eat from it? Through this also our nature was changed" (11.1–3). After Eve returns from the failed quest, again Adam asks the accusatory question: "Why have you wrought destruction among us and brought upon us great wrath, which is death gaining rule over all our race?" (14.2–3)

At this point, the narrative shifts into Eve's own telling of the story of the fall. In this narrative, the devil makes a pact with the serpent, that they might make Adam "to be cast out of Paradise through his wife" (16.3). Approaching Eve

---

dated more accurately than between 200BCE and 100CE, but there may well have been a version prior to Paul, and its midrashic rather than allegorical treatment suggests a provenance within the land of Israel. Our current texts could therefore reflect traditions and speculations about Adam and Eve known to Paul." Dunn, *The Theology of Paul the Apostle*, 87 n.32. For extended arguments on dating see Michael Stone, *A History of the Literature of Adam and Eve*, SBL Early Judaism and Its Literature 3 (Atlanta, GA: Scholars Press, 1992), 53–58.

29. John L Sharpe asserts that in The Apocalypse of Moses the "fallen Adam" and "Adam restored to glory in the eschaton" represent a parallel to Paul's treatment of the old and new Adam. We will return to this theme in the next chapter. While clearly aware of Eve's central role in The Apocalypse, typical of so many biblical scholars, he makes no note about Eve's absence in Paul's narrative. See John Sharpe, "The Second Adam in the Apocalypse of Moses," *The Catholic Biblical Quarterly* 35, no. 1 (January 1973): 35–46. On the central role of Eve's sin, see M.D. Johnson's introduction to the text in Charlesworth, *The Old Testament Pseudepigrapha, Vol. 2*; Fitzmyer, *Paul and His Theology*, 73. See also Dunn, *The Theology of Paul the Apostle*, 87–88.

from beyond the walls of paradise, the devil tempts Eve and Eve opens the gate to let him in (19.1).[30] After eating of the tree (19.3) she speaks to Adam "unlawful words of transgression such as brought us down from great glory" (21.2–3). Upon realizing what has happened when he eats of the tree, Adam exclaims: "O evil woman! Why have you wrought destruction among us?" (21.6)

As her telling of the narrative concludes, Eve falls to the ground, saying, "I have sinned, O God; I have sinned, O Father of all; I have sinned against you, I have sinned against your chosen angels, I have sinned against the cherubim, I have sinned against your steadfast throne; I have sinned, LORD, I have sinned much; I have sinned before you, and all sin in creation has come about through me" (32.1–3).

The text concludes with the promise of resurrection. Even if relief from suffering does not take place in this life, God has mercy upon the dead. In turn both Adam and Eve are taken up to heaven and buried in paradise to await the recreation of the world (37–43).

The issue of responsibility for sin in the Apocalypse is not entirely clear cut. Narratively, the devil bears some responsibility.[31] And Adam, for all his blaming of Eve, eventually admits to his own sin. Before his death, he goes as far as to claim to "alone have sinned" (27.2). And he is explicitly convicted of his own sin by God (39.1–2). These indications of Adam's guilt, however, come late in the text and are best understood in the light of his immanent redemption. The

30. Though, this verse may be a later mistranslation. See S. T. Lachs, "Some Textual Observations on the Apocalypsis Mosis and the Vita Adae et Evae," *Journal for the Study of Judaism in the Person, Hellenistic, and Roman Period* 13, no. 1/2 (December 1982): 175.

31. John Levison, Marinus de Jonge, and Johannes Tromp have all rightly argued that the issue of responsibility for sin in this text is complex. See John R. Levison, "The Exoneration of Eve in the Apocalypse of Moses," *Journal for the Study of Judaism in the Person, Hellenistic, and Roman Period* 20, no. 2 (December 1989): 135–150; Marinus de Jonge and Johannes Tromp, *The Life of Adam and Eve and Related Literature*, Guides to Apocrypha and Pseudepigrapha (Sheffield, UK: Academic Press, 1997), 52–54. The devil is doubtless the agent behind much of the action; eliciting an oath from Eve to feed the fruit to Adam before she has done it herself (19.1–2) and being cast by Eve's narrative as having spoken to Adam through her (21:3). Levinson argues that such qualifications mark chapters 15–30, which he sees as an earlier text which "exonerates" Eve, in contrast to the surrounding texts (later additions) which "denigrate" her. The claim of "exoneration" is overstated. Even if Eve's character is softened in 15–30, she is still located as playing the key role in the narrative of the fall. She is deceived first. She swears the oath to the devil. She keeps her oath to the devil while violating the commandment of God. She begins her deception of Adam before the devil is said to speak through her (21.1–2). For Levison's later treatment of the same theme using a more fine grained analysis of different versions of the text, see his "The Exoneration and Denigration of Eve in the Greek Life of Adam and Eve" in Gary A Anderson, Michael E Stone, and Johannes Tromp, *Literature on Adam and Eve Collected Essays*, Studia in Veteris Testamenti Pseudepigrapha 15 (Boston: Brill, 2000), 251–276.

completeness of his confession is a sign of the goodness of his "true contrition."[32] God's explicit condemnation is voiced in the same sentence with his promise to turn Adam's sorrow to joy.

Eve too is redeemed by God's forgiveness in the end of the narrative. But her redemption story receives far less attention than did Adam's while the condemnations of Eve are, as shown above, numerous and consistent.[33] While there is no single figure that bears all the responsibility for sin in the Apocalypse, there is far more material in the text laying the blame on Eve than upon Adam or the devil.[34]

Vita Adae et Evae (The Life of Adam and Eve)

The Life of Adam and Eve (*Vita*) is a sister text to the Apocalypse of Moses. Both draw upon a common source for some chapters but add to this independent material. Given the emphasis on the sin of Eve in the Apocalypse, it may come as a surprise that of the two texts, the *Vita* offers the more negative portrayal of Eve.[35]

The narrative starts with Adam and Eve cast out of Eden and in need of food.[36] Eve asks Adam to kill her that he might be allowed back into paradise "for it is because of me that the Lord God is angry with you" (3.1–2). Adam rebukes her, not because she is wrong, but because it would be wrong for him to kill "his own flesh." What follows is, as Gary Anderson has pointed out, a parallel of the story of the fall locating Eve as the responsible partner.[37] Adam suggests that the two do penance. Eve, consistently pictured as ignorant in the text, asks what

32. Levison, *Portraits of Adam in Early Judaism*, 171.

33. Marinus de Jonge and Johannes Tromp suggest that the story of Adam's redemption "counterbalances" Eve's story of the beginning of death. Jonge and Tromp, *The Life of Adam and Eve and Related Literature*, 47, 49.

34. "Both texts [The Apocalypse and the Vita] repeatedly assert that sin has come to the human race through a woman." M. D. Johnson, "Introduction to the Life of Adam and Eve" in Charlesworth, *The Old Testament Pseudepigrapha, Vol. 2*, 252.

35. Levison, *Portraits of Adam in Early Judaism*, 171. Gary Anderson contends that later, likely Christian influenced versions of the text attempt to balance the responsibility for sin between Adam and Eve. This leaves the earlier versions as clearly placing the blame on Eve. See Gary Anderson, "The Penitence Narrative in the Life of Adam and Eve," in Anderson, Stone, and Tromp, *Literature on Adam and Eve*, 22–23.

36. Levison has argued that the denigration of Eve starts even here, where she is more motivated by hunger and Adam is more motivated by the wish for forgiveness. Levison, *Portraits of Adam in Early Judaism*, 175.

37. Gary Anderson, "The Punishment of Adam and Eve," in Anderson, Stone, and Tromp, *Literature on Adam and Eve*, 79–80.

this could mean. At this time, Adam (like God in Eden) gives Eve a command. The command is to do penance by standing neck deep in the Tigress River for thirty-seven days. In this command, Adam notes that, as an acknowledgement of Eve's weakness, he is not requiring her to do as much as he himself will do in penance. He will stand in the Jordan for 40 days, although as soon as he enters the Jordan river and confesses to sin, all the creatures of the Jordan come around him to protect him from the water. Adam, it appears, maintains his dominion over the world from the garden.[38] Eve receives no similar help.

Paralleling a common reading of the story of Eden (if one identifies Satan with the serpent), Satan now comes to Eve and tricks her. Making himself to look like an angel, he tells Eve she is forgiven and may cease her time of penance. Eve emerges from the water and goes to Adam. He is not deceived by Satan, but recognizes him immediately. Eve is then judged by Adam (as she and Adam were judged by God in Eden). "O Eve, Eve," Adam cries, "where is the work of your penitence? How have you again been seduced by our enemy by whom we have been deprived of our dwelling in Paradise and of spiritual joy?" (10.3–4). Eve has sinned a second time, violating her husband's command and thus violating God's given order after the fall ("your desire shall be for your husband, and he shall rule over you" [Gen 3:16b]). Eve then asks the devil why he pursues them so. The devil tells of his expulsion from heaven. When Adam was created, God commanded the angels to worship Adam as the image of God. Filled with envy, Satan refused, and thus was expelled. When this narrative is complete, Adam banishes the devil and completes his time of penitence.

Continuing the parallel to the Genesis narrative, now Eve leaves Adam (as Adam and Eve had left paradise), walking to the west and building a structure to live in. She leaves because of her sin. "You live on, my lord," says Eve to Adam. "Life is granted to you, since you have done neither the first nor the second error, but I have been cheated and deceived, for I have not kept the command of God. And now separate me from the light of such life, and I will go to the sunset and stay there until I die" (18.1–3).

At this point, the story gives up its last reference to Eden. Eve, pregnant, goes into labor and is afflicted with severe pain (echoing her punishment in Genesis 3:16—"I will greatly increase your pangs in childbearing; in pain you shall bring forth children"). Eve appeals to God for mercy. "But neither was she heard, nor was the mercy of God around her" (19.2). It is only when Adam prays for her that she is given relief. And, just to make the point explicit, the Angel Michael tells her, "Blessed are you, Eve, because of Adam. Since his prayers and utterances are many, I am sent to you that you might receive our help" (21.2–3).

As the story continues, it comes to overlap with the Apocalypse of Moses. But at several points the failure of Eve is stressed even more. Where Adam in

38. Levison, *Portraits of Adam in Early Judaism*, 176.

the Apocalypse charges Eve with bringing death, the Adam of *Vita* charges her with bringing not only death, but sin (Apocalypse 14, Vita 44). There are also hints in his condemnation that Adam finds himself guiltless.[39] In Eve and Seth's encounter with the beast in *Vita*, the beast is said to be a serpent, suggesting Satanic identity.[40] Yet again, Eve is unable to identify the enemy, calling him "cursed beast" and asking how he has the courage and strength to attack her son, the image of God (37.3). Seth, in contrast, has no problem recognizing Satan. He rebukes the beast, calling it the "cursed enemy of truth, chaotic destroyer" (39.2). In contrast to the Apocalypse, where Seth and Eve were simply denied oil, here they receive immediate promises that Adam's soul will be saved after death (43.2–3). The narrative ends with the death of Adam and Eve. For Adam, there is an extended narrative in which the sun, moon, and stars are darkened (46.1) and his son is able to witness the ascent of his soul to heaven. For Eve, we learn only that in the middle of prayer she gave up the spirit (52.3). There can be no question in the *Vita* that the sin of Eden is assigned primarily to Eve.[41]

2 Enoch

2 Enoch is a late Second Temple text which for most of its modern life had only been known to exist in medieval Slavonic translations. But recently, a version was also found in Coptic.[42] Andrei Orlov argues that the original dates from the turn of the era between BCE and CE,[43] and there are many reasons to think that it was highly influential in early Christianity.

Scholarly study of the Genesis narrative in relation to 2 Enoch has typically focused on the contrast between Adam and Enoch. Because this is a potential source for a first/second Adam model, we shall have to return to this in the next chapter. However, for current purposes, we need to focus on a point that is consistently overlooked in this area of scholarship. While Enoch is often located by scholars as renewing humanity after Adam's fall, the text of Enoch does not foreground Adam in the story of the fall.

39. Levison, 176.

40. Levison, 176; M. D. Johnson note on 39.1 in Charlesworth, *The Old Testament Pseudepigrapha, Vol. 2*, 274.

41. Michael Stone, *The Penitence of Adam*, Corpus Scriptorum Christianorum Orientalium 430 (Lovanii: Peeters, 1981), xvi–xvii; Jonge and Tromp, *The Life of Adam and Eve and Related Literature*, 58–61.

42. See Joost L. Hagen, "No Longer Slavonic Only: 2 Enoch Attested in Coptic from Nubia" in A. Orlov, Gabriele Boccaccini, and Jason Zurawski, eds., *New Perspectives on 2 Enoch: No Longer Slavonic Only*, Studia Judaeoslavica 4 (Boston: Brill, 2012), 7–36.

43. Andrei Orlov, "The Sacerdotal Traditions of 2 Enoch and the Date of the Text," in Orlov, Boccaccini, and Zurawski, *New Perspectives on 2 Enoch*, 103–116.

In the story of the creation of Eve, 2 Enoch sets the stage: "I imposed sleep upon him, and he fell asleep. And while he was sleeping, I took from him a rib. And I created for him a wife, so that death might come by his wife" (30.17). And in the story of the originating sin, the book emphasizes the guilt of Eve and at least partially exonerates Adam. The text tells us of the devil's fall and scheming against Adam. The devil "corrupted Eve. But Adam he did not contact. But on account of [her] nescience I cursed him" (31.5–7).[44]

Philo of Alexandria

For only the second time in our survey, we find a text for which we have concrete information on both dating and authorship. Philo was a diaspora Jew who lived in Alexandria, Egypt. He was born in the last two decades of the first century BCE and lived until the middle of the first century CE. While Philo treats Adam and Eve in multiple texts, an exposition of one will be sufficient to make our points here. *On the Creation of the Cosmos According to Moses* was written sometime between 30 and 40 CE.[45]

Deeply influenced by Greco-Roman philosophy, Philo's approach to Adam and Eve was significantly different from the other authors in this survey. He was focused on an allegorical reading of the text, in which Adam, Eve, and the Serpent represented different facets of the human self. In fact, Philo leaves his account so abstract that he does not even use Adam and Eve's proper names.[46] For ease of reference, I will insert the names.

For Philo, Adam represents the highest human faculty and power: mind and reason. In his creation, he was glorious. According to Philo, he named the animals with absolute precision:

> the rational nature in his soul was still uncorrupted, and not a single weakness or disease or passion had found its way in. So he took in wholly unblemished impressions of things material and immaterial, and made appellations that were accurate, taking aim in excellent fashion at what was revealed, so that their natures were pronounced and understood at the very same time (§149).

---

44. The "her" in this passage is not found in all manuscripts. But even without this word, as Brevard Child notes: "The point is emphasized that the devil seduced Eve, but did not touch Adam." Brevard Childes, "Adam," in *Interpreter's Dictionary of the Bible* (Nashville, KY: Abingdon Press, 1962), 43.

45. "Introduction" in Philo of Alexandria and David T. Runia, *On the Creation of the Cosmos According to Moses: Introduction, Translation and Commentary*, Philo of Alexandria Commentary Series 1 (Boston: Brill, 2001), 4. All translations of On the Creation are taken from this source.

46. Philo of Alexandria and Runia, 333.

Corruption, however, was on its way. And it was on its way in the form of Eve. Philo foreshadows what is to come, writing that the "starting-point of a blameworthy life becomes for him woman" (§151). This is because Eve represents sensation. This creates a set of contrasts. Adam is associated with the higher world of intellect, Eve with the inferior material world: Adam with action, Eve with passivity. (Notably, an exact inversion of their qualities in the Genesis narrative!) Yet, sensation is not in itself evil. Indeed, it is a "faculty inferior to reason but most necessary to mankind,"[47] and is a good inasmuch as it is controlled by the mind.[48] Thus, when Eve "modestly responded" to Adam's first greeting, Adam and she began a (apparently non-sexual) loving relationship.[49] But corruption is in the offing.

> The love that ensues brings together the two separate halves of a single living being as it were, and joins them into unity, thereby establishing in both a desire for union with the other in order to produce a being similar to themselves. But this desire also gave rise to bodily pleasure, which is the starting-point of wicked and lawbreaking deeds, and on its account they exchange the life of immortality and well-being for the life of mortality and misfortune (§152).

It is notable that in this telling, pleasure (which will be identified with the Serpent) is produced by the slippage from love to desire between mind and sensation.

Now, the trees in the garden are taken to be potential objects of attraction, and God is using two of them to test Adam and Eve. The Tree of Life represents the highest good: "reverence for God." The Tree of the Knowledge of Good and Evil represents the lower good of "practical insight" or "cunning" (§154, 155). Turning toward the one is turning upward toward the highest good of contemplation of the intellectual world, while turning toward the other is turning toward the lower, material world of contingency and change.

Now pleasure (the Serpent) enters the story to trick Eve.[50] He focuses Eve on the ephemeral appearance of taste and sight of the fruit. "Without further

47. Mireille Hadas-Lebel, *Philo of Alexandria: A Thinker in the Jewish Diaspora*, Studies in Philo of Alexandria 7 (Boston: Brill, 2012), 132.

48. Maren Niehoff, *Philo of Alexandria: An Intellectual Biography*, The Anchor Yale Bible Reference Library (New Haven, CT: Yale University Press, 2018), 131–132, 202.

49. Maren Niehoff notes that this is a more positive image of Eve than Philo presents elsewhere. Niehoff, 138–139.

50. On the nature of the serpent as pleasure, see §157–166; Philo of Alexandria, Albert C. Geljon, and David T. Runia, *Philo of Alexandria, On Cultivation: Introduction, Translation,*

reflection, as the result of an unstable and unsettled conviction, she consented to the idea, ate of the fruit and shared it with her husband" (§156). (Again, contrast with Eve's perception and desire for wisdom in Genesis).

In Philo's later expansion on this part of the story, he explains:

> Pleasure does not dare to offer her tricks and deceits to the man, but rather to the woman and through her to him. This is said quite suitably and appropriately, for in us the intellect has the role of man, while sense-perception has that of woman. Pleasure encounters and consorts with the senses first, and through them she deceives the ruling intellect as well (§165).

He goes on to liken pleasure (the Serpent) to a "shameless prostitute" who seeks out a "pimp" (sensation/Eve) to help lure the intellect (Adam) in (§166). In other texts, he suggests that the order of control may have been reversed, referring to the snake as "Eve's serpent."[51]

Philo's is certainly a different reading from the other offerings in this survey, but his appeal to allegory does not lead him to formulate an account in which Eve is removed from the chain of sin or Adam is solely culpable. John Levison concludes that in Philo's work, "The onus for the entrance of evil . . . falls upon the first woman rather than upon the first man."[52] When we return to this text in our discussion of Paul, we will find reason to qualify this conclusion. But there is no doubt that Philo fails to produce a formula similar to Paul's own, claiming that sin came into the world through one man. If the man had been left on his own, he would have been perfect.

The Wisdom of Solomon

The final two texts in this survey serve to test our thesis. At points each one of them in some sense omits Eve from the narrative of sin and foregrounds Adam.[53]

---

and Commentary, Philo of Alexandria Commentary Series 4 (Boston: Brill, 2013), 64, 185, 189, 196; Philo of Alexandria and Runia, *On the Creation of the Cosmos According to Moses*, 377.

51. See *Leg All*, 2.79. Philo of Alexandria, *Philo, Volume 1*, trans. F. H. Colson and G. H. Witaker, The Loeb classical library 226 (Cambridge, MA: Harvard University Press, 2004), 275.

52. Levison, *Portraits of Adam in Early Judaism*, 75.

53. H.C. Kee translation The Testament of the Twelve Patriarchs includes references to Adam in Testament of Simeon 6.6 and Testament of Levi 18.10. Charlesworth, *The Old Testament Pseudepigrapha. Vol. 1*. If these translations reflected the earliest versions of The Testament, they would mark a very early reference to Adam that appears to be in the tradition of Paul's later letters. But the Testament of Levi 18 is likely a later, Christian addition. See Robert A. Kugler,

Ultimately, however, they fail to go as far as Paul in claiming that sin entered the world through Adam. And they still contain traces of the theme of blaming Eve. Thus, they leave a significant step for Paul's formula in erasing Eve from the narrative.

Suggested dates for the Wisdom of Solomon can run as early as the third century BCE to as late as the second century CE. However, most scholars see it as having been written prior to any Christian scriptures, and many see it as directly influencing Christian thought from its earliest stages.[54]

In Wisdom we find the most developed account in this survey pointing to mortality being a punishment for sin. Created for immortality (2.23), "the ungodly by their words and deeds summoned death; considering him a friend, they pined away and made a covenant with him, because they are fit to belong to his company" (1.16).[55] At stake here is a form of spiritual life or death; life or death beyond death. According to Wisdom, "the righteous live forever, and their reward is with the Lord; the Most High takes care of them" (5.15). Further, Wisdom is comfortable setting the responsibility for sin with each individual who must choose for themself whether to follow God. So, yet again, we do not have a statement of original sin.

But Wisdom is interested in the Genesis narrative and refers to it obliquely several times. Eve's absence in the text is notable. "She [Lady Wisdom] protected the first formed father of the world, when he alone had been created; she delivered him from his transgression, and gave him strength to rule all things" (10.1). Elsewhere, the author of Wisdom uses creation from the earth as a metaphor relating to the development of idolatry. "With misspent toil, these workers form

---

The Testaments of the Twelve Patriarchs, Guides to Apocrypha and Pseudepigrapha (Sheffield, UK: Sheffield Academic Press, 2001), 52. The manuscript of The Testament of Simeon that Kee is translating 6.6 from includes the proper name Ἀδὰμ. At stake here is probably an original Hebrew text that used the term hā'āḏām (הָאָדָם). As R. H. Charles noted on the original Greek manuscripts "Tὸν 'Aδάμ is here used of the human race—a use intelligible in a translation from Hebrew but not in a piece of original Greek." R. H. Charles, *The Greek Version of the Testament of the Twelve Patriarchs* (Oxford: Clarendon Press, 1908), 24, n.41.

54. Joseph Dodson, *The "Powers" of Personification: Rhetorical Purpose in the "Book of Wisdom" and the Letter to the Romans*, Beihefte Zur Zeitschrift Für Die Neutestamentliche Wissenschaft 161 (New York: De Gruyter, 2008), 3–4; Francis Watson, *Paul and the Hermeneutics of Faith*, T&T Clark Cornerstones (London: Bloomsbury T&T Clark, 2016), 405; David A. DeSilva, *Introducing the Apocrypha: Message, Context, and Significance* (Grand Rapids, Michigan: Baker Academic, 2018), 150; C. Marvin Pate, *The Reverse of the Curse: Paul, Wisdom, and the Law*, Wissenschaftliche Untersuchungen Zum Neuen Testament 114 (Tübingen: Mohr Siebeck, 2000), 233; Richard B. Hays, "Wisdom according to Paul," in Stephen C. Barton, ed., *Where Shall Wisdom Be Found? Wisdom in the Bible, the Church, and the Contemporary World* (Edinburgh: T&T Clark, 1999), 112.

55. Translations of The Wisdom of Solomon are taken from the NRSV.

a futile god from the same clay — these mortals who were made of earth a short time before and after a little while go to the earth from which all mortals are taken, when the time comes to return the souls that were borrowed" (15.8).

There is no doubt here that the sin of Adam is foregrounded in this telling. But this must be qualified in several ways. First, the responsibility for Adam's sin is shared. Though verse 1.16, noted above, appears to put the onus for the "summoning" of death on wicked humans, Death (here personified) and the Devil also play key roles in instigating sin. "God created the man for incorruptibility and he made him to be the likeness of his own eternity; but through the envy of the Devil, Death entered into the cosmos, and those worthy of him experienced him" (2.23–24). Two important subpoints emerge here. First, there is a sense in which Adam is not the focus of the story of originating sin. Adam plays a part in a wider narrative of cosmic conflict between the Devil/Death and God/ Lady Wisdom.[56] Second, the reference to the devil's "envy" here appears to refer to the tradition, discussed in the Apocalypse of Moses, that the devil refused to bow down before Adam when God commanded it. As such, the author of Wisdom assumes that his reader knows a longer narrative of Adam, the Devil, and (presumably) Eve.[57]

Perhaps this is in part why Adam's trespass does not seem to bear the same weight as many others who have sinned. While Adam was saved by Lady Wisdom, his son Cain was not: "an unrighteous man departed from her [Wisdom] in his anger, he perished because in rage he killed his brother" (10.3). As several scholars have noted, the contrast between Adam and Cain begins a repeated pattern in the following verses where a righteous figure is saved while a wicked figure perishes.[58] Noah is saved while the wicked of the world perish, the same for Abraham/ the builders of the tower of Babel, Lot/the evil cities, Joseph/his brothers, and, ultimately, Israel/Egypt. This pattern does not exonerate Adam. Unlike most of the others who are saved, he is noted as having transgressed and is not labeled as righteous. Yet, his trespass is significantly qualified. He is saved by Lady Wisdom.

This leads to a final consideration. It is possible that, especially in the context of the established narrative, Eve's absence here is intended to indicate her faultiness. Wisdom is personified as a female. It is "She" who protects Adam. Is

56. Dodson, *The "Powers" of Personification*, 51–118; Ernst Käsemann, *New Testament Questions of Today* (Philadelphia: Fortress Press, 1969), 136; Yehoshua Amir, "The Figure of Death in the 'Book of Wisdom,'" *Journal of Jewish Studies* 30 (1979): 157; Collins, *Jewish Wisdom in the Hellenistic Age*, 189.

57. Dodson, *The "Powers" of Personification*, 65–68.

58. Moyna McGlynn, *Divine Judgement and Divine Benevolence in the Book of Wisdom* (Tübingen: Mohr Siebeck, 2001), 127–130. See also Francis Watson, *Paul and the Hermeneutics of Faith*, 386–391.

there an implicit contrast here between the faithfulness of Lady Wisdom and the failure of Eve? Andrew Glickman suggests that the "absence of the first woman from the retelling of Genesis 1–3 seems to stress the idea that Lady Wisdom and not Eve is the true 'suitable partner' for Adam since Wisdom delivered him from his sin and made him strong, while Eve did the opposite."[59] After all, the text locates Lady Wisdom as the ideal "bride, throne companion, and lover" (8.2, 9, 16).[60] Thus, rather than simply erasing Eve and locating the first sin with Adam, her absence from the story may function implicitly to incriminate her yet again.

Liber Antiquitatum Biblicarum, or Pseudo-Philo's Biblical Antiquities

The second text that tests our thesis is *Liber Antiquitatum Biblicarum* (LAB). While commonly transmitted through history with the works of Philo of Alexandria, it is by an anonymous author often labeled Pseudo-Philo. Dates assigned to the text range from the late second century BCE to the end of the first century CE with major arguments about whether it should be dated before or after the destruction of the temple in 70 CE. For the purposes of argument, I will count it in the pre-70 tradition that has set the limit of this survey, though nothing of immense importance rests on this assumption.

The depiction of sin in LAB is key to the text, and consistently foregrounds Adam's role. Amid a discussion between God and Moses about the Tent of Meeting (suggesting the Temple) and the establishment of holy days, there is a break where God reveals to his interlocutor the beauties of creation and paradise.

> And he said, "This is the place concerning which I taught the first man, saying, 'If you do not transgress what I have commanded you, all things will be subject to you.' But that man transgressed my ways and was persuaded by his wife; and she was deceived by the serpent. And then death was ordained for the generations of men." (13.8–9).[61]

Later in the text there is an extended story about Kenaz, a figure mentioned only briefly in the Bible (Judg 1:13). In this story a set of powerful precious stones

59. Andrew T. Glicksman, *Wisdom of Solomon 10: A Jewish Hellenistic Reinterpretation of Early Israelite History through Sapiential Lenses*, Deuterocanonical and Cognate Literature Studies 9 (Berlin: De Gruyter, 2011), 155, see also 110.

60. The quote here is taken from Sarah Tanzer as she summarizes the noted verses, "The Wisdom of Solomon," in Newsom and Ringe, *Women's Bible Commentary*, 296.

61. All translations of LAB are taken from Charlesworth, *The Old Testament Pseudepigrapha, Vol. 2.*

and books has been captured from the Amorites (LAB 25.10). The power of these relics is so great that they resist destruction by natural means, and only God is able to deal with them. At this point, Kenaz thanks God that humans have been protected from dealing with such power. Alluding to the idea that Adam had been given a view of the glories and powers of the world in paradise, Kenaz states, "Blessed be God, who . . . made Adam as the first created one and showed him everything so that when Adam sinned thereby, then he might refuse him all these things (for if he showed them to the whole human race, they might have mastery over them)" (26.6–7).[62]

A third substantive treatment of Adam can be found in chapter 37, which explores the effect of sin in corrupting the world. For, "when the first-formed was condemned to death, the earth was condemned to bring forth *thorns and thistles*" (37.3; see Gen 3:18). The text uses this phrasing to draw a contrast between Adam and Moses, who met God through a "thicket of thorns" (i.e., the burning bush).

There can be no doubt that each of these passages show, as C. T. R. Hayward states, "the abiding significance of Adam lies in his transgression."[63] The first passage lays blame on Adam before even mentioning Eve and the Serpent. The second suggests that Adam was tested on behalf of all humanity and failed. This is not the final word, as new opportunities for righteousness are offered through Noah and Moses. Thus again, this is not original sin. But there is a sense in which Adam's sin stands in for the potential sin of all humanity. Hayward further points out that the Adam passages tend to come up in cultic contexts, where Adam represents the curse that can be overcome by participation in the cult. And, perhaps in a rejection of earlier tradition, LAB never suggests that Adam performs a sacrifice or takes on the role of priest.[64]

LAB also appears to wish to vindicate the creation of Eve. In the only substantive passage dedicated to a discussion of the first woman, the text states: "Rejoice, earth, over those dwelling in you, because the knowledge of the Lord that builds a tower among you is present. Not unjustly did God take from you the rib of the first-formed, knowing that from his rib Israel would be born. Your forming will be a testimony of what the Lord has done for his people" (32.15–16).

As many scholars have noted, LAB often seems concerned to present positive views on women.[65] Mary Therese DesCamp has argued that these

62. On this passage, see Frederick J. Murphy, *Pseudo-Philo: Rewriting the Bible* (New York: Oxford University Press, 1993), 123–124.

63. C. T. R. Hayward, "The Figure of Adam in Pseudo-Philo's Biblical Antiquities," *Journal for the Study of Judaism in the Person, Hellenistic, and Roman Period* 23, no.1 (June 1992): 6.

64. Hayward, 6.

65. Pieter Willem van der Horst, "Portraits of Biblical Women in Pseudo-Philo's Liber Antiquitatum Biblicarum*," *Journal for the Study of the Pseudepigrapha* 3, no. 5 (October 1989):

positive views are developed in relation to the image of good Jewish mothers, wives, and daughters.[66] Here, as mother of Israel itself, Eve is made to fit into this mold.

Thus, LAB does present a more negative picture of Adam and a more positive picture of Eve than many other Second Temple texts. But, given the polemic interests of the author, perhaps we should be surprised that LAB does not take the further step that Paul will make; claiming that "sin came into the world through one man."

Even while minimizing Eve's role, LAB includes her and the devil in the story of the fall. As Frederick Murphy notes, here the "'feminism' of Pseudo-Philo, striking as it is, has its limitations."[67] And positive as the depiction of Eve is in 32.15–16, there is potentially a darker underbelly to the passage. As DesCamp suggests, the passage defends God against criticism: "Not unjustly did God take from you the rib of the first-formed." The implied criticism is that God should never have created Eve, given the trouble she made. The defense of God does not deny Eve's failings. It suggests that even with those failings, the creation of Eve was worthwhile because she became the mother of Israel. "This line acknowledges the complaint against Eve—and women—while making it clear that the taking of the rib was worth whatever trouble or difficulty it caused. The female capacity to give birth—specifically, birth to Israel—makes up for any difficulty or suffering that her presence brought about."[68]

So, rather than constituting a break with the tradition of foregrounding Eve's sin, LAB may be an example of how hard it was to break with this tradition.

Conclusions

Eve has lived a long literary life, but it has clearly not been an easy one. In this chapter we have traced out the first way in which her offspring betrayed her: by assigning to her disproportionate blame for originating sin. This theme does not die with the destruction of the Second Temple. It resurfaces many times in later

---

29–46; Cheryl Anne Brown, *No Longer Be Silent: First Century Jewish Portraits of Biblical Women*, Gender and the Biblical Tradition (Louisville, KY: Westminster/John Knox Press, 1992), 212–220; Mary Therese DesCamp, "Why Are These Women Here? An Examination of the Sociological Setting of Pseudo-Philo Through Comparative Reading," *Journal for the Study of the Pseudepigrapha* 8, no. 16 (July 1997): 53–80.

66. Mary Therese DesCamp, *Metaphor and Ideology: Liber Antiquitatum Biblicarum and Literary Methods through a Cognitive Lens*, Biblical Interpretation Series 87 (Boston: Brill, 2007), 314.

67. Murphy, *Pseudo-Philo: Rewriting the Bible*, 74. n. 77.

68. DesCamp, *Metaphor and Ideology*, 334–335.

Judaism and Christianity. Having traced it thus far, however, we will take leave of it for a while to look at our other noted alternative: erasing Eve.

Given the prevalence of blaming Eve, the emergence of a tradition omitting her from the narrative should be somewhat shocking to us. I have argued in this chapter that Paul presents us with the earliest extant writings representing this tradition. This does not necessarily mean that he was inventing this alternative. But even if his statement of the tradition is the proverbial tip of the iceberg, it is the visible bit with which we must start.

There is no doubt that patriarchy and misogyny played a significant role in the blaming of Eve in the sources treated in this chapter. Paul's formula was not intended as a feminist corrective to this tradition. So why did Paul decide to formulate his picture of sin coming into the world in the way that he did? And what new theological dangers did that formulation open up? These are the questions to which we turn in the next chapter.

CHAPTER TWO

Erasing Eve

> She is key to the situation. Take the snake, the fruit tree and the woman from the tableau, and we have no fall . . . hence no need of a Savior. Thus the bottom falls out of the whole Christian theology.
>
> —Elizabeth Cady Stanton. *The Woman's Bible*, xi.

WHILE WRITING *DE Civitate Dei* 14.11, Augustine came across a problem. There was, he perceived, a conflict between 1 Timothy 2:14 and Romans 5:12–21. The one stated that "Adam was not deceived, but the woman was deceived and became a transgressor." The other that "sin came into the world through one man." One text vindicates Adam and condemns Eve. The other, as Gary Anderson writes, "pins all the blame on Adam" and mentions Eve not at all.[1] Yet, holy scripture could not contradict itself. Augustine's solution was to read the two texts as distinguishing between two distinct kinds of sin. Eve ("the lower part of the human couple")[2] was deceived by the serpent/Satan. Adam was not deceived. But Adam did sin. He *knowingly* sinned so as to remain with his wife.

Augustine's solution to the problem is not of primary interest to us, nor is his understanding of the shape of the problem. What Augustine's analysis raises up for us is the strange disappearance of Eve in Romans 5. In the last chapter, I surveyed pre-Pauline, Second Temple texts to show that Eve was universally located as a key figure in the story of originating sin. Where has she gone?

That Romans 5:12–21 is a shocking and innovative piece of early Christian theology is universally attested in contemporary scholarship. It has been the site of multiple scholarly debates in just the last few decades. These concern whether Paul was the first to claim that all humanity sins "in Adam," whether Paul was the first to suggest that humans were created immortal and lost this quality with sin, and whether the passage includes an early statement on the full humanity of Christ. But the absence of Eve has rarely been noted as a novel facet of the passage, and never to my knowledge explored in any depth.[3]

---

1. Anderson, *The Genesis of Perfection*, 106.

2. Translations taken from Augustine, *The City of God: 11–22*, trans. William Babcock, Works of Saint Augustine 7 (Hyde Park, NY: New City Press, 2013).

3. There has been very interesting work done suggesting that Eve is represented in Romans 7. I will not have the opportunity here to engage with this argument, but see Austin Busch, "The

Alongside Augustine and Gary Anderson we can include Beverly Gaventa, Douglas Moo, Leander Keck, and George Kretchmar among those who have noted the issue. Gaventa, writing in the *Women's Bible Commentary*, notes: "Women may sense their exclusion" when reading Romans 5:12–21. But she suggests that the passage mixes universalistic and historical/particular concerns and concludes that in any case "it is difficult to imagine that Paul, a product of his age, could have chosen for his argument any representative figures other than two males."[4] Douglass Moo writes provocatively that the "fact that Paul attributes this sin to Adam is significant since he certainly knows from Genesis that woman, Eve, sinned first (2 Cor 11:3; 1 Tim 2:14)." But then, without any supporting citation or argument, Moo goes on to write that "Paul's claim that 'sin came into the world through one man' would have been nothing new to anyone who knew their OT or Jewish tradition."[5] One wonders where in the Old Testament he finds this idea. Keck raises the issue in one sentence and then tries to resolve it in a parenthetical remark before placing a period. "Nor does Paul blame Eve . . . (probably because it would have seemed odd to say that a woman was a 'type' of Christ, v. 14)."[6] This parenthetical is at least worthy of expansion to articulate why the common humanity of Eve and Christ was not sufficient to create a typological relationship. Georg Kretschmar goes further, seeing the erasure of Eve as a continuing theme in early Christianity from the point of Romans 5 on. "In Jewish legend, Adam and Eve almost always stand next to one another. Christian narratives, on the other hand, generally focus completely on Adam, the type of Christ. . . . at Golgotha in Jerusalem, nobody looked for the grave of Eve!"[7]

Kretschmar is not quite right here. As scholars like Paula Fredrickson and Daniel Boyarin have recently reminded us, we should not underestimate the diversity of first century Judaism or the extent to which early Jewish Christians

---

Figure of Eve in Romans 7:5–25," *Biblical Interpretation* 12, no. 1 (2004): 1–36; Dunning, *Christ without Adam*, 87–113; Nicholas Elder, "'Wretch I Am!' Eve's Tragic Speech-in-Character in Romans 7:7–25," *Journal of Biblical Literature* 137, no. 3 (2018): 743–763.

4. "Romans" in Carol A. Newsom and Sharon H. Ringe, eds., *Women's Bible Commentary*, Expanded ed (Louisville, KY: Westminster John Knox Press, 1998), 408.

5. Douglas J. Moo, *The Letter to the Romans*, 2nd ed., The New International Commentary on the New Testament (Grand Rapids, MI: Eerdmans, 2018), 347.

6. Leander E. Keck, *Romans*, Abingdon New Testament Commentaries (Nashville: Abingdon Press, 2005), 149.

7. Georg Kretschmar, "'Natus ex Maria Virgine': Zur Konzeption und Theologie des Protevangelium Jacobi," in *Anfänge der Christologie: Festschrift für Ferdinand Hahn zum 65. Geburtstag*, ed. Cilliers Breytenbach, Ferdinand Hahn, and Henning Paulsen (Göttingen: Vandenhoeck und Ruprecht, 1991), 426. Translation mine.

were drawing from elements within this diversity.[8] Within half a century after Paul, we do have two Jewish sources that include sections bearing striking resemblances to Paul's thought in Romans 5: 4 Ezra and 2 Baruch. Both are likely written between the destruction of the Second Temple in 70 and the end of the century. They each identify Adam with sin and omit Eve in their formulas discussing the originating sin.[9] Similar moves are found in some later Rabbinic sources.[10] We can't entirely rule out relations of influence among these different documents.[11] But nothing in the later texts requires direct literary dependence on Paul.[12]

We are left, then, with a bit of ambiguity. Either Paul is originating a tradition that sin enters the world through Adam (omitting Eve), or Paul is drawing upon an inchoate tradition that was forming during this period or pre-existed Paul in some form that we do not have access to today. Tracking down the origins of this posited earlier tradition in a wider exploration of Jewish scriptures, culture, and motivation may be a worthwhile project. However, that project moves beyond what can be achieved in the context of the present work. I am interested in tracing out the problems of locating Eve as these problems developed eventually in the Christian tradition. As such, the analysis of this chapter shall be focused on Paul. If Paul originated this tradition, the following exploration can be read as an analysis of why he might have done so. If Paul was drawing on a pre-existent tradition, it can be read as an exploration of why he adapted this

8. Daniel Boyarin, *The Jewish Gospels: The Story of the Jewish Christ* (New York: The New Press, 2012); Paula Fredriksen, *When Christians Were Jews: The First Generation* (New Haven, PA: Yale University Press, 2018).

9. 4 Ezra: "you led him into the garden which your right hand had planted before the earth appeared. And you laid upon him one commandment of yours; but he transgressed it, and immediately you appointed death for him and for his descendants (3.6–7) and "O Adam, what have you done? For though it was you who sinned, the fall was not yours alone, but ours also who are your descendants" (7.48[118]-49[119]). 2 Baruch: "what did it profit Adam that he lived nine hundred and thirty years and transgressed that which he was commanded? Therefore, the multitude of time that he lived did not profit him, but it brought death and cut off the years of those who were born from him" (17.2–4) Translations taken from Charlesworth, *The Old Testament Pseudepigrapha. Vol. 1.*

10. See Robin Scroggs, *The Last Adam: A Study in Pauline Anthropology* (Philadelphia, PA: Fortress Press, 1966), 18, 36.

11. 4 Ezra and 2 Baruch are closely related and potentially one is dependent on the other. See Michael E. Stone and Matthias Henze, eds., *4 Ezra and 2 Baruch* (Minneapolis: Fortress Press, 2013).

12. By the time of the writing of The Apocryphon of John in the mid second century it was possible to claim that Eve was not even created when Adam ate the fruit (II 22.3–9). For translation see, Karen L King, *The Secret Revelation of John* (Harvard University Press, 2006).

tradition for his own purposes. In the process of answering this question about Paul, many of the suggestions might shed light on why the tradition originated even if it was not Paul's work.

My primary concern here is not whether Paul originated the tradition, but whether the formula that Paul articulates is adequate for theological investment. Does it achieve what Paul wanted? Does it achieve what we want? To formalize these concerns, I aim to address three questions. First, what is Paul's intent in developing the Adam/Christ scheme in Romans 5? Second, why does Paul claim that "sin comes through one man" when he knows the Eve tradition? Third, is Paul's formula in Romans 5 (1) adequate to achieve his own intentions in the passage, and (2) adequate to stand as the basis for doctrinal statements of later Christians? In asking the third question, I am going beyond exegesis of the passage. My goal here is theological. It is accepted today that the formulas that blame Eve for sin are inadequate for theological development. I will argue that Paul's omission of Eve is also problematic, both for achieving what Paul wanted this passage to do and for the development of doctrine.

Paul's Intent in Developing the Adam/Christ Formula in Romans 5

A complete exegesis of Romans 5:12–21 is beyond the scope of the current chapter. Thankfully, such is not necessary to get to Paul's central message. We only need recognize that the passage is shot through with a repeating pattern that even the anacoluthon in verse 12 cannot obscure. This pattern concerns the "one man" (both of them), and dominion over the many/all.[13] To bring this pattern out, it is helpful to schematically paraphrase the passage. Brackets mark where I have filled in implied key terms.

> 5:12 Through the sin of one man (ἑνὸς ἀνθρώπου), [Adam]
>> death spread to all (πάντας) because all human beings (πάντας ἀνθρώπους) had sinned
>
> 5:14 Death exercised dominion [over the many]
>> from [the one man] Adam (Ἀδὰμ)
>
> 5:15 The many (πολλοὶ) died
>> through the one man's [Adam's] trespass (τῷ τοῦ ἑνὸς παραπτώματι)

---

13. Moo, *The Letter to the Romans*, 321–322; Robert Jewett, *Romans: A Commentary*, Hermeneia (Minneapolis, MN: Fortress Press, 2007), 370–377; N. T. Wright, "Romans," in *The New Interpreter's Bible Commentary, Volume X* (Nashville, KY: Abingdon Press, 2015), 533; James D. G. Dunn, *Romans 1–8*, Word Biblical Commentary 38 (Dallas, TX: Word Books, 1988), 283–84, 293; Keck, *Romans*, 146.

[But] the grace of the one man (τοῦ ἑνὸς ἀνθρώπου), Jesus Christ
abounded for the many (πολλοὺς)
5:16 And the free gift [from the one man, Jesus]
is not like the effect of the one man's [Adam's] sin (δι' ἑνὸς ἁμαρτήσαντος)
5:17 Because of the one man's [Adam's] trespass (δι' ἑνὸς ἁμαρτήσαντος)
death exercised dominion [over many]
through the one (ἑνός), [Adam]
More surely will those (οἱ) [many]
exercise dominion in life
through the one (διὰ τοῦ ἑνὸς), Jesus Christ
5:18 Just as one [man's/Adam's] trespass (δι' ἑνὸς ἁμαρτήσαντος)
led to condemnation for all human beings (πάντας ἀνθρώπους)
So one [man's/Jesus Christ's] act of righteousness (δι' ἑνὸς δικαιώματος)
leads to justification and life for all human beings (πάντας ἀνθρώπους).
5:19 By the one man's [Adam's] disobedience (διὰ τῆς παρακοῆς ἑνὸς ἀνθρώπου)
the many (πολλοί) were made sinners
By the one [man's/Jesus Christ's] obedience (διὰ τῆς ὑπακοῆς τοῦ ἑνὸς)
the many (πολλοί) will be made righteous[14]

This pattern clarifies several things. First, while the common humanity of Adam and Jesus is doubtless assumed, that is not a main point of the passage.[15] Rather, the text is concerned primarily to show that what the two share is that

14. One positive of focusing on this pattern is that it allows one to sort out Paul's comments about the Torah, which I take to be qualifications within the broader scheme of the passage.

15. Here I disagree with Gordon Fee who claims that in both 1 Cor. 15:21–22 and in Romans 5:12–21 "Paul brings Christ into the picture to emphasize his genuine humanity, a humanity that he shared fully with Adam and thus with us, but without sin." Gordon D. Fee, *Pauline Christology: An Exegetical-Theological Study* (Peabody, MA: Hendrickson Publishers, 2007), 272. Fee's claim works better with 1 Cor. than it does with Romans. But, as I will argue below, the two passages are quite different in emphasis. Ernst Käsemann moves too far in the opposite direction when the writes: "For in Paul Adam and Christ are antipodes unrelated by any original consubstantiality. Not Adam who is only earthly protoplast, not a fallen heavenly being, but the world implicated in Adam's fall, is redeemed. Christ is not Adam redivivus; he is the eschatologically manifested Son of God. Adam and Christ are commensurable, not in terms of nature, but solely in terms of function; the world is changed by both." Ernst Käsemann, *Commentary on Romans*, trans. Geoffrey William Bromiley (Grand Rapids, MI: William B. Eerdmans, 1980), 144. Paul is not here denying human identity to Adam or Jesus (they are both ἀνθρώπους), but

they each inaugurate a dominion. Adam inaugurates the dominion of sin and death (here personified). Jesus Christ inaugurates a dominion of righteousness and life. What have the two done to inaugurate these dominions? Adam has brought sin and death into the world through his disobedience. Jesus has brought the gift of righteousness by grace through his obedience. For whom do these dominions exist? For all/the many. Through Adam's action the dominion of sin and death fell upon all, as all sin and all die. Jesus' dominion is available to all, as all might be made righteous by grace.[16] How do people become caught up in these dominions? Paul does not seem overly concerned about this question in this passage.[17] Adam's disobedience causes the spread of sin and death to all people, who sin and die, but we gain little clarity on the mechanism, agency, or mix of agencies by which this works.[18] Jesus's obedience allows people to gain the gift of righteousness by grace. But again, the mechanism for gaining this gift is not filled out in this passage. What is clear is that all have existed under the dominion inaugurated by Adam, and they should now want to enter and/or stay within the dominion inaugurated by Jesus.

There is no doubt here that Paul's intention in the passage is to articulate a scheme that is adequate to cover all people. Indeed, the scheme is adequate to cover all people twice, capturing all first in the dominion inaugurated by Adam, then opening the alternative to all to enter the dominion inaugurated by Christ. But there is no need here to posit metaphysical speculation about Adam

---

Paul is, as Käsemann rightly notes, focused on the function of each rather than their nature or substance. See Moo, *The Letter to the Romans*, 321–322, 343.

16. I set aside here questions about whether Paul thinks that "all" could be saved. Nothing in my argument hangs on this issue. See Jewett, *Romans*, 385–387; Dunn, *Romans 1–8*, 283–284, 293.

17. Dunn, *Romans 1–8*, 298.

18. In relation to such a claim one must acknowledge the massive arguments about how to interpret Romans 5:12 "ἐφ' ᾧ" and to what extent Paul has corporate sin in view in this passage. See Moo, *The Letter to the Romans*, 349–355; Jewett, *Romans*, 373–376; Wright, "Romans," 526–27; Brendan Byrne, *Romans*, Sacra Pagina Series 6 (Collegeville, MN: Liturgical Press, 2007), 175–77; Joseph A. Fitzmyer, "The Consecutive Meaning of ΕΦ' Ω in Romans 5.12," *New Testament Studies* 39 (July 1993): 321–339; Karl Kertelge, "Adam und Christus: Die Sünde Adams im Lichte der Erlösungstat Christi nach Röm 5,12–21," in *Anfänge der Christologie: Festschrift für Ferdinand Hahn zum 65. Geburtstag*, ed. Cilliers Breytenbach, Henning Paulsen, and Christine Gerber (Göttingen: Vandenhoeck & Ruprecht, 1991), 141–145; Dunn, *Romans 1–8*, 271–274; Käsemann, *Commentary on Romans*, 146–149. For present purposes, following Joseph Fitzmyer's comments in 1989, I would like to sidestep the whole debate: "Paul attributes to Adam not only the condition of total death that affects every human being, but even the contagion of sin that is ratified by personal sins. This sense of Rom 5:12 does not depend on the vb. hēmarton, 'have sinned,' being understood of some 'habitual' sin, or on the prep. phrase eph' hō understood as connoting some incorporation of all human beings in Adam. Rather, the context of vv. 13–14 indicates such a causal connection." Fitzmyer, *Paul and His Theology*, 73; Dunn, *Romans 1–8*, 271–274.

corrupting the substance of humanity. Nor is there reason to read into the text any concept of Jesus saving the substance of humanity through incarnation. Both are ideas that will find a home among early church theologians. Here, if there is anything we could call recapitulation, it would be limited to the central act: Adam disobeys, Christ obeys.[19]

What is at stake then are these two ends of the story. Adam disobeys and thus inaugurates the dominion of sin and death. Christ obeys and inaugurates the dominion of righteousness and life through grace. Given the Genesis narrative, the problem here is glaring. As Robert Jewett notes: "To speak of sin as 'entering' the world and death as 'reaching' all persons clearly implies that neither was present prior to Adam's act."[20] Inauguration, by definition, marks a beginning, a start, a first.

The problem is that no one reading Genesis 3 would attribute this role to Adam. As we have seen, Eve is the primary agent in the Genesis narrative. She is first to look at the tree and find its fruit to be nourishing, appetizing, and a source of potential wisdom. She is the first to eat. She was also aware of the command from God not to eat. In fact, the version of the command that she recounts includes two prohibitions: not to touch and not to eat. She broke both before handing the fruit to Adam.

Paul's goal was to cover the entirety of humanity; to claim that "two men between them cover the whole of the human story from start to finish."[21] "All people," Paul wished to say, "stand in relationship to one of two men."[22] But this intention is frustrated by its incompatibility with the source material. Given the constraints of the Genesis narrative, two men are insufficient to cover the territory. At least one person has fallen outside: Eve the mother of all living. And if Eve falls out, women have good reason to feel excluded from this passage. So, why has Paul chosen a scheme with such a significant plot hole?

He Has Not Erased Eve

We can anticipate a first set of responses to this query in various forms of denying the premise.[23] Despite the appearance of having excluded Eve, critics

---

19. "Although some commentators have suggested that this obedience entailed Christ's entire life, the comparison with Adam's single act of obedience suggests that Christ's obedience unto death is implied." Jewett, *Romans: A Commentary*, 386.

20. Jewett, *Romans*, 374–375.

21. Dunn, *Romans 1–8*, 289.

22. Moo, *The Letter to the Romans*, 343.

23. The below examples of objections were not phrased as such because no one appears to have raised the problem previously. Thus, they are necessarily taken partially out of context.

may claim, Paul has not in fact done this. These responses might rely on various aspects of the pericope. Here it is useful to take up five possibilities in turn. First, the idea that Paul intends to use "Adam" in the passage as a metonym for "Adam and Eve." Second, the possibility that Paul's use of ἀνθρώπους (anthropos) is inclusive in a way that should alleviate our concerns. Third, that the name Ἀδάμ (Adam) is synonymous with humankind in a way that should alleviate our concerns. Fourth, that Paul's statement that he is using Adam as a τύπος (type) should alleviate our concerns. Finally, that the general sense of the passage requires us to take Adam as a "representative" of humanity. Each of these responses, I will argue, fails to address the central concern of erasing Eve.

The Metonym Solution

A metonym is a figurative use of language or a cognitive process where one word or phrase (or concept) stands in for another word or phrase (or concept) with which it is associated. Thus, to talk about the royal family in England, one can speak of "the crown." A synecdoche is a kind of metonym where a word or phrase referring to a part of a whole is used to refer to a whole.[24] So one might refer to their "wheels" by which they mean their car. The use of these kinds of phrases is so common that competent speakers of a local language often do not even notice that they are using figurative language when they are deployed.

Metonymy is a common occurrence across languages, and it is a common occurrence in biblical texts. In fact, Jewish usage includes an established set of metonyms that use proper names as referents for groups of people, which is not common in most other languages. Thus, Paul can quote Isaiah: "Out of Zion will come the Deliverer; he will banish ungodliness from Jacob" (Rom 11:26; Isa 27:9). Here the name "Jacob" is a metonym for the Jewish people. By the time of Paul, the name Israel had become such a common metonym for the same purpose that it functionally became the name for the Jewish people.

Could Paul's use of "Adam" in Romans 5 function something like a metonym, such that the reference to Adam is actually a reference to "Adam and Eve" or perhaps the whole Genesis narrative? This seems to be assumed by several biblical interpreters. For instance, while discussing Romans 5, N. T. Wright pens: "Paul clearly believed that there had been a single first *pair*, whose *male*, *Adam* had been given a commandment and had broken it. Paul was, we may be sure, aware of what we would call mythical or metaphorical dimensions to the story, but he would not have regarded these as throwing doubt on the existence, and

24. Jeannette Littlemore, *Metonymy: Hidden Shortcuts in Language, Thought and Communication* (New York: Cambridge University Press, 2015), 23.

primal sin, of the first historical *pair*."[25] It is not entirely clear how to interpret this set of claims. One could read it as suggesting that Adam had special responsibility for sin because it was he who received the command, but this does not explain how Wright transitions so quickly from the pair, to Adam, back to the pair. Perhaps he is assuming that the reference here is the same the whole time because Adam is a figurative representative of "the pair."

One can draw a similar conclusion from the writing of James Dunn. At one point, Dunn writes that "Paul here [in Romans 5] shows himself familiar with and indeed to be a participant in what was evidently a very vigorous strand of contemporary Jewish thinking about *Adam* and the origin of evil and death in the world." He then cites a set of Second Temple works that clearly blame Eve and often exonerate Adam, even explicitly quoting Sir. 25.24: "From a woman sin had its beginning and because of her we die."[26] Dunn appears to be assuming a use of "Adam" here that is figurative in a way similar to a synecdoche or a metonym such that a reference to "Adam" can be a reference to "Eve."

One finds the thesis most explicitly stated by Louise Schottroff, who claims that there is a Jewish tradition in which "Adam represents humanity and Eve is included within this. If one speaks of Eve then this concerns women only, whether this has to do with sin or any other theme."[27] As we have seen, there is no evidence of this tradition being applied to sin in any extant literature prior to Paul. But could Paul be appealing to some broader tradition, or appealing to a developing tradition in his own time that uses Adam as a synecdoche?

What shall we make of such a reading? Two arguments can be made in favor of reading "Adam" here as a synecdoche for "Adam and Eve." First, it is unlikely that Paul means explicitly to deny Eve's role in originating sin.[28] He is clearly aware of the broader narrative (see 2 Cor 11:3), as is his audience. As I have shown in the last chapter, Eve is usually foregrounded in Second Temple treatments of Genesis. As such, the argument would go, the cultural and literary context should lead us to assume that when he refers to Adam, he *must* be referring to the broader known narrative. This is a conclusion with much to recommend it.

25. Wright, "Romans," 526. Italics mine.

26. Dunn, *Romans 1–8*, 272.

27. Louise Schottroff, "The Seduction of Eve and Adam's Sin: Social Historical Feminist Interpretation of Pau's Understanding of Sin and Freedom," in *Text and Logos: The Humanistic Interpretation of the New Testament*, ed. Theodore W. Jennings and Hendrikus Boers (Atlanta, GA: Scholars Press, 1990), 166.

28. However, below I will explore one option in which he might do so because a "benevolent patriarchal" reading of the Genesis narrative locates Adam as primarily responsible for originating sin because it was his job to oversee Eve.

The second argument depends on the relation between Adam and Eve. In the order of creation, Adam comes first, as such, Eve is a "part" of Adam. This kind of primacy in the order of creation may make Adam a good figure to function as a synecdoche for the pair. More on this below.

Despite the strength of such arguments, their conclusion is not as obvious as many seem to have assumed. As we have noted, several careful readers of the text have not seen a metonym or synecdoche at work here. Classically, we can cite Augustine's concern about the passage placing all the blame on Adam. Contemporarily, as noted in the introduction to this chapter, Anderson, Moo, Keck, Kretchmar, and Gaventa each seems explicitly to take an alternative reading of the passage. Since the disagreement has remained implicit, it is hard to know how many others share their position.

These later scholars are, at least, not clearly wrong. There are good reasons to think that Adam is not functioning synecdochally. For one, the passage contains none of the common grammatical[29] or truth conditions[30] indicating a synecdoche. Metonyms are usually "clearly anomalous or incongruous against the surrounding discourse."[31] Take, for instance, the reference to Jacob as the Jewish people in Romans 11:26 in just a slightly broader context: "Out of Zion will come the Deliverer; he will banish ungodliness from Jacob. And this is my covenant with them (αὐτοῖς) when I take away their (αὐτῶν) sins." Immediately, one who was unsure if Jacob was a metonym would note the shift from singular to plural. Jacob is a single person, but in the next verse it refers to taking away *their* sins. Add to this another significant signal: that Jacob has been dead for many, many years, and yet is treated here as if he is going to be acted upon by God in the present. Such signals tell the reader that something other than literal discourse is happening, thus pointing to the metonym.

Romans 5 contains no grammatical signs, and the claim there does not necessarily violate any factual constraint. Further, it is usual for metonyms to follow established cultural patterns. As noted, the use of "Israel" was an established metonym, "Jacob" was less common, but still easily recognizable to any person familiar with Jewish scripture. Beyond this, the practice of referring to a tribe by reference to a famous ancestor or patriarch follows a more general cultural

29. Katja Markert and Udo Hahn, "Understanding Metonymies in Discourse," *Artificial Intelligence* 135, no. 1–2 (February 2002): 145–98; Littlemore, *Metonymy*, 138, 142; Alice Deignan, *Metaphor and Corpus Linguistics*, Converging Evidence in Language and Communication Research 6 (Amsterdam ; Philadelphia: J. Benjamins Pub, 2005), 145–67.

30. Littlemore, *Metonymy*, 45.

31. Littlemore, 124.; Lynne Cameron, *Metaphor in Educational Discourse*, Advances in Applied Linguistics (London and New York: Continuum, 2003), 106, also 59. This is usual, but not necessary. As such it can only contribute to a cumulative argument on interpretation.

pattern. As we have seen, extant pre-Pauline, Second Temple texts reveal no such tradition using Adam as a metonym for Adam and Eve regarding originating sin. And those texts we have from after Paul's time with similar formulas face interpretive problems akin to those we face in reading Paul.

More than this, reading Adam as a metonym runs against the broader logic of the pericope in which the name is set. Paul's argument depends upon Adam being taken as a single person. Christ is clearly one person and is not functioning synecdochally. As the type of Christ, the logic of the passage requires that Adam parallels Christ. As such, the argument seems to fix "Adam" as referring to one person.[32]

How are we to assess the two sides of this argument? There is not a clear answer. Either Paul has deployed a strained metonym or has made a claim that would strike his readers as remarkably strange (unless one of the accounts of his reason I provide below softens the blow significantly). Thankfully, for the purposes of this chapter, we need not resolve the dispute because there is a compelling case to be made that we can talk intelligibly about the erasure of Eve on either account. If Paul has used the term "Adam" as a proper name, referring to one person, then the sense in which Eve has been erased is straightforward. She has somehow entirely disappeared from the narrative. If this is the proper reading, the claim is jarring.

If Paul intends a metonymical usage of the term *Adam* for Adam and Eve, it seems a half-hearted metonym. It must be weak enough to allow the logic of the passage to hold. This itself would suggest that even in proffering the metonym, Paul effaces Eve's role at least partially. But we can go further than this. The structure of metonyms is not random. In a metonym one term (the vehicle) is used to refer to another (the target). In this case, "Adam" would be the vehicle while "Adam and Eve" would be the target. But why choose Adam as the vehicle? There are, it turns out, standards that usually govern the selection of the vehicle. Usually one term "is seen as being more salient than the other and is therefore selected as the vehicle."[33]

Some of the frequent criteria determining saliency include "important over less important," "central over peripheral," "typical over non-typical," and "ideal over non-ideal."[34] These rules are not deployed consciously, but they are established patterns when people employ metonyms. As such, if Paul is constructing a metonym, the metonym might tell us something about Paul's assumptions

---

32. Keck, *Romans*, 145.

33. Günter Radden and Zoltán Kövecses, "Towards a Theory of Metonymy," in *Human Cognitive Processing*, ed. Klaus-Uwe Panther and Günter Radden, 4 (Amsterdam: John Benjamins Publishing Company, 1999), 19. See also Littlemore, *Metonymy*, 35–40.

34. Radden and Kövecses, "Towards a Theory of Metonymy," 49.

about Adam and Eve, even if he was not consciously aware of the choice. Günter Radden and Zoltán Kövecses even note one point at which gendered thought might influence the choice of vehicle. One of the rules that they note in such choices is "dominant over less dominant." They note that this rule may explain tendencies in many cultures to select male generics like "mankind, postman or you guys."[35]

Whatever implicit criteria Paul might have been using if he was constructing a metonym, it should be registered that it is strained in the given context. I noted above that one might argue that Adam is an apt vehicle for Adam and Eve because Adam comes first in the order of creation. This is true, but the immediate context does not focus on the order of creation. It focuses on the order of sin. In this context Eve clearly comes first. Choosing Adam as the vehicle to talk about sin thus must require some significant overriding justification.

To make the point, take an example from the writing of James Dunn. As I have suggested above, he seems to assume a metonymical reading of "Adam" in Romans 5. He carries this over into his analysis of other points where he sees an "Adam Christology" in Paul's writings. In his examination of Philippians 2:6–11, he finds much evidence to suggest Paul was thinking of "Adam" as he wrote. "In the second contrast 'equality with God' probably alludes to Adam's temptation (Genesis 3.5—. . . you will be like God/the gods) . . ." Musing on the parallels between the Philippians hymn and "Adam," he later writes: "What did Adam seek to grasp and what did he lose? Adam was already in the image of God (Genesis 1.26f.) . . . But he chose to grasp at the opportunity to be (completely) like God . . ."[36]

Note the strain this puts on the metonym. The serpent tempted *Eve* with the possibility of becoming like God. *Eve* grasped the fruit from the tree.[37] Adam just sat there and ate when it was handed to him. If this is a metonym, it is a strange one indeed. The target is the one who is active while the vehicle is passive, yet the metonym makes the vehicle the immediate reference for the activity. This runs directly contrary to what one would expect for a metonym. Either it would be better to reject the claim that it is a metonym (say, accept that the Philippians hymn is an "Eve Christology" or reject the claim that it constructs an Adam/Christ parallel at all) or to accept that it is a metonym that relies on some extremely strong criteria to override what seems the obvious choice of the vehicle.

---

35. Radden and Kövecses, 47.

36. James D. G. Dunn, *Christology in the Making: A New Testament Inquiry into the Origins of the Doctrine of the Incarnation*, 2nd ed. (Grand Rapids, MI: Eerdmans, 1996), 115–116.

37. Austin Busch notes similar problems with attempting to expand "Adam" as the focus of Romans 7. See Busch, "The Figure of Eve in Romans 7:5–25," 15.

All the plausible criteria for overriding the choice of Eve as the vehicle involve gendered presuppositions if not immediate gendered judgments. These may be related to "rhetorical effects"[38] or "social-communicative effects,"[39] two considerations that often open the way to overriding general rules of metonym construction. But they all employ gender in ways that should strike us as problematic. All of them have the effect of erasing Eve. Below, I will consider several of the forces that might have led Paul to make such a decision about the metonym if that is what he was doing. At this point it is sufficient to conclude that either Paul is using "Adam" to refer only to Adam in Romans 5, or he is deploying a metonym that has a similar impact in marginalizing Eve.

The ἀνθρώπους Solution

Beverly Gaventa presents us with the most clearly stated version of the ἀνθρώπους (anthropos) solution. After noting that women may feel excluded from the passage, she goes on to note: "The Greek word *anthropos*, which means human being or person rather than male, appears consistently in this text." She later adds the qualification: "Perhaps 'man' was left as the [English] translation of Anthropos when referring to Adam and to Jesus Christ because those two historical figures were men."[40]

There can be no doubt that there is something to this. Paul has used the term ἀνθρώπους here instead of the term ανηρ (anēr), which would have fixed the referent as a male. We should not make too much of this word choice, because Paul is drawing the wording from Genesis in the LXX.[41] But at least he did not use language that would explicitly exclude women.

We cannot end our analysis here, though. The primary meaning of ἀνθρώπους is human being. But it is overly simple just to claim that ἀνθρώπους means "human being" or "person" as opposed to "man." The translation depends on the context. For a clear example take Galatians 5:3, "I testify to every ἀνθρώπῳ who lets themselves be circumcised that they are obliged to obey the entire law." The problems with translating this as "person" are many, not least that it might suggest to some reader that Paul is concerned with female circumcision. Translation is always dependent on context.

In the case of Romans 5, the NRSV, NIV, and ESV, for instance, all translate ἀνθρώπους as "man" throughout the pericope. They do so for exactly the reason

38. Radden and Kövecses, "Towards a Theory of Metonymy," 52–53.

39. Radden and Kövecses, 53–54.

40. "Romans" in Newsom and Ringe, *Women's Bible Commentary*, 408.

41. Lee, *Death Warning in the Garden of Eden*, 148.

that Gaventa notes. The term obviously refers to Adam and Jesus, both of whom are males. If Paul had here contrasted Eve and Jesus, then the term ἀνθρώπους would clearly mean "person" or "human being" because that is what the two exemplars would have shared. But in this case, especially by excluding Eve, Paul's formula makes clear that for some reason he is interested in contrasting two males. The two men are the only referents in the passage for the term.[42]

Thus, even if a translation does take a more inclusive approach, as the NABRE does, it makes no difference to the meaning of the passage. Women are right to feel excluded whether ἀνθρώπους is translated as "man" or as "person." Either way, Paul "does not use ἀνθρώπους here to characterize humankind as a whole."[43] Eve has disappeared from the narrative. Paul has provided referents for the term that break with the tradition of including a woman in the narrative, leaving only males to be the Alpha and Omega of the story of sin. The fact that ἀνθρώπους could mean "person of unspecified gender" in a different context will not save us from the root of the problem here.

The Ἀδάμ Solution

But if Adam as referent is the problem, perhaps Adam as referent is also the solution. The Hebrew "וְאָדָם" (ha-'āḍām) and "אָדָם" ('āḍām) are terms that commonly refer to humankind rather than function as a proper name. Paul does not write in Hebrew, but in Greek. Thus, the word he uses is Ἀδάμ, but C. K. Barrett writes that "Paul learnt to think in Hebrew, and knew that the name Adam ('āḍām) means" human.[44] Is it then possible that when Paul writes "Ἀδάμ" he does not mean to specify the referent of ἀνθρώπους as a particular man, but is instead drawing on the deep roots of Hebrew thought to use Ἀδάμ as a cypher for "the human person" or some such?

This line of thought is problematic for several reasons. First, it is not at all clear that we should accept that Paul is "thinking in Hebrew." No doubt Paul was fluent in Hebrew language, history, and culture. But he was at the very least thoroughly bilingual. While there are significant arguments about Paul's

42. "The fact that Paul uses the more generic term Anthropos gives grounds for a more gender-inclusive translation, 'through the person.' But since Paul clearly regards Adam as a historical individual, the 'type' of the (equally historical) Jesus (v. 14), it seems best, for the sake of the argument, to retain the more precise reference." Byrne, *Romans*, 183. Note also the significance of this claim also under the argument concerning τύπος below.

43. Dunn, *Romans 1–8*, 272.

44. C. K. Barrett, *From First Adam to Last: A Study in Pauline Theology* (New York: Scribner, 1961), 6.

Greco-Roman education, no scholar reading Paul doubts his facility with basic Greek. Even when working with originally Hebrew terms, his ability to translate to a non-Jewish audience is quite good. He was at least also, as Paula Fredriksen notes, a "Greek thinker."[45] He frequently drew directly from the Septuagint.[46] And his language when talking about Adam and Christ reflects the language in the Septuagint.

It should also be noted that Romans is written to a mixed church, with the majority being Gentiles. Paul states in the opening of the letter that his apostleship is to bring obedience of faith "among all the Gentiles . . . including yourselves" (1:5). Later he wishes that he may "reap some harvest among you as I have among the rest of the Gentiles," noting that he is a "debtor both to Greeks and barbarians" (1:13–14). As such, his audience clearly includes many who speak only Greek. Even if Paul's thought were primarily in Hebrew, he would not be able to assume that his audience would be able to grasp the Hebrew hiding beneath Greek rendered in entirely different terms.

It is here that the Ἀδάμ solution runs into a problem, because while וְאָדָם is ambiguous, Ἀδάμ is not. Nowhere in the New Testament is Ἀδάμ properly translated as anything other than the proper name Adam. The Septuagint, on which Paul regularly drew, is quite subtle with its translation of אדם in Genesis. It translated וְאָדָם as ἀνθρώπον in cases where it wanted to render the term as "person" or "man." But it switches to translating וְאָדָם as the proper name Ἀδάμ in verse 2:16. This is before the Hebrew states the term as the proper name אָדָם, but there is no doubt in the Greek that the transition has been made. The only way to make sense of the capitalized word Ἀδάμ is as a proper name.[47] In fact, in cases like Genesis 2:18, when God says that "it is not good for וְאָדָם to be alone," the Septuagint reverts to the term ἀνθρώπον to indicate that the statement is not specifically about Adam the individual. If "human beings" or even "men" are in view, the term Ἀδάμ is not used.[48]

In the end, we must conclude with James Dunn that in this passage "Paul is hardly concerned to make use of the Hebrew meaning of 'Adam,' and the bulk

45. Paula Fredriksen, *Paul: The Pagans' Apostle* (New Haven: Yale University Press, 2017), 35.

46. Christopher G. Norden, "Paul's Use of the Psalms in Romans: A Critical Analysis," *Evangelical Quarterly* 88, no. 1 (April 26, 2016): 74.

47. "Even in places where Ἀδάμ appears with he article (ὁ), the capitalization of Ἀδάμ indicates its use as a proper name." Susan Ann Brayford, *Genesis*, Septuagint Commentary Series (Boston: Brill, 2007), 230.

48. Brayford, 231.

of his Greek-speaking readership would probably have been unaware of it even if they knew the LXX."[49]

The τύπος Solution

The third way of challenging the premise that Paul has excluded Eve concerns a term that Paul uses to describe his understanding of Adam in Romans 5. Adam, he says, is a "type (τύπος) of the one who was to come." On this basis, Richard B. Hays writes of "Paul's portrayal in Romans 5:12–21 of Adam as the source of sin and typological representative of sinful humanity."[50] If Adam is used typologically here, even though his proper name does not refer to humanity in general, is Paul not using him as a symbol that simply means "all humanity"?

The problem here is that Hays' comment does not arise from a careful exegesis of Romans. Paul does not say that he is using Adam as "a typological representative of sinful humanity." Rather he says that Adam is a type of "the one who was to come." This "one" is Jesus, not humanity. So, what does Paul mean by saying that Adam is a "τύπος" of Christ? The word τύπος originally derives from a verb meaning "to strike" and came to refer to the mark left by the striking implement. So, a coin would be the τύπος of the mold with which it was struck.

Richard Davidson, in his broader study of typology, has analyzed Romans 5 as a form of "horizontal (earthly/historical) τύπος structure."[51] This structure depends upon "a *historical correspondence* between the OT events and the NT realities."[52] The abstraction involved in the typology arises in relation to this correspondence. One being the type of the other, the abstraction can be found in the overlap between the two characters. This is why Davidson starts his analysis of the typology in Romans 5 by securing the claim that Paul is "undoubtedly thinking of Adam as an historical individual."[53]

---

49. Dunn, *Romans 1–8*, 289.

50. Richard B. Hays, *The Moral Vision of the New Testament: Community, Cross, New Creation: A Contemporary Introduction to New Testament Ethics* (San Francisco: HarperSanFrancisco, 1996), 67.

51. Richard M Davidson, *Typology in Scripture: A Study of Hermeneutical Typos Structures* (Berrien Springs, MI: Andrews University Press, 1981), 191.

52. Davidson, 280.

53. Davidson, 299. Here he is citing Matthew Black, *Romans*, New Century Bible Commentary (London: Oliphants, 1973), 86. I am not particularly interested here in whether Paul actually needs an historical Adam in order to make the typology work. Most scholars hold that Paul did believe in an historical Adam, though James Dunn argues that all he needs is a definite, socially accessible, but potentially mythical character "Adam" to make his point. Dunn, *Romans 1–8*, 289.

The greatest question about the typology in Romans 5 concerns not of whom Adam is a type, but how he functions as a type of Christ. What the two have in common is that they each inaugurate a dominion. They are both, to use James Dunn's terminology when discussing typology, "epochal figures."[54] Beyond that, the comparison immediately turns to contrast. While Adam inaugurates the dominion of sin and death, Christ inaugurates the dominion of righteousness and life by grace. And, again contrasting, Christ's act and dominion overflow in power and glory in ways that leave Adam's looking definitively puny. As such, Leonhard Goppelt describes the word τύπος as indicating that "Adam and Christ are related to one another as a photographic negative is to its positive print, or as a mold to the plastic shaped by it."[55] Adam is a "hollow mold," one where the mold creates an "opposite impression" on that which it strikes.[56] Many biblical interpreters have preferred terms like "antithetical correspondent"[57] or even "antitype."[58]

But at this point Paul's use of typology in Romans does not solve the problem of the absence of Eve. It serves to reinforce the structure of the whole passage. It does nothing to change the fact that "Adam" refers to a specific male individual. Adam's action has a causal effect on everyone after him. But typology does not abstract in a way that makes his identity synonymous with humanity.

Regardless, Does Not Adam "Stand for" Humanity?

Yet, many biblical scholars when engaging with Romans 5 eventually make the claim that Adam is a "representative man"[59] or that Adam's identity is "corporate"[60] so that he stands for the whole of humanity. "In Adam, as first ancestor, is told the sin story of the entire race—a story that leads to death," writes Brendan

---

54. Dunn, *Romans 1–8*, 292.

55. Leonhard Goppelt, *Typos: The Typological Interpretation of the Old Testament in the New* (Grand Rapids, MI: Eerdmans, 1982), 129.

56. Davidson, *Typology in Scripture*, 302.

57. Jewett, *Romans*, 378.

58. Calvin J. Roetzel, *Paul, a Jew on the Margins* (Louisville, KY: Westminster John Knox Press, 2003), 34; Fitzmyer, *Paul and His Theology*, 73; Hans Conzelmann, *1 Corinthians: A Commentary on the First Epistle to the Corinthians*, ed. George MacRae, trans. James Weitch, Hermeneia (Philadelphia: Fortress Press, 1975), 248; Käsemann, *Commentary on Romans*, 115.

59. Dunn, *Christology in the Making*, 118; Davidson, *Typology in Scripture*, 305.

60. Moo, *The Letter to the Romans*, 344.

Byrne.[61] "When Paul speaks of or alludes to 'Adam,'" writes James Dunn, "he speaks of humankind as a whole."[62]

I am not inclined to endorse the claim that Adam's identity is "corporate" here. This imports too much of a later theory of original sin into Paul's writing. The closest Paul comes to suggesting a "corporate" identity for Adam is in 1 Corinthians 15:22: "all die in Adam." Such claims on Paul's part should be read in the light of the comparison that he is making between Adam and Christ. For Paul, there is certainly a sense in which Christ *can* be a corporate person. Believers can be "in Christ," "have the mind of Christ," and so forth. Adam seems to take on similar characteristics when being compared to Christ. But Paul's focus in these passages is always on Christ rather than Adam.[63] So, I do not think we should make too much of the "corporate" nature of Adam's identity.

Even so, let us grant that there is a sense in which Adam is representative of humanity. Adam sins and dies and brings about a new dominion in which all sin and die. What is important here for our current argument is to keep the direction of the relationship straight. Saying that Adam is representative of humanity is not saying that Adam loses his particularity, becoming an anonymous sinner. It is to say that each human is somehow caught up in Adam's particularity as the source of sin and death. It is humanity that follows Adam, not the other way around. This must be the way that the relationship runs because if it were not, the comparison with Christ would not work. To say that humans could be "in Christ" is not to say that Christ loses Christ's particularity, but rather that those humans would lose the particularity of their current position under the dominion of sin and death because of what Christ has done and is doing.

Thus, the sense in which Adam is a "representative man" does not alleviate our concerns here. Rather, it may give women even more reason to be uncomfortable. They are joined together under the dominion of one or another male in the light of his actions. Eve is still nowhere in sight.

Why Did Paul Erase Eve?

Having argued that Paul's scheme in Romans 5 does in some sense exclude Eve, we can now progress to explore potential reasons why Paul might have done so. Below I offer several different possible reasons for Paul's particular formulation, whether we conceive of it as a strained metonym or a straightforward claim.

---

61. Byrne, *Romans*, 182.

62. James D. G. Dunn, *The Theology of Paul the Apostle*, 83.

63. "Paul's interest is not in developing a doctrine of Adam's sin but rather to employ the Adamic material as a foil to explain the abundant life in Christ that overturns the legacy of sin and death." Jewett, *Romans*, 383. See also Kertelge, "Adam und Christus."

Some are more speculative than others, and none needs stand entirely on its own. There may be some mix of all the reasons bearing on Paul's decisions. I am not arguing for or against any of them as being the "right" account. I am interested in whether any of these accounts provide us with either an adequate justification for the erasure of Eve or a reason not to be concerned about its implications.

Paul Is Led by Rhetorical Convention

Whatever else he was, Paul was a rhetorician. The arguments of his letters are constructed not only to move his audience, but to embrace a certain style while doing so. There has been a lively argument in recent decades about what level of Greek education Paul achieved. But thankfully we need not enter this fray to draw out the points that we want to make.[64]

Those who assume that Paul was highly educated, or at least picked up much of the style of the highly educated, point out that Romans 5 fits with the rhetorical trope called a (σύγκρισις) synkrisis.[65] Literally referring to "judging together," a synkrisis offered a comparison, often a moral comparison, of two figures. Romans 5:12–21 fits this model.[66] The synkrisis came with strictures. As Aelius Theon would write in the late first century:

> Comparison [σύγκρισις, *synkrisis*] is a form of speech which contrasts the better and the worse. Comparisons are drawn between people, and between things: between people, for example Ajax and Odysseus . . .

---

64. We need not choose between "oral" or "literary" culture. The first century had overlapping cultures and various levels of literacy. See, Stanley Porter and Bryan Dyer, "Oral Texts? A Reassessment of the Oral and Rhetorical Nature of Paul's Letters in Light of Recent Studies," *Journal of the Evangelical Theological Society* 55, no. 2 (2012): 323–341. For arguments about Paul's education, see Ryan S. Schellenberg, *Rethinking Paul's Rhetorical Education: Comparative Rhetoric and 2 Corinthians 10–13*, Early Christianity and Its Literature 10 (Atlanta, GA: Society of Biblical Literature, 2013); Ronald Hock, "Paul and Greco-Roman Education," in *Paul in the Greco-Roman World: A Handbook Volume I*, ed. J. Paul Sampley (London: Bloomsbury T&T Clark, 2016), 230–253.

65. Christopher Forbs suggests that Paul had observational knowledge of upper-level rhetoric. Christopher Forbs, "Paul and Rhetorical Comparison," in *Paul in the Greco-Roman World: A Handbook Volume I*, ed. J. Paul Sampley (London: Bloomsbury T&T Clark, 2016), 214. Similarly, see Stanley E. Porter's claim that Romans is best categorized as a "diatribe" (though this is a loose designation in the study of ancient rhetoric) which features such "characteristics" as "parallelism and antitheses (5:12–21)." Stanley E. Porter, "Paul of Tarsus and His Letters," in *Handbook of Classical Rhetoric in the Hellenistic Period (330 B.C.– A.D. 400)*, ed. Stanley E. Porter (New York: Brill, 1997), 575–576.

66. Forbs, "Paul and Rhetorical Comparison," 219.

> First, it should be noted that comparisons are not drawn between things which are vastly different from each other. It would be ridiculous to debate whether Achilles is more courageous than Thersites.[67]

Notable here is Aelius' qualification. While the synkrisis is meant to contrast a better and a worse example, it should not overstep. Achilles was a hero. Thersites was a known coward. The two were not worthy of contrast. Paul lived in a society that was deeply patriarchal. Christianity often challenged this patriarchy, at least on its edges, for example with a baptismal formula that includes the claim that in Christ there is "no male and female" (Gal 3:28).[68] But Paul is not consistent in this effort. There were problems in Corinth, for instance, that led Paul to significantly qualify challenges to patriarchy. He had to deal with members of the church rejecting the institution of marriage and women failing to veil in church (1 Cor 7:1–24, 11:2–16). When repeating the formula eliminating opposites in the letter, he omits that there is "no longer male and female."

Within his culture, would the structure of synkrisis even allow a contrast between Eve and Christ? A tradition of the glorification of Adam had been developed in Second Temple literature, so that a comparison between Adam and Christ could fit. (More on this below). But would a comparison of Eve and Christ have come off as unbelievable to Paul's audience? Here, Gaventa's point may be well taken: "it is difficult to imagine that Paul, a product of his age, could have chosen for his argument any representative figures other than two males."[69]

If this seems too "elite" a concern for Paul, one can also find rhetorical traditions in less literary grounds that might have influenced Paul. As Walter Ong and others have noted, the world in which Paul lived was dominated by orality, which came with its own formulas.[70] Paul's letters were often dictated orally

---

67. Quoted in Forbs, 214.

68. There has been a great deal of debate about how to read this passage. For a review of relevant literature, see Shelly Matthews, "A Feminist Analysis of the Veiling Passage (1 Corinthians 11:2–16): Who Really Cares That Paul Was Not a Gender Egalitarian After All?," *Lectio Difficilior* 2 (2015): 1–20.

69. "Romans" in Newsom and Ringe, *Women's Bible Commentary*, 408.

70. Though produced by a chirographic culture, "the Bible, from Genesis through the entire New Testament including its epistolary parts, registers the oral culture still so dominant when the Bible came into being." Walter J. Ong, *The Presence of the Word: Some Prolegomena for Cultural and Religious History* (New Haven, CT: Yale University Press, 1967), 188–89; Walter J. Ong and John Hartley, *Orality and Literacy: The Technologizing of the Word* (New York: Routledge, 2002); Ben Witherington, *What's in the Word: Rethinking the Socio-Rhetorical Character of the New Testament* (Waco, TX: Baylor University Press, 2009), 7–8.

and read aloud to his intended audience.[71] As such, it is not surprising that they reflect oral rhetorical structures.[72] Oral cultures tend to produce language that is rhythmic and formulaic (34), aggressive rather than analytic (using "clusters of integers, such as parallel terms or phrases or clauses, antithetical terms or phrases or clauses, epithets" 38), agonistic (engaging the reader in "intellectual combat" 43), situational rather than abstract (referring to concrete objects rather than abstractions 48); it also deploys the use of "heavy figures" (outsized, heroic figures 68).[73] All of these tendencies mark Paul's rhetoric in Romans 5:12–21.

Unfortunately, as James Dunn notes, Paul sometimes "sacrificed precision of language for rhetorical effect."[74] Is Paul's agonistic treatment of Adam and Christ an example of this? Was the draw of parallel between "one man" and "one man" too good of a formula to give up, rhetorically? There is doubtless something to this. If Paul had written that "sin came into the world through two people" and then continued to contrast Adam and Eve with one man, Christ, it would not have had the same rhetorical effect.

Yet, if we step back, it is important to note that the driving force behind either of these reasons for excluding Eve is not rhetoric per se, but a rhetoric shaped by patriarchal presuppositions. Eve was the protagonist of the Genesis narrative: the mother of all living. Outside of gendered assumptions (the same kind that saw Adam glorified and Eve blamed in pre-Pauline literature, see below), there is no reason that one could not compare Eve and Christ. And while contrasting Adam and Eve to Christ might have thrown off Paul's rhythm, it was entirely possible to say that sin came through one ἀνθρώπους, Eve. While this may at first look like simply a reiteration of the "blaming Eve" theme, it would have led to the construction of Christ as the "second Eve."

Rhetoric then, provides at best a partially satisfactory answer to our ultimate questions. While gendered rhetorical presuppositions were a part of Paul's world, and worked with Paul's intent for his immediate audience, this does not provide a good reason for a continued embrace of Paul's formula.

Paul Is Drawing on the Glorification of Adam

The case of synkrisis above presents us with another question. If Eve was ruled out as too different from Christ based on gender, why was Adam not ruled out

---

71. Porter, "Paul of Tarsus and His Letters," 538, 540; Witherington, *What's in the Word*, 9.

72. "Since Paul's letters were intended to be read aloud, not silently, it is typical of Paul's prose to express contrasts or analogies by way of balanced, poetic lines." Fee, *Pauline Christology*, 115 n.84.

73. Page references in this paragraph are to Ong and Hartley, *Orality and Literacy*.

74. Dunn, *Romans 1–8*, 297.

because the contrast between the "first sinner" and the "righteous man" is too obvious? Part of the answer here could be provided by a tradition that had developed in the Second Temple period: the tradition of glorifying Adam.[75]

This tradition has its origin in God's command in Genesis: "have dominion over the fish of the sea and over the birds of the air and over every living thing that moves upon the earth" (1:28). This became linked with Psalm 8:

> what are human beings (אֱנוֹשׁ man/humankind) that you are mindful of them, mortals (בֶן־אָדָם son of ʾāḏām/a human) that you care for them? Yet you have made them a little lower than God (מֵאֱלֹהִים) and crowned them with glory and honor. You have given them dominion over the works of your hands; you have put all things under their feet, all sheep and oxen, and also the beasts of the field, the birds of the air, and the fish of the sea, whatever passes along the paths of the seas (vv. 4–8).[76]

From this beginning, authors near the turn of the millennia, just as they denigrated Eve for sin, speculated about the power and privilege given to Adam prior to originating sin. In *Vita Adae et Evae* (The Life of Adam and Eve) we find a story in which Eve is not mentioned, Adam is created in the image of God, and God commands the angels to bow down and worship Adam as the image of God (12–16). Envious, the devil refuses and is cast out of heaven. In *Liber Antiquitatum Biblicarum* (The Biblical Antiquities of Pseudo Philo- LAB) we find the tradition that God had "made Adam as the first created one and showed him everything" (26.6–7). This seems to refer to allowing Adam to see all the esoteric powers and glories of creation while in the garden. In 2 Enoch 30.8–10, 13 and the Sibylline Oracles 3.24–25, Adam is created as a microcosm of the world, named after the four cardinal directions.[77]

Some of these accounts saw Adam's glory as continuing beyond originating sin and expulsion from the garden. This can be seen especially in *Vita Adae et Evae* where the creatures of the Jordan river gather around Adam to protect him

---

75. Gary A. Anderson, "The Exaltation of Adam and the Fall of Satan," in *Literature on Adam and Eve: Collected Essays*, ed. Gary A. Anderson, Michael E. Stone, and Johannes Tromp, Studia in Veteris Testamenti Pseudepigrapha 15 (Boston: Brill, 2000), 83–110; Scroggs, *The Last Adam*, 21–28. The above section only draws out representative samples of this tradition, I do not pretend to present a comprehensive account.

76. The LXX translates אֱנוֹשׁ as ἄνθρωπος, and "son of ʾāḏām" as ἀνθρώπου. The LXX translates אֱלֹהִים as ἀγγέλους (angels). This translation is still reflected in the King James version of the Bible.

77. Scroggs, *The Last Adam*, 113–114.

during his time of penance after being expelled from the garden. Seth, Adam's son is also located as the image of God (37, 39). Seth (39) and Adam (17), retain the ability to recognize the devil and to banish him. These instances point to Adam's (and Seth's) continued dominion over creation and extend this to power over the devil. Eve, who also takes part in penance and is with her son Seth when he recognizes and banishes the devil, is given none of these powers and is not said to be made in the image of God.

Other sources from the same period see Adam losing his special status after the originating sin. The Apocalypse of Moses, a sister text to *Vita Adae et Evae*, emphasizes Adam's pain and mortality after his expulsion from Eden. When LAB tells of the mysteries of paradise being revealed to Adam, it tells this story to thank God that God did not allow all humans to see these mysteries. Adam was, it seems, a test case. He failed the test as later humans would have if God had tested them. By testing Adam, God avoided the damage that could have been done if other humans had been allowed such opportunities. These were not traditions that uniquely identified Adam with sin. They did not claim that Adam brought sin and death into the world by himself. Usually, these traditions placed blame disproportionately on Eve for originating sin. But, especially in the light of the glorified aura that Adam was taking on in his Edenic life, they emphasized the degradation of Adam's life, and the life of all humanity after expulsion from Eden.

Another development in this tradition was the tendency to see figures that re-establish hope for, or even the realization of, a return to Adamic glory. In LAB, God's covenant with Noah includes God's promise to destroy "all the things that grow on earth" (3.3) and "to destroy all those inhabiting the earth" (3.4), thus emphasizing the completeness of Noah's new beginning.[78] As in the biblical account, it is now Noah's children who will spread across the earth. God's promise not to destroy the earth again stands as a partial corrective to the curse on creation that came after Adam. God's promises in reigning in the curse of creation is reaffirmed with Moses, the next great man on the scene, after he has built the tent of meeting (13.7).

The parallel with Adam is made explicit as God tells Moses that he has brought him to the location of Eden (13.8–9). God then provided Moses with a command "regarding the salvation of the souls." All God required is that God's people "walk in my ways." If they do so, God would "bless their seed; and the earth will quickly yield its fruit, and there will be rains for their advantage, and it will not be barren" (13.10). In this passage Moses has been located as a new Adam. God is offering a solution to the curse of the soil that was God's

78. See Hayward, "The Figure of Adam in Pseudo-Philo's Biblical Antiquities," 7–9. All translations of LAB taken from James H. Charlesworth, ed., *The Old Testament Pseudepigrapha, Vol. 2* (Garden City, NY: Doubleday, 1985).

punishment for Adam. LAB does anticipate a more final end to evil. The end of the world and a general resurrection are yet to come (3.10). But, short of that, it has constructed a scheme with figures functioning as "new Adams," giving new opportunities to the creation long before the eschaton.

In 2 Enoch, we see Enoch take the place of Adam. In chapter 21, Enoch is brought to the seventh heaven, where God tests the angels by glorifying Enoch, allowing him to stand in front of God's face. In an implied reversal of the failure of the angels to bow down to Adam, the angels now venerate Enoch. Enoch is then clothed in glory and becomes like an angel himself.[79]

Did the tradition of the glorification of and expectation for a new Adam shape Paul's thought? This is quite plausible. We cannot know if Paul read the above texts, but it is likely that he was at least familiar with these traditions. As James Dunn has argued, Paul's Christology links Christ with Psalm 8, which appears to have been a conduit for the tradition glorifying Adam.[80] Dunn further claims that Paul linked Psalm 8 to Psalm 110 and, on this basis, developed a wide-ranging Adam Christology.[81] In this, Paul emphasized that Christ laid claim to the glory, dominion, and image of God that were originally intended for Adam before the fall. By Christ's humble obedience, Adam's rebellious disobedience was reversed.

Similarly, Stephen Hultgren argues that the origin of Paul's doctrine of the two Adams is found in his use of εἰκόν (image/likeness) language, which is related to the doctrine in 1 Corinthians 15:49: "Just as we have borne the image of the man of dust, we will also bear the image of the man of heaven." Such language, Hultgren argues, is based upon Paul's own conversion experience, where he felt himself being remade in the image/likeness of Christ.[82] This in turn overlaps with prophetic language about the likeness of God's glory, and ultimately with the language of the creation of humanity in Genesis. "So God created humankind in his image" (Gen 1:27). "Once these fundamental identifications had been made," Hultgren writes, "it was only natural that Paul should be led back to the creation of Genesis, and specifically, to the creation of man."[83]

79. Anderson, "The Exaltation of Adam and the Fall of Satan," 99–102.

80. Dunn, *Christology in the Making*, 107–110.

81. Dunn, 107–110. For a similar account see C. K. Barrett, *A Commentary on the First Epistle to the Corinthians* (New York: Charles Scribner's Sons, 1962), 376 and Barrett, *From First Adam to Last: A Study in Pauline Theology*. For a critical view of this kind of interpretation, see Fee, *Pauline Christology*, 513–23.

82. Stephen Hultgren, "The Origin of Paul's Doctrine of the Two Adams in 1 Corinthians 15:45–49," *Journal for the Study of the New Testament* 25.3 (2003): 367.

83. Hultgren, 369.

So, does such an account of the source of Paul's scheme in Romans 5 resolve our concern? Far from it. As any careful reader of Genesis will note, despite Hultgren's statement, Genesis 1:27 does not refer to "the creation of man." If one finishes out the passage it states: "in the image of God he created them; male *and female he created them*" (italics mine). While looking for the origin of Paul's two Adams scheme, Hultgren has imposed part of the scheme on the source material that he believes Paul is drawing from.

The whole tradition of the glorification of Adam is built on what is a patriarchal, if not a misogynistic, reading of Genesis 1:28. God's command to "subdue" the creation was delivered not to Adam, but to the "male and female" created in Genesis 1:27. Even in the Septuagint there is no confusion on this point. In 1:27 God created ἄνθρωπον (humankind), ἄρσεν (male) and θῆλυ (female). The tradition of glorifying Adam is tied to the contingent and culturally shaped refusal to glorify Eve and to the tradition of blaming Eve. If Paul is drawing on the tradition of glorifying Adam, he is only extending this patriarchal tradition to include the erasure of Eve from the narrative of originating sin.

Paul's Logic Slips between Schemes

Of course, perhaps he was drawing on a different source. Romans 5 was not Paul's first recorded effort to explicitly compare Adam and Christ. In 1 Corinthians 15, Paul offers a scheme that is related to his formula in Romans 5; however, the two pericopes assume quite different pictures of the relation between created nature and death. In 1 Corinthians, Paul's claim that death came with Adam is matched with the implied claim that death is a part of created human nature. But Romans 5 posits that death was not natural but was a new phenomenon that came only after sin. Could Paul's assertion that "sin came into the world through Adam" be a result of Paul eliding the two schemes?[84]

---

84. It is not clear exactly where Paul's thought in 1 Corinthians emerges from. Some have posited that Paul is there responding to a piece of speculative theology that exists in Corinth, and is borrowing terms from his opponents to create his own position. Arguments for and against various versions of this thesis have produces a massive amount of literature in recent decades. Here I will point toward some of the summaries which can serve as an opening to the rabbit hole for those interested. See Gordon D. Fee, *The First Epistle to the Corinthians*, Revised Edition, The New International Commentary on the New Testament (Grand Rapids, MI: William B. Eerdmans Publishing Company, 2014), 857; Joseph A. Fitzmyer, *First Corinthians: A New Translation with Introduction and Commentary*, The Anchor Yale Bible 32 (New Haven, CT: Yale University Press, 2008), 592; Hultgren, "The Origin of Paul's Doctrine of the Two Adams in 1 Corinthians 15:45–49," 343–370. If Paul did develop this scheme for 1 Corinthians, it would be interesting, because we might even be able to posit a development of his thought

What is the shape of Paul's Adam/Christ comparison in 1 Corinthians? Paul begins the comparison in a way that seems to parallel the comparison in Romans: "For since death came through a human being, the resurrection of the dead has also come through a human being; for as all die in Adam, so all will be made alive in Christ" (1 Cor 15:21–22). But unlike in Romans, Paul's focus in Corinthians is not on sin. He does not state here that Adam brought death into the world through sin, nor is there any reason to presuppose this is his position based on this pericope alone. He certainly holds that Christ died for the sins of humanity (15:3), that if Christ has not risen the Corinthians are still in sin (15:17), that the Corinthians should stop sinning (15:34), and that "the sting of death is sin" (15:56). But none of these necessitate that death started with sin.[85]

Christianity eventually develops the doctrine that humans were created immortal and lost this status on the occasion of sin.[86] This doctrine, however, is not found in Genesis and only rarely and obscurely in any Second Temple sources.[87] Most pre-Pauline literature had taken for granted that humans were created mortal. In Second Temple literature, post-Edenic mortality came to be linked to sin first because of Adam and Eve's expulsion from the garden, which made it impossible for them to eat from the Tree of Life. In this middle-ground position, humans have always been mortal but lost their chance at immortality with sin. Eventually mortality came to be seen as an independent punishment on

related to the scheme between here and Romans 5. Pursing this possibility is, at the very least, beyond the current argument.

85. Fee reads 15:56 as suggesting that "death is not simply the result of decay through normal human processes. Rather it is the result of the deadly poison, sin itself." Fee, *The First Epistle to the Corinthians*, 806. But if this is right, the verse would effectively derail Paul's argument up to this point: "it is not the spiritual that is first, but the physical [i.e. mortal/perishable], and then the spiritual." The verse appears out of context as it sits, and some have suggested that it is an interpolation or a later comment written in by Paul. It's meaning is opaque by itself. Fitzmyer, *First Corinthians*, 607. As Fee does, most interpreters move immediately to Romans to fill in the empty spaces. As I have noted here, there are significant differences between Paul's scheme here and his thought in Romans. This might make us want to take a beat before calling in Romans as an interpretive key.

86. See Lee, *Death Warning in the Garden of Eden*; Kelly, "Adam Citings before the Intrusion of Satan," 13–28; Barr, *The Garden of Eden and the Hope of Immortality*.

87. Wisdom of Solomon 2.23 records that "God created us for incorruption and made us in the image of his own eternity, but through the devil's envy death entered the world, and those who belong to his company experience it." Philo comes similarly close to articulating this doctrine in Questions on Genesis 1.51 where he interprets Gen. 3:19 in terms of Adam having turned away from his heavenly nature toward his earthly nature. But one must hedge there because Philo is not interested in articulating a doctrine of original sin where Adam hands this condition on to his descendants. He is providing an allegorical interpretation in which each person has a choice of whether to turn toward God or toward the things of this world.

originally immortal beings. The slow evolution of this doctrine from "naturally mortal," to "originally mortal and continuing mortal because of sin," to "originally immortal and now mortal because of sin" took hundreds of years, and the shifts between positions are not always clear.

Paul seems not to have an entirely settled position on the issue. Summarizing a claim he finds in Bultmann, and with which he agrees, Hans Conzelmann writes that Paul holds "three conceptions side by side without being harmonized: (a) the juristic view of death as punishment; (b) the idea that death grows organically out of sin; and finally (c) the notion that man as a creature is earthly and mortal."[88] 1 Corinthians 15 and Romans 5 represent two of these different options.

First Corinthians suggests that the "death" that comes to all through Adam is associated with Adam's created nature. "God," Paul writes, "gives it [each seed/being] a body as he has chosen, and to each kind of seed its own body. Not all flesh is alike, but there is one flesh for human beings, another for animals, another for birds, and another for fish" (15:38–39). Paul goes on to reference Genesis in claiming that the "first man was from the earth, a man of dust" (15:47). By receiving the breath of God, "The first man, Adam, became a living being" (15:46). As Joseph Fitzmyer writes, "There is not even a hint here that Adam is being considered 'a sinner' . . . he is simply the first human being created."[89] Nothing in Paul's account of the creation of humanity speaks of original immortality, or of mortality coming only with the originating sin. If it did, it would ruin his argument that "it is not the spiritual that is first, but the physical, and then the spiritual" (15:46). Humans were created with mortal bodies.

Paul goes on to contrast the first Adam with the last Adam, Christ. But the comparison is between Adam's created body and Christ's resurrected body. As Adam is associated with weakness, physical body, earth, and perishability, Christ is associated with glory, spiritual body, heaven, and imperishability. As in Romans, the emphasis here is not primarily on the commonality between the two, but upon what distinguishes them (at least when we are comparing the originally created body of Adam to the resurrected body of Christ).

It is important to note how the focus on original bodily status fits with Adam rather than Eve. Adam is first in the order of creation, and Adam is associated most closely with dust in Genesis (2:7). Further, it is Adam who is explicitly told that he will have to work the cursed land, "until you return to the ground, for out of it you were taken; you are dust, and to dust you shall return" (Gen 3:19). In Genesis this did not refer to a punishment of mortality. It was only a

88. Conzelmann, *1 Corinthians*, 293 n. 45.

89. Fitzmyer, *First Corinthians*, 597.

note that Adam's toil will last *until* he dies. His death is a product of his nature.[90] Finally, in the Septuagint, the expulsion from the Garden is addressed specifically to Adam.[91] Here, the erasure of Eve came long before Paul.

As such, Paul's Adam/Christ comparison in 1 Corinthians does not face the problem of erasing Eve from the narrative in the same way that his comparison in Romans does. When dealing with the order of creation, Adam is the originating point in the Genesis narrative. It is in the order of sin that Eve fits better as the originating point. Paul does not claim in 1 Corinthians that Adam is the source of sin. He associates Adam with death. But how hard would it be once one begins down Paul's line of thought in Corinthians to collapse the order of creation and the order of sin if one shifted the frame?

An especially tantalizing possibility here is that Paul's thought in Romans 5, when he did focus on sin as the origin of death, was influenced by The Wisdom of Solomon 2.23. There the author writes that "God created us for incorruption, and made us in the image of his own eternity, but through the devil's envy death entered the world, and those who belong to his company experience it." This articulates a doctrine of creation, sin, and death that is absent from Paul's first letter to the Corinthians.[92] But it is a doctrine that fits well with Paul's scheme in Romans 5 where he writes that "death came through sin" (5:12). Even more interestingly, as Robert Jewett notes, the wording "through the devil's envy death entered the world" offers the closest earlier parallel to Paul's claim that "sin came into the world through one man" (Rom 5:12).[93] Is it possible that Paul's scheme in Romans represents a mixing of his scheme from 1 Corinthians with The Wisdom of Solomon? Did he in Romans 5 maintain the centrality of Adam drawn from the order of creation from 1 Corinthians, eliding this with the order of sin, thus replacing Satan's role with Adam?

If such an elision, whether influenced by The Wisdom of Solomon or not, contributed to Paul's formula in Romans 5, the rhetorical slippage stands as an explanation for why Paul wrote this but not as an excuse. The erasure of Eve from the narrative comes only if one overestimates the importance of Adam's priority in creation in a way that allows Adam to come to represent everything

90. However, again, the reading of this passage as punishment of death was developing by the time of Paul. It is unclear what (or whether) he thought of this verse when writing 1 Corinthians.

91. The Hebrew text is הָאָדָם, which has been translated as the proper name Ἀδάμ in the LXX.

92. Keck, *Romans*, 150.

93. See Jewett, *Romans*, 373–374. For a fuller discussion of the parallels between the two texts, see Lee, *Death Warning in the Garden of Eden*, 169–173. James Barr suggests that one can trace all the differences between Genesis and Paul's interpretation of Genesis to The Wisdom of Soloman. James Barr, *Biblical Faith and Natural Theology: Gifford Lectures for 1991* (Oxford: Clarendon Press, 1993), 61.

that happens to humanity in the first three chapters of Genesis. Even if this made sense in Paul's patriarchal context, it is not the kind of precedent that we should want to perpetuate in our own theological language.

Paul Does Not Think Eve Capable of Originating Sin

The last in our list of possible "sources" contributing to Paul's erasure of Eve is the darkest of the bunch. Paul, as we know, was a part of a deeply patriarchal society, and he was perfectly capable of creating entirely novel misogynistic readings of scripture on his own. What if Paul did not include Eve in the narrative of originating sin because it gave her a key role in the story—a role that he did not think a woman worthy of?

In 2 Corinthians 11:3, Paul names Eve for the only time in his extant letters. He uses his reading of her role in Genesis to warn his readers: "I am afraid that as the serpent deceived Eve by its cunning, your thoughts will be led astray from a sincere and pure devotion to Christ." In this context, it is notable that Paul does not speak of Eve as sinning. Nor does he say she rebelled. Rather, she was deceived. As noted in the introduction to this chapter, Augustine suggested that this may be a different kind of failure than one might assign to Adam.[94] Much more recently, Edwin Zulu has noted that in his native patriarchal culture in Zambia, people read Genesis as pinning the primary responsibility for the fall on Adam for failing to do his duty to protect his family.[95] Was Eve, as the weaker sex, "a manipulated victim" where Adam, as the stronger sex and the proper protector of Eve, was "the sinner"?[96]

We should be extremely careful here given the history of arguments about Paul and the role of women. Paul clearly does acknowledge the role of women in ministry (Rom 16). And the baptismal formula that he cites in Galatians includes the apparently egalitarian claim that "there is no longer male and female; for all of you are one in Christ Jesus" (3:28). Further, some of the most misogynistic claims in the Pauline corpus (1 Cor 14:33–36) are later, non-Pauline additions.[97] As such, one cannot accurately paint Paul as opposed to women participating, and even leading, in the Christian movement.

But, even when Paul is trying his best, he sometimes articulates sexist arguments drawn from the same source texts that we have been examining. Take,

94. Augustine, *De Civitate Dei*, n.d., 14.41.

95. Edwin Zulu, "Sin, Gender, and Responsibility," 60.

96. For an expanded exploration of Eve as passive, manipulated victim, see Busch, "The Figure of Eve in Romans 7:5–25," 2–3.

97. Fee, *The First Epistle to the Corinthians*, 699–709.

for instance, 1 Corinthians 11. When arguing that women should wear head coverings, he alludes multiple times to Adam and Eve.

> For a man (Ἀνὴρ) ought not to have his head veiled, since he is the image and reflection of God; but woman (γυνὴ) is the reflection of man (ἀνδρός). Indeed, man (ἀνὴρ) was not made from woman (γυναικός), but woman (γυνὴ) from man (ἀνδρός). Neither was man (ἀνὴρ) created for the sake of woman (γυναῖκα), but woman (γυνὴ) for the sake of man (ἄνδρα) (vv. 7–9).

Here Paul, as Richard B. Hays writes, leads himself into a "theological quagmire."[98] It is one of the worst imaginable readings of Genesis by a person with facility in the original languages. Paul endorses the idea that men reflect God's image and glory in a way that women do not.[99] This idea can be found nowhere in Genesis 1:27, which is clearly supposed to be Paul's starting point. Paul then collapses this into a reading of Genesis 2:18 and 22 to justify a gender differentiation that is nowhere in view in those texts.

Paul's backpedal in 1 Corinthians 11:11–12[100] may leave the modern reader thinking that Paul wished he had an eraser at hand. And doubtless Paul's arguments here are meant for a specific social location.[101] But we should not

98. Richard B. Hays, *First Corinthians*, Interpretation (Louisville, KY: John Knox Press, 1997), 186.

99. As Hans Conzelmann notes "the woman is here, indirectly, excluded from being an image, or she is only in a derivative sense. This cannot be derived from gen 1:26f either—quite the contrary!" Conzelmann, *1 Corinthians*, 186; Jouette Bassler, "1 Corinthians," in Newsom and Ringe, *Women's Bible Commentary*, 416–417.

100. "Nevertheless, in the Lord woman is not independent of man or man independent of woman. For just as woman came from man, so man comes through woman; but all things come from God." Richard Hays does not believe that Paul is aiming to produce a general picture of female subordination here. He doesn't mean to violate the spirit of the baptismal formula: "There is no longer Jew or Greek, there is no longer slave or free, there is no longer male and female; for all of you are one in Christ Jesus" (Gal 3.28) (though he does cut "neither male and female" from his statement in 1 Cor 12:13). What Paul has in mind is a kind of complementarian equality between males and females, at least until the eschaton; equality with gender distinctions. See Hays, *First Corinthians*, 183. Hans Conzelman sees Paul as contradicting himself with his retreat in verses 11–12, and emphasizes the qualification "in the Lord" in these verses. Conzelmann, *1 Corinthians*. Fitzmyer sees here an explicit appeal to Gen. 3:16 and an established "hierarchy" between genders, which is then "qualified" by Paul's comments in v. 11–12, again emphasizing the qualification "in the Lord". See Fitzmyer, *First Corinthians*, 409, 420.

101. See Fitzmyer, *First Corinthians*, 406–407.

underestimate the sense in which the "ontological priority"[102] of the male is set in Paul's mind and associated with Adam and Eve. Paul does not introduce his argument in 1 Corinthians 11 as *ad hoc* but rather as a special teaching drawn deeply from "the treasury of his knowledge" or as an expression of esoteric truth.[103]

It is, at the very least, interesting that Paul's association of the image of God with Adam and Adam's son and not with Eve fits with the themes we saw in *Vita Adae et Evae* above.[104] It also echoes the reading of Paul by Stephen Hultgren above, where he argued that Paul started with the concept of the image of God, and then associated this specially with the creation of man.[105]

Paul would not have been the first to think that priority in the order of creation gave Adam a different status from Eve. Philo of Alexandria, a contemporary of Paul, writes that as Eve was produced from Adam's "side" we should understand that Adam was literally and figuratively more than the female: "the moulding of the male is more perfect than, and double, that of the female" (*Quaest in Gn* 1.25).[106]

Philo's views of Adam and Eve also fit with the kind of interpretation that might have found in Adam the primary sin in Eden. Allegorically identifying Adam with mind and Eve with sensation, Philo's reading of Genesis ultimately placed the blame on Eve for weighing Adam down, carrying the mind into the dirty world of sensation and pleasure. But many of his depictions of Eve suggest that she was not capable enough to be held fully responsible.

> And woman is more accustomed to be deceived than man. For his judgment, like his body, is masculine and is capable of dissolving or destroying the designs of deception; but the judgment of woman is more feminine, and because of softness she easily gives way and is taken in by plausible falsehoods which resemble the truth (*Quaest in Gn* 1.33).[107]

---

102. Hays, *First Corinthians*, 187.

103. Conzelmann, *1 Corinthians*, 183.

104. This idea can also be found in 2 Enoch, 30.10.

105. Hultgren, "The Origin of Paul's Doctrine of the Two Adams in 1 Corinthians 15:45–49," 369.

106. Philo of Alexandria, *Quaest in Gn*, n.d., 1.25. Translations from Philo of Alexandria, *Philo: Questions and Answers on Genesis*, trans. Ralph Marcus, The Loeb classical library 380 (Cambridge, MA: Harvard University Press, 2007).

107. For a list of similar claims in Philo, see Dorothy Sly, *Philo's Perception of Women* (Providence, RI: Brown Jewdaic Studies, 2020), 97. Throughout this section I draw upon this work.

The theme of Eve's incapability to perceive deception can also be traced back to *Vita Adae et Evae*. But Philo comes closest to explicitly qualifying Eve's moral accountability because of her incapacity. When answering the question: Why did God call to Adam and not Eve when he could not find the two in the garden? Philo responds that "being irrational, she has no capacity derived from herself to receive reproof" (*Leg All* 3.50). The primary problems in Eden were that Adam failed to lead, and Eve failed to follow. While Philo does place blame on Eve, the case could easily be made that the primary problem was really Adam failing to properly control his wife.

This leads us to a third theme that Philo and other contemporary accounts of Adam and Eve share: the sexualization of Eve's engagement with the serpent. In the original Hebrew, when Eve claims that the serpent deceived her (הִשִּׁיאַנִי), the claim is straightforward. The serpent caused her to accept a false belief. But when the passage was translated into Greek, things took a turn.[108] In the Septuagint the word used is ἠπάτησέ. This word could much more easily be taken in the sense of "seduce." By the turn of the age, interpreting Eve's "deception" as involving a sexual liaison with the serpent was becoming popular. In The Apocalypse of Moses, a sister text to *Vita Adae et Evae*, Eve's punishment of pain in childbearing seems to be linked to her sin. When in pain, God says, she will cry out "save me and I will never again turn to the sin of the flesh" (25.3–4).[109] More allegorically, Philo paints a similar picture. The serpent represents pleasure, Eve is sensation. She falls to the temptations of pleasure and then brings Adam along.[110]

In this context, it is notable that Paul accepts something like this account of Eve's "deception."[111] As noted above, in 2 Corinthians, Paul likens his readers to Eve. They are in danger of being deceived. But before he draws this comparison, he suggests that what is at stake is something like sexual purity. He reminds his readers: "I promised you in marriage to one husband, to present you as a chaste virgin to Christ" (2 Cor 11:2). The implicit contrast is to Eve's "deception" in the next verse. Thus, we know that Paul is familiar with traditions that are represented in Philo and other patriarchal first-century texts, and at times, as in 1 Corinthians 11, is at the very least willing to use them in his arguments. But did Paul implicitly take the further step of foregrounding Adam's sin in the light of Adam's patriarchal priority and primary responsibility when he says that "sin comes through one man"? Has he drawn on the picture of women as unable to

108. On this development, see Anderson, *The Genesis of Perfection*, 89–93.

109. John R. Levison, *Portraits of Adam in Early Judaism*, 169.

110. Sly, *Philo's Perception of Women*, 109.

111. For a more complete analysis, see Busch, "The Figure of Eve in Romans 7:5–25," 10–12.

control their own desires and make their own decisions, so that Adam is the only one who could really be responsible for sin?

As I have suggested in my qualification on Paul's views of women in leadership, there is good reason to find this account of Paul's motivations in Romans 5 unlikely.[112] Most evidence suggests that Paul's thought in 1 Corinthians 11 is not in keeping with his more consistent message. All of humanity has lost the image of God through sin.[113] In Christ there is no male and female. Unfortunately, we cannot entirely rule out that there was a darker side to Paul's thought—one that we glimpse only occasionally in his extant letters.

Regardless, it seems clear that if this is the reason, or one of the reasons, behind Paul's claim that "sin came into the world through one man" we have exceptionally good reasons to reject the formula. Paul's reading of Genesis as bestowing the image of God upon men and not women cannot be sustained exegetically, morally, or theologically. While one must recognize an "ontological priority" belonging to Adam in the sense that he was created first, this entails nothing regarding gender roles or hierarchy. If anything, the Bible reminds us constantly that God is in the business of reversing "ontological priority."[114] Jacob and Joseph take favor in God's plans despite being born after their brothers. And for Jesus, "the first must be last" (Mark 9:35). Nor will it do to claim that patriarchy is a system of servant leadership. Benevolent patriarchy is as sure to undermine the agency and value of women as any other kind of patriarchy. If that is what lay behind Paul's formula, we are well rid of it.

Conclusion

In this chapter, I have argued that while Paul's intent in Romans 5:12–21 is to paint a picture in which the whole of the world can be caught up into the new creation through Christ, the formula that he used to paint that picture is problematic. I have argued that in Paul's claim that "sin came into the world through one man," the gendering is significant. It has a clear referent in Adam, who is a male and whose identity is not lost in a process of abstraction. This is especially true in the light of the fact that Paul's formula erases Eve from the narrative of Eden. While this may at first seem to be a better option than blaming Eve, as almost all sources had done in the Second Temple period, it is ultimately

---

112. One does fear, to quote Daniel Boyarin, that "on the issue of gender, as on several other matters of equal significance, Paul seems to have produced a discourse which is so contradictory as to be almost incoherent." Daniel Boyarin, *A Radical Jew: Paul and the Politics of Identity*, Contraversions 1 (Berkeley, CA: University of California Press, 1997), 183.

113. Dunn, *Christology in the Making*, 105.

114. Anderson, "The Exaltation of Adam and the Fall of Satan," 99–102.

unsatisfactory. Erasure is a patriarchal alternative to blame. Both stand as ways that women have been marginalized throughout history. And in this case, erasing the primary agent in the story of sin raises questions about how women will be treated through the rest of the narrative of sin and salvation.

I then explored several possible sources or motivations for Paul's formula in Romans 5:12–21. Paul's formula is not found elsewhere, but there are near traditions that could help us understand how Paul alighted on his formula. My goal in articulating these sources and motivations was not to argue that one or another was true. It was only to explore to what extent these background accounts might address our concerns about sex/gender in the passage. Unfortunately, none of these provide a redeeming account for why one would erase Eve from the narrative.

At this point, if my argument has succeeded, we also find a tension between Paul's intention and his final formula. The formula might have been chosen for effectiveness in a patriarchal society. In such a context, the problems with the formula might have been obscured from view. Even then, however, the problems in matching this formula with the universal possibility of salvation through Christ existed. In a society that is more sensitive to issues of gender difference and gender justice, it is all the more clear that Paul's formula cannot achieve what he himself set out to achieve with it. If we are going to honor Paul, we would at least need to adjust his formula to achieve his own end.

We are not the first ones to think that Paul's formula was missing something, or the first to think that Eve needed to be reinserted into this narrative. Several early Christians appear to have similarly sensed a lack. Their answer was to add onto each side of the formula. Adam *and Eve* are to sin what *Mary and* Jesus are to salvation. This attempted patch to the tradition, I will argue, led to even more theological issues without adequately addressing the problems we have raised here. It is to this argument that we now must turn in the next chapter.

CHAPTER THREE

The Mary Solution

> If the first woman God ever made was strong enough to turn the world upside down all alone, together women ought to be able to turn it rightside up again.
>
> —Sojourner Truth

THUS FAR, WE have looked at two patriarchal narratives drawn from Genesis in Second Temple Judaism. We have seen Eve blamed and erased. But in the process, a more complex pattern has been emerging, and we need to flesh it out to make sense of the next stage in our exploration. In the last chapter, I investigated the relationship between Paul's arguments in 1 Corinthians 15 and Romans 5. There I argued that the two focus on different topics: 1 Corinthians on body, Romans 5 on sin. In the light of this difference, the formula in Romans 5 presents problems that are not in sight in 1 Corinthians. This is because the Adam/Christ typology in 1 Corinthians depends on the order of creation. In the order of creation, Adam comes first, Jesus comes last. As such, a soteriology that covers everything from Adam forward includes Eve.

The Order of Creation

- →

Adam   Eve   Jesus

In contrast, when focused on the order of sin, a soteriology that covers everything from Adam forward leaves Eve outside. This is a fundamental theological problem raised by Romans 5.

The Order of Sin

          - →

Eve   Adam   Jesus

Since Paul's decision to make the Adam-Jesus connection in Romans is influenced by gendered considerations, when we look at this visualization, we may find ourselves asking with Rosemary Radford Reuther: Can a male savior save women?[1] Reviewing the development of Mariology in the early church, Tina Beattie has wondered if women in that period did not ask similar questions.[2]

One of the earliest themes in Mariology may suggest that they did. Early Christians developed what appears to have been an augmentation of or alternative to Paul's typology. Instead of focusing on Adam and Christ, they focused on Eve and Mary the mother of Christ. The earliest statements of this theme can be seen in the *Protoevangelium of James* and the work of Justin Martyr. But neither of these sources coordinated the Eve/Mary typology with the Adam/Christ typology. This work was left to Irenaeus of Lyons, the greatest theologian of the second century. Indeed, Irenaeus seems to have thought that together the two typologies might offer a more adequate scheme than either of them on their own. If the Adam/Christ typology left Eve outside the narrative of fall and salvation, the Eve/Mary typology might offer a second strand of the narrative, one that could be thrown as a soteriological lifeline back to Eve.

The Order of Sin (with the Mary solution)

Eve Adam Mary Jesus

That it was Irenaeus who made this connection is fitting. Greatly concerned with the economy of salvation, he paid close attention to the ordering, steps, and parallelisms in God's plan to bind alpha to omega. But this was, even for Irenaeus, a troublesome project. It was only undertaken at the "risk of creating serious theological difficulties for the tradition."[3] Still, it was, Irenaeus saw, a necessary risk if one were to address the problems that already existed.

Unfortunately, Irenaeus ends up playing a tragic role in our story. While he was the first who seems to have taken the full measure of the problem, in the form that he attacked it, the problem was insoluble. He was destined to fail in producing a scheme that would pass muster for both consistency and

1. Rosemary Radford Ruether, *Sexism and God-Talk: Toward a Feminist Theology: With a New Introduction*, 10th anniversary ed (Boston: Beacon Press, 1993), 116–38. See also Margaret Daphne Hampson, *Theology and Feminism*, Signposts in Theology (Cambridge, MA: Blackwell, 1990), 50–80; Elisabeth Schüssler Fiorenza, *Jesus: Miriam's Child, Sophia's Prophet: Critical Issues in Feminist Christology*, Second edition, Cornerstones (New York: T&T Clark, 2015), 35–70.

2. Tina Beattie, *God's Mother, Eve's Advocate: A Marian Narrative of Women's Salvation* (New York: Continuum, 2002), 167.

3. Sarah Parvis and Paul Foster, "Introduction: Irenaeus and His Traditions," in *Irenaeus: Life, Scripture, Legacy*, ed. Sarah Parvis and Paul Foster (Minneapolis, MN: Fortress Press, 2012), 8.

theological orthodoxy. First, while the new scheme was internally coherent as a way to address the order of sin, it was extremely hard to square with the order of creation. Adam was created first, and Eve from Adam. Mary came first (at least in human form) and gave birth to Christ. Adam and Eve were husband and wife, and sexual partners. Mary and Christ were mother and son. If confusing the order of creation and the order of sin had caused problems for Paul, it would create even more massive issues for the Christian theologians who followed.[4] Resolving these problems would require rhetorical gymnastics that pushed the credibility of the typology almost, if not completely to breaking.

But more important for our purposes was the theological problem with the augmented typology. The whole project of early Christianity started out as a way to show the unique offering of salvation that came through Christ, the God-man. Indeed, most of the invocations of Mary in early theology were for the purposes of shoring up this central claim. But if this central claim were maintained, the Mary solution could only provide what was at best a second-class soteriological lifeline for Eve. And if it were abandoned, it led to the idolization of Mary as a second savior. Either solution raised significant questions about whether Christ was necessary to salvation. Irenaeus teetered between the two, never resolving the tension.

Moving beyond Irenaeus, we will review two other theologians who similarly try and fail to patch the problem of locating Eve via appeals to Mary: Tertullian and Gregory of Nazianzus. Tracing the problem through these two theologians reveals that the problem continued in different forms in both the Latin and Greek traditions. Exploring the different routs they took to address the problem also highlights just how intractable the problem turns out to be if one accepts the basic premises that gave rise to it.

There was, of course, another solution: to make Christ alone the answer for both Eve and Adam. Christ could have become the new Adam *and* Eve, or the new Eve. None of the authors we will explore contemplated this route. It was likely not a live option for them. This is doubtless partly because they are attempting to maintain the formula that Paul put forward. As I have argued in the last chapter, gendered assumptions played a key role in that formula. As such, these authors had no option but to maintain a gendered order established by tradition. As Benjamin Dunning writes, the "specter of Paul haunted . . . theological imagination in ways that were not easily resolved."[5] But beyond this, we can also see, at least for Tertullian and Irenaeus, that they had their own reasons for maintaining sex/gender as key categories in their theology. Both posited

4. Stephen O. Presley, *The Intertextual Reception of Genesis 1–3 in Irenaeus of Lyons*, The Bible in Ancient Christianity 8 (Boston: Brill, 2015), 113.

5. Benjamin H. Dunning, *Specters of Paul: Sexual Difference in Early Christian Thought*, Divinations (Philadelphia: University of Pennsylvania Press, 2011), 135.

that sexual/gender difference was built into the creation and would last into the eschaton in some form. As such, they had multiple reasons not to simply expand the gendered Christ to sufficiently cover Eve and her sin without remainder.

Before we can return to these issues, however, we must start at the beginning of the Eve/Mary tradition, and to get to that we shall need to look at the early development of popular Mariology.

Protoevangelium of James

The origins of the early cult of Mary are lost to the fog of history. What we do know is that it appears to have developed quickly, at least in some segments of the Christian population. Formal theologians had their own reasons for emphasizing the role of Mary as the human mother of Christ, but Mary's status in some popular expressions of Christianity seems early on to have exceeded what was necessary for this supporting role. The rapidity of Mary's rise suggests that her elevation was in some way related to pre-Christian traditions. Some theorize that pagan women who converted to Christianity promoted Mary as a way of holding onto practices and beliefs in their previous goddess cults.[6] Others suggest that Mary's role was enlarged as she became associated with a rejection of the goddess cults. Mary evolved into a paragon of Christian femininity as an alternative to the goddesses.[7] The valorization of Mary may also have been in part in response to smear campaigns against the mother of Jesus by pagan apologists.[8]

What is clear is that by the middle of the second century it was possible to hold a remarkably high Mariology. This possibility is represented in the *Protoevangelium of James,* a pseudonymous, noncanonical text from the middle to end of the second century. While the text presents itself as written by James the brother of Jesus, the author has little knowledge of Jewish law, Jewish cult, or Palestinian geography. As such, the text is of no value in providing historical information about Mary, and yet it has had a deep influence on Christian tradition. While the *Protoevangelium* includes the story of Jesus's birth, it is a text primarily about Mary as "a human creature totally enclosed in sacred

6. Stephen Benko, *The Virgin Goddess: Studies in the Pagan and Christian Roots of Mariology*, Studies in the History of Religions 59 (New York: Brill, 1993); Rosemary Radford Ruether, *Mary, the Feminine Face of the Church* (Philadelphia: Westminster Press, 1977), 13–18.

7. Beattie, *God's Mother, Eve's Advocate*, 62 suggests that this is at least the view that the "fathers" of the Church may have taken. See her wider review of the literature (60–63).

8. Stephen J. Shoemaker, *Mary in Early Christian Faith and Devotion* (New Haven: Yale University Press, 2016), 54.

space."[9] Indeed, the text is so fixed upon Mary that "a reader who knew only the *Protoevangelium* might reasonably conclude that Mary is the holy figure and that Jesus' holiness derives from her."[10]

The text begins by relating the story of Mary's miraculous birth to a wealthy but previously barren couple named Joachim and Anna. Mary is born, auspiciously, in the seventh month of Anna's pregnancy and learns to walk by the age of six months. For three years, she lives in the sanctuary of her bed chamber, cared for by the "undefiled daughters of the Hebrews," (6)[11] never touching the ground. During this time, she receives superlative blessings from the priests of Israel. Eventually she is transferred to live in the Temple and is only removed from the Temple when she reaches the age of menstruation. At this point, Joseph is selected (by a miraculous sign) from the widowers of Judea to be Mary's betrothed caretaker. Generally following the Gospel of Luke, the nativity story follows. When Mary and Joseph are separated for some months, Mary receives news from an angel that she will give birth, and the baby grows in her womb. When Joseph finds out, he fears that she has violated her virginity but is corrected by an angel. When the pregnancy becomes public, Mary and Joseph are tested by being required to drink "waters of conviction" that are said to harm adulterers. Both pass the test unharmed. On their way to Bethlehem Mary begins labor and they are forced to stop in a cave. While Joseph leaves to find a midwife, time halts as Mary gives birth. Joseph returns to the cave with a midwife only to be greeted first by a great cloud and then a great light as they come near. Mary, Joseph, and child are then joined by a woman named Salome, who doubts Mary's continued virginity. Seeking to test whether Mary is still intact, Salome "puts forth her finger" and her hand is promptly burned and "falls away" from her (20.1). The narrative concludes with what is probably a later addition, the story of the wise men's visitation.

Though rarely emphasized in studies of the *Protoevangelium*, evidence suggests that the text was written to reflect an underlying comparison between Eve and Mary.[12] The echoes of the Genesis narrative begin with Anna, before Mary

---

9. Peter Brown, *The Body and Society: Men, Women and Sexual Renunciation in Early Christianity* (London: Faber and Faber, 1989), 273; Ronald Hock, *The Infancy Gospels of James and Thomas*, The Scholars Bible 2 (Santa Rosa, CA: Polebridge Press, 1995), 14.

10. Beverly Roberts Gaventa, *Mary. Glimpses of the Mother of Jesus*, Personalities of the New Testament (Edinburgh: T&T Clark, 1999), 119.

11. Translations and original language taken from Bart D. Ehrman and Zlatko Pleše, eds., *The Apocryphal Gospels: Texts and Translations* (New York: Oxford University Press, 2011).

12. Kretschmar, "Natus ex Maria Virgine,' 417–428. My argument here expands on Kretchmar's insight.

has arrived on the scene. While barren, Joachim leaves Anna to go and pray in the wilderness. This is a parallel of the tradition found in The Apocalypse of Moses (7.2–3), when Adam left Eve alone before her temptation. While Joachim is gone, Anna's maidservant offers her a headband as a kind of talisman to aid in her becoming pregnant. To this Anna, suspicious, responds, "For all I know, some scoundrel (πανοῦργος) has given this to you, and you have come to implicate me in your sin" (2.3). The word translated as "scoundrel" here is the same as the word used in Theodotion's mid–second century revision of the Septuagint to translate "clever" (עָרוּם / ʿārûm) in the claim that the serpent was the most "clever" of the animals in Genesis 3:1.[13] Here Anna is tempted with a solution to her barrenness but saved by her suspicion. She will rely upon God alone.

Anna then goes to her garden (παράδεισον/parádeison) to pray. The word here is the same as that found in the LXX for the garden of Eden. By the time of the New Testament, the term had taken up a double meaning, serving both for "garden" and "paradise." In the garden, Anna sits under a "laurel tree." The Greek is more specific here, labeling the tree as δαφνιδέαν (dafnidéan). This is a laurel tree that is associated with the Greek myth of Daphne, who was transformed into a tree while attempting to escape Apollo's coercive, amorous pursuit. Apollo, unwilling to give up his love, assigned the tree a special place as the source of the laurel wreaths of victors. "And as my head is ever young and my locks unshorn, so do thou keep the beauty of thy leaves perpetual."[14] In short, Anna sits down under a tree of life in a garden to contemplate and pray to God about her fruitlessness.

In the process, Anna laments that she is "not like this soil, for even this soil (γῆ) produces its fruit in its season . . ." The immediate reference here is to Psalm 1:3. Those who do not follow the advice of the wicked "are like trees planted by streams of water, which yield their fruit in its season, and their leaves do not wither." Again, this imagery invokes an ever-living tree. But the subject of the sentence has been changed from trees to soil, possibly referring to the creation of Adam, formed from the dust of the earth (γῆς) (Gen 2:6 LXX).

This makes it appropriate that, upon Mary's first birthday, after hearing the priests' blessing for her daughter. Anna proclaims: "The Lord my God has given me the fruit of his righteousness" (3). The immediate reference here appears to

---

13. John William Wevers, *Notes on the Greek Text of Genesis*, Septuagint and Cognate Studies Series 35 (Atlanta, GA: Scholars Press, 1993), 36 n. 3; The LXX translates עָרוּם as φρονιμώτατος in Gen 3:1. But it translates the same term as πανοῦργος in Job 5:12, Prov 12:16, 13:16, 14:8, 22:3, and 27:12. Brayford, *Genesis*, 38, 236.

14. Ovid, Metamorphosis, 1.553–567. Translation from Publius Ovidius Naso, *Ovid. 3: Metamorphoses Books I–VIII*, trans. Frank Justus Miller, The Loeb Classical Library 42 (New York: G.P. Putnam's Son's, 1916).

be Proverbs 11:30: "The fruit of the righteous is a tree of life."[15] Thus, a line is drawn between Mary and the tree of life.

The allusions to Genesis continue in Mary's story. As Anna wished for fertile soil, Mary is prohibited from coming in contact with soil. When Mary takes her first steps, Anna swears, "As the Lord my God lives, you will not walk at all on this ground (γῆ) until I have taken you up to the Temple of the Lord." At stake here is clearly Mary's purity, but if this is a reference to Adam, the concern becomes more clearly associated with sex and reproduction.

As a child, Mary is raised at the Temple, a location that, at least since the time of the writing of the Book of Jubilees, had been identified with the garden of Eden (Jub. 3:9–14).[16] Mary is required to leave the temple when she loses her childlike state, that is, when she begins menstruating. Thus, she is transferred to a sexless betrothal to Joseph.

Again, in a parallel of Second Temple Adam and Eve tradition, Joseph now leaves Mary alone as he goes off to construct buildings.[17] From this point, as Georg Kretschmar has argued, the comparison to Eve becomes more earnest and more focused. These comparisons have one telos: the virgin birth. For contemporary Christians, this will not seem surprising. But as Kretschmar points out, this is a significant shift from the Gospel narrative. In the canonical Gospels the miracle at stake is a virgin conception. If this is where the tradition stayed, it would not have made a good inversion of the Eve story. Eve is primarily associated with the punishment of painful childbirth. Thus, any adequate reversal must address this key issue. In the *Protoevangelium* we find a shift in emphasis "from conception to birth."[18]

This does not mean that the author of the *Protoevangelium* rejects the virgin conception. The most explicit parallel with Eve still focuses on this miracle. When Joseph returns to find Mary pregnant, he echoes God's question to Eve (Gen 3:13):[19] "Why have you done this?" (τί τοῦτο ἐποίησας). Then he laments: "Who has done this wicked deed in my home and defiled the virgin? Has not the entire history of Adam been summed up in me? For just as Adam was singing praise to God, when the serpent came and found Eve alone and led her astray, so too has this now happened to me" (13.1). This draws upon the tradition

15. Wilhelm Schneemelcher and R. McL Wilson, eds., *New Testament Apocrypha. Vol. 1*, Revised Edition (Louisville, KY: Westminster John Knox, 2003), 428, 437 n.24 makes this connection.

16. Kretschmar, "Natus ex Maria Virgine," 424.

17. Kretschmar, 423.

18. Kretschmar, 420. Translations mine.

19. LXX: "τί τοῦτο ἐποίησας" Brayford, *Genesis*; Hock, *The Infancy Gospels of James and Thomas*, 21.

that claims that Eve was sexually seduced by the serpent. It also makes explicit the comparison between Eve and Mary and Adam and Joseph. While Joseph complains that he has become the new Adam, the reader knows that what has happened is exactly the opposite. When Joseph is soon visited by an angel, the "instructions to Joseph implicitly reject [Joseph's] typology and rescue Mary from the taint of Eve."[20] By this point, "the use of the Adam and Eve story to interpret Mary's story" is established.[21]

While the focus on virgin conception is not abandoned, its significance is reduced. Like Eve's, Anna's husband had been away when she received the message about her pregnancy, and most manuscripts of the *Protoevangelium* say that, when angels come to Joachim while he is away from his wife, they tell him that his "wife Anna has conceived a child" (4.2). Thus, Anna experiences a virgin conception just as Mary will later on. Repeating a similar miracle over two generations relativizes the impact of Mary's virgin conception.

After the conception, the theme of hiding shame enters the narrative. When Mary returns home from Elizabeth's, she "hid (ἔκρυβεν) herself from the sons of Israel" (12.3). This parallels Adam and Eve, who hid (LXX: ἐκρύβησαν/ἐκρύβην) from God in the garden (Gen 3:8, 10). When Joseph finds out about Mary's pregnancy, he suggests that she has "humiliated [her] soul" (ἐταπείνωσας τὴν ψυχήν) (13.2) Like Eve, he is suggesting, she has brought shame upon herself. Though Genesis does not speak of shame, it was widely accepted by the second century that Adam and Eve were hiding to cover their shame after the first sin. When Mary is brought before the High Priest, the High Priest repeats the accusation that Mary has brought shame on herself (15.3). Finally, when Mary requests to halt their journey to Bethlehem to give birth, Joseph asks: "Where can I take you to hide your shame (ἀσχημοσύνην)?" (17.3). Each time the intimation of shame is followed by a reversal. Mary passes the tests that show she has suffered no shame in her conception. And even in the process of giving birth, her nakedness is covered by the glory of God.

As virgin conception is marginalized, virgin birth takes center stage.[22] Mary's first reaction to the angel who informs her of her special role is not to marvel at the virgin conception, but to ask herself whether she will give birth like other women (11.2). To this unspoken query the Angel responds, "Not so, Mary. For the power of God will overshadow you. Therefore, the holy one

20. Gaventa, *Mary. Glimpses of the Mother of Jesus*, 116.

21. Gaventa, 116.

22. If Georg Zervos is right, the addition of the virgin birth is a later redaction of the text. Here I have not assumed Zervos theory of redaction. George Zervos, *The Protevangelium of James: Greek Text, English Translation, Critical Introduction*, vol. 1 (New York: Bloomsbury Publishing, 2019), 171–73.

born from you will be called the Son of the Highest" (11.3). The words here are a reference to the Angel's communication in Luke 1:35, but their meaning has been transformed by the context. In Luke, the angel responds to Mary's question about how she can conceive while still a virgin. In the *Protoevangelium*, the angel responds to a question about how Mary can give birth and still be a virgin.

In case readers missed this shift, the narrative reinforces it at the time of Jesus's birth. In the Gospel of Luke, the Holy Spirit was to come upon Mary, and she was to be "overshadowed" (ἐπισκιάσει) by God in the process of conception. But the *Protoevangelium* says that when Joseph returned to Mary after the birth of Jesus, he is confronted by a bright cloud that "overshadowed" (ἐπισκιάζουσο) the cave.[23] The cloud is a clear reference to God's presence (Exod 16:10; 19:9; 24:15–16).

Salome's test of Mary's postpartum virginity finishes out the shift in emphasis from conception to birth, but to what end? The tradition that Mary gives birth without pain will be expressed explicitly in the Odes of Solomon (19.8).[24] However, as Kretschmar argues, the logic of the painless birth is contained in the *Protoevangelium*, even if it is not explicitly stated. Mary is the inversion of Eve. She has been loyal to God even while her husband was away, and she is saved from Eve's *punishment*.

Determinations

If the above analysis is correct, we have an instance of an early, popular manifestation of the Mary/Eve typology. What was driving this development? Some of the same motives that drove the origins of Mariology in general. We know that some early gnostics took Eve as a positive role model.[25] Rejecting the evil God of material creation, Eve defiantly sought gnosis from the tree. If Eve came to be tied to pagan goddesses or a positive gnostic portrayal of her role in Genesis, Mary might have been seen by proto-orthodox Christians as a healthy alternative. Thus, the contrast between Eve and Mary would have been a narrative parallel of a sociological situation in early Christianity. The parallel may also have developed in part as a rejection of pagan criticism of Mary. Celsus, a pagan critic of Christianity, claimed Mary was seduced by a Roman soldier and gave birth to Jesus as a bastard. Other claims by Celsus, that Mary and Joseph were poor and not of royal lineage and that Mary had to work as a spinner because

23. Kretschmar, "Natus ex Maria Virgine," 421.

24. Shoemaker, *Mary in Early Christian Faith and Devotion*, 44.

25. Elaine Pagels, *Adam, Eve, and the Serpent* (New York: Penguin Books, 1990), 69–71, 77.

of her poverty, are clearly countered in the *Protoevangelium*.[26] It may be that placing Mary as the inversion of Eve was a way of rejecting the claim that Mary had given into seduction, which was securely associated with Eve.

How would these developments be related to the Pauline tradition of the Adam/Christ typology? Kretchmar argues that it is extremely unlikely that the two traditions developed independently of one another.[27] But the *Protoevangelium* reveals no interest in maintaining the Pauline tradition. It is Joseph who takes on the role of the new Adam in this text. This may be, as noted in the introduction to the chapter, a simple product of the problematic relation between the Adam/Christ and Eve/Mary typologies. Given that Mary and Christ are mother and son, while Eve and Adam are spouses, there is a structural problem that irritates every effort to harmonize the two typologies.

Kretchmar, however, suggests another alternative.[28] We know that the Pauline tradition was the source of some controversy in the early church, exactly over the treatment of women. The pseudonymous Pastoral Epistles (1 Tim, 2 Tim, and Titus) presented a Paul that was clearly in favor of accommodation to established Greco-Roman gender roles, with the woman finding her place underneath the paterfamilias in marriage. On the other hand, the Acts of Paul and Thecla, a non-canonical text from the same period, emphasized Paul's endorsement of asceticism and celibacy, thus granting women spiritual and material autonomy from men.[29] Linked with this, such texts saw women as independent leaders in the early church.

Within this context, the idea of a painless birth is significant. 1 Timothy 2:15 suggests that Eve is uniquely guilty of sin and presents the position that following Eve, women are "saved through childbearing." Undergoing the punishment of Eve becomes a soteriological act for women. Could it be the *Protoevangelium* represents another perspective in this argument, one that did not seek to reclaim Paul's authority for liberating women, but that offered an alternative typology to the one that Paul had put forward? If so, this would be a tradition orthogonally

26. See Ehrman and Pleše "The Proto-Gospel of James: The Birth of Mary, the Revelation of James" Ehrman and Pleše, *The Apocryphal Gospels*, 34–35; Shoemaker, *Mary in Early Christian Faith and Devotion*, 54. For a full analysis of Celsus' arguments, see Margaret Y. MacDonald, *Early Christian Women and Pagan Opinion: The Power of the Hysterical Woman* (New York: Cambridge University Press, 1996), 95–102. However, note that Hock warns against assuming that the text is a direct response to Celsus. Hock, *The Infancy Gospels of James and Thomas*, 11–12.

27. Kretschmar, "Natus ex Maria Virgine," 426.

28. Kretschmar, 426.

29. Dennis Ronald MacDonald, *The Legend and the Apostle: The Battle for Paul in Story and Canon* (Philadelphia: Westminster, 1983); Dale B Martin, *New Testament History & Literature* (New Haven, CT: Yale University Press, 2012), 277–308.

related to either of the above alternatives. It does not directly celebrate the rejection of marriage or celibacy. But neither does it suggest that women should accept the punishment of Eve, living their lives in hierarchical family relationships. Rather, it sees a path forward for women that follows that of Mary, who becomes glorified through her own faithfulness and obedience to God.

If something like this is the correct interpretation, Tina Beattie is right to wonder whether early Christian women were struggling with how to locate themselves in relation to a male savior.[30] And, the Pauline Adam/Christ typology was playing a vital role in these struggles, even if its primary role was inspiring alternative formulations.

Justin Martyr

Though the *Protoevangelium* gives us a view into an early form of popular Mariology, it was not alone in the second century in thinking about the relationship between Mary and Eve. Early Christian theologians whether reflecting the same popular *movement*, or for their own reasons, were developing formulas relating the two.

We must be careful, however, to take different statements in their own contexts. The earliest is found in Justin Martyr's Dialogue with Trypho. Interestingly, Justin's statement of the relationship does not appear to share any of the same concerns as those driving the *Protoevangelium*. We do not find in Justin's short comments any emphasis on Mary's holiness or any suggestion of her virginity postpartum. In fact, in the comparison of Mary *and* Eve we do not find an emphasis on the miraculous nature of Mary's virginity at all, in relation to either conception or birth.

Justin does not mean to diminish the importance of the virgin conception.[31] At other points in the Dialogue with Trypho, Justin specifies that Mary's virginity is a "sign" that God has used to point to the significance of Jesus' birth (84.1–3). But even here what is important about the miracle has nothing to do with Mary. What is important is that it makes the birth of Christ distinctive, and distinctive in a way that fits with Justin's reading of Hebrew scripture.

The Dialogue is ostensibly aimed at a Jew named Trypho, with the goals of articulating the relationship between "Judaism" and "Christianity" and winning Trypho over to the latter[32] In the process, Justin wishes to avoid the "heresies" of both judaizers, who required obedience to Torah law, and those he sees as

30. Beattie, *God's Mother, Eve's Advocate*, 167.

31. See Justin Martyr, The First Apology, *32.14–34.2*

32. Daniel Boyarin, "Justin Martyr Invents Judaism," *Church History* 70, no. 3 (September 2001): 427–461.

wayward Christians. Especially important here are the Marcionites, who claimed the God of the Hebrew scriptures was evil in contrast with the God of Jesus and the New Testament. In a rejection of Marcionism and an appeal to interested Jews, Justin emphasized the continuity of Christianity with the Hebrew Scriptures. At the same time, he attempted to show that the "Jews" rejected the Messiah that God had foretold and sent to them, and that gentile Christians had become the new Israel.[33]

It is in this context that Mary's virginity is a "sign," not primarily because it is a miracle, but because it is a distinctive form of birth that Justin finds predicted in the LXX translation of Isaiah 7:14. Elsewhere Justin's references to the "virgin" focus more on the fact that she is a true descendent of the patriarchs of Israel than on the miraculous nature of her conception (*Dial. 100*.2–3).

This is also the context in which we should read Justin's short comments on Mary and Eve.

> He is become incarnate of the Virgin, in order that the disobedience caused by the serpent might be destroyed in the same manner in which it had originated. For Eve, an undefiled virgin, conceived the word (λόγον) of the serpent, and brought forth disobedience and death. But the virgin Mary, filled with faith and joy, when the angel Gabriel announced to her the good tidings that the Spirit of the Lord would come upon her, and the power of the Most High would overshadow her, and therefore, the holy one born of her would be the Son of God, answered, 'Be it done unto me in accordance with your word (ῥῆμά).' And, indeed, she gave birth to him, concerning whom we have shown so many passages of Scripture were written, and by whom God destroys both the serpent and those angels and men who have come to resemble the serpent but frees from death those who repent of their sins and believe in Christ.[34]

In this passage the miraculous nature of Mary's conception only receives a wink. What is important is the way in which the parallel between the two

33. Susan J. Wendel, *Scriptural Interpretation and Community Self-Definition in Luke-Acts and the Writings of Justin Martyr*, Supplements to Novum Testamentum 139 (Boston: Brill, 2011); Matthijs den Dulk, *Between Jews and Heretics: Refiguring Justin Martyr's Dialogue with Trypho* (New York: Routledge, 2020); David E. Nyström, *The Apology of Justin Martyr: Literary Strategies and the Defence of Christianity*, Wissenschaftliche Untersuchungen Zum Neuen Testament. 2. Reihe 462 (Tübingen: Mohr Siebeck, 2018), 120.

34. Justin Martyr, *Dialogue with Trypho*, 100.5. Trans. Thomas B Falls. Selections from the Fathers of the Church, vol. 3. Ed. Michael Slusser. (Washington, DC: Catholic University of America Press. 2003). Greek text available at: https://scaife.perseus.org/library/urn:cts:greek-Lit:tlg0645.tlg003/

women binds together the Hebrew scriptures and the New Testament so that the New Testament is the fulfillment of the old. Both women are virgins (παρθένος) who conceive the "word" of a superhuman agent. Justin is restrained here because he is tied to the word choice in the Gospel of Luke, which set (ῥῆμά) as the term for "word" in the annunciation. But there can be no doubt, especially with Justin's Logos Christology,[35] that he means to present a parallel between the logos of the serpent and the Logos of God. The ultimate payoff of this parallel is to bring attention to another passage that Justin can locate as a prophetic anticipation of Christ's work.

Genesis 3:15 is an etiological verse, meant to explain the animosity between humans and serpents. Because of the serpent's role in originating sin, God makes there to be enmity between Eve and the serpent, and between their offspring: "he will strike your head, and you will strike his heel." By the second century, the identification of the serpent with the devil was well established. From here it took the least of figurative reading for Christians to see this as a prophecy of the battle between Christ and Satan. In this form the verse became a "protoevangel" or "proto-gospel" foretelling the end of the story in the beginning.[36] Eventually, in Mariological texts, Mary will be located as active in the bashing of the snake. But here in Justin we find an early allusion that attributes the activity directly to God through Christ.[37]

Determinations

How does this use of the Mary/Eve typology relate to our concerns about the fit of the typology and the relation to Paul's Adam Christ typology? The parallel between Mary and Eve is, we must say, "precarious."[38] The two are likened in being virgins. Though the Genesis account does not say that Adam and Eve remained celibate within Eden, the parallel is certainly necessary to get the

35. Nyström, *The Apology of Justin Martyr*, 101–115.

36. Jaroslav Pelikan, *Mary through the Centuries: Her Place in the History of Culture* (New Haven, CT: Yale University Press, 1996), 26; Robert Fastiggi, "Mary in the Work of Redemption," in *The Oxford Handbook of Mary*, ed. Chris Maunder, Oxford Handbooks (New York: Oxford University Press, 2019), 304.

37. Justin Martyr, *Dialogue with Trypho*, 94.2. Trans. Thomas B Falls. Selections from the Fathers of the Church, vol. 3. Ed. Michael Slusser. (Washington, DC: Catholic University of America Press. 2003). Greek text available at: https://scaife.perseus.org/library/urn:cts:greekLit:tlg0645.tlg003/

38. Dunning, *Specters of Paul*, 207; Helen Rhee, "Irenaeus and Paul: Sexuality, Virginity, and Women," in *Irenaeus and Paul*, ed. Todd D. Still and David E. Wilhite (London: T&T Clark, 2020), 212.

comparison off the ground.[39] Having both conceive by the word of a superhuman agent requires one to embrace the tradition that Eve was "seduced" rather than simply "deceived" by the serpent and accept that the serpent represents Satan. Both were, at Justin's time, secure enough as readings of the Genesis narrative, even if they sit on dubious exegetical foundations.

But even allowing for these traditional bits of eisegesis, there are significant problems with the typological parallel between the two "births." Eve births (ἔτεκε) disobedience and death, whereas Mary gives birth to a god-man. The comparison is, at best, a stretch. Especially in later uses of Mary's role in theology, where she is used to secure the humanity and materiality of Christ, will the metaphorical birth from Eve not raise problems?

As we shall see in a moment, it is not clear at all whether Justin is constructing his Eve/Mary parallel with the Adam/Christ model in mind. But, even if the Eve/Mary scheme is independent, we can already here identify some of the pressures building toward making an idol of Mary. Eve is the source of disobedience and death. Mary is *the mother of* the source of obedience and life. This distinction is crucial to maintaining the uniqueness and utter necessity of Christ's role.

Mary's will (her choice to accept God) plays a significant role in the story of the annunciation and conception. But acknowledging this, we reach a problem. If we locate her acceptance of God as the parallel to Eve's acceptance of the serpent's temptation, then just as Eve is the source of disobedience and death. Mary is the source of obedience and life.[40] We have already solved the problem of disobedience and death, even before Christ enfleshed has reached the scene. As with the *Protoevangelium*, though from a quite different starting point, Justin's treatment shows us how easy it is once one starts down this road to land oneself with a serious theological problem.

Things will only become more complicated when relating this typology to the Adam/Christ typology. But is Justin not already doing this? Unfortunately, the answer is far from clear. Justin was based in Rome, the city of the church to which Paul had *written* when he elaborated his Adam/Christ typology almost a century before. Paul's letters seem to have been accessible in Rome by Justin's time.[41] They were used by the author of 1 Clement, and they played a key role in

39. Beattie, *God's Mother, Eve's Advocate*, 175.

40. Lanne makes the inverse point: "If Mary's role in redemption is only passive, the same could be said about the role of Eve in disobedience." Emmanuel Lanne, "Marian Doctrine and Piety up to the Council of Chalcedon: The Fathers and the Liturgy," ed. Anglican/Roman Catholic International Commission, Nicholas Sagovsky, and Adelbert Denaux (New York: T&T Clark, 2007), 40.

41. Paul Foster, "Justin and Paul," in *Paul and the Second Century*, ed. Michael F. Bird and Joseph R. Dodson, Library of New Testament Studies 412 (New York: T&T Clark, 2011), 109.

Marcion's theological project.[42] Like Justin, Marcion was working out of Rome. And yet, Justin nowhere mentions Paul in any of his extant writings.

It seems unlikely that Justin is unfamiliar with Paul, so accounting for the absence of explicit reference has exercised some scholastic effort. It may be that Justin does not reference Paul because Paul has been so thoroughly co-opted by Marcion that Justin would rather avoid the association or would rather avoid Paul entirely.[43] Oscar Skarsaune has argued that Justin does draw upon Paul, but he does not do so explicitly. Rather, we can find Paul's influence in the form of some of Justin's citations of Hebrew scripture, which at times more closely follow Paul's quoted versions than the LXX.[44] However, Paul Foster has countered that even when the linguistic parallels are quite close, Justin's argumentation usually departs significantly from Paul's. Thus, it is better to assume that the parallels are the product of either inherited traditions or collections of testamonia that have been excerpted from Paul.[45]

Whatever the exact situation, Justin does not appear to take Paul's *writings* as authoritative scripture. For example, in the Dialogue 80.5, Justin claims that he and "all other wholeheartedly orthodox Christians" believe in the resurrection of the flesh (σαρκὸς ἀνάστασιν). Though Justin cites this as orthodox belief, and though this will eventually become part of the rule of the faith, Claudia Setzer and Jennifer Strawbridge record this as the earliest statement of its kind in extant Christian literature.[46] This is to be contrasted with Paul's claim in 1 Corinthians 15:50 that "flesh (σὰρξ) and blood cannot inherit the kingdom of God." It may be that Justin is here explicitly attempting to correct, or at least clarify, a point that he sees Paul as having muddled.[47]

---

42. Todd D. Still, "Shadow and Light: Marcion's (Mis)Construal of the Apostle Paul," in *Paul and the Second Century*, ed. Michael F. Bird and Joseph R. Dodson, Library of New Testament Studies 412 (New York: T&T Clark, 2011), 91–107.

43. Foster, "Justin and Paul," 109, 124.

44. Oskar Skarsaune, *The Proof from Prophecy: A Study in Justin Martyr's Proof-Text Tradition: Text-Type, Provenance, Theological Profile*, Supplements to Novum Testamentum 56 (Leiden: E.J. Brill, 1987), 92–100; See also Rodney Werline, "The Transformation of Pauline Arguments in Justin Martyr's 'Dialogue with Trypho,'" *The Harvard Theological Review* 92, no. 1 (1999): 80.

45. Foster, "Justin and Paul."

46. Jennifer R. Strawbridge, *The Pauline Effect: The Use of the Pauline Epistles by Early Christian Writers*, Studies of the Bible and Its Reception 5 (Boston: De Gruyter, 2015), 102 n.29; Claudia Setzer, *Resurrection of the Body in Early Judaism and Early Christianity: Doctrine, Community, and Self-Definition* (Boston: Brill, 2004), 75.

47. Setzer, *Resurrection of the Body in Early Judaism and Early Christianity*, 75.

Given the absence of explicit references to Paul, and Justin's willingness to move in different directions from Paul, it is interesting that most contemporary treatments of Justin's Eve/Mary parallel assume that it is a direct and unproblematic expansion on Paul's Adam/Christ typology.[48] In fact, one looks in vain to find a clear statement of the Pauline Adam/Christ typology in Justin's extant works.

It is possible to find statements about Adam that sound like Paul's. Take, for instance, Justin's claim that Jesus died for humanity, which "from the time of Adam had become subject to death and the deceit of the serpent, each man having sinned by his own fault" (*Dial.* 88.4). One can explore this synoptically with Romans 5:12: "sin came into the world through one man, and death came through sin, and so death spread to all because all have sinned." The two are comparable, but far from identical. For Justin, people have been subject to death "from (ἀπὸ) Adam," they are not said to be subject to death "through (δι') Adam." And Justin is clearer than Paul that he is not endorsing any concept of all sinning in Adam. As with other passages, there does not seem to be any direct textual dependence here, even if Justin's thought is similar to Paul's. And there is no sign of Paul's Adam/Christ typology. When explicitly assigning blame for originating sin, Justin refers to Adam and Eve (*Dial.* 124.3–4) or to Eve alone as he does in our above passage.

The closest Justin comes to articulating a Pauline Adam/Christ typology is when he considers the devil's motivation for tempting Jesus. "For since the Devil had deceived Adam, he fancied that he could in some way harm [Christ] also" (*Dial.* 103.6). This certainly posits a parallel between the two and a contrast in terms of their ability to resist temptation. And, as in Paul, Eve is neatly effaced from the narrative. Skarsune has argued that this is a part of a broader Adam/Christ typology built around the temptation of Christ in the wilderness.[49] But this is not Paul's typology. No one reading Paul could doubt that by Christ's "obedience" Paul is referring to his obedience "to the point of death—even death on a cross" (Phil 2:8). So, the point of comparison in the narrative of Christ's activities is different in the two typologies, even if both point to similar issues of temptation, obedience, and disobedience. Again, Paul Foster's point holds, even while this may show a familiarity with a tradition found in Paul, the difference in the details of the argument prevents us from asserting a direct textual dependence between the two.

---

48. Luigi Gambero and Thomas Buffer, *Mary and the Fathers of the Church: The Blessed Virgin Mary in Patristic Thought* (San Francisco: Ignatius Press, 1999), 47; Lanne, "Marian Doctrine and Piety up to the Council of Chalcedon," 39; Johannes Quasten, *Patrology. 1: The Beginnings of Patristic Literature* (Westminster, MD: Newman Press, 1962), 211.

49. Skarsaune, *The Proof from Prophecy*, 221–223.

Ironically, the closest parallel for Paul's text in Romans 5 is found not in a Justinian Adam/Christ typology, but in his Eve/Mary typology. Justin claims that Eve brought forth (ἔτεκε) disobedience (παρακοὴν) and death (θάνατον). This is similar to Paul's claims in Romans 5:12, 19 "sin came (εἰσῆλθεν) into the world through one man, and death (θάνατος) came through sin, and so death spread to all because all have sinned— . . . just as by the one man's disobedience (παρακοῆς) the many were made sinners, so by the one man's obedience the many will be made righteous." For Justin, Eve births disobedience and death just as for Paul sin came through Adam. Both Adam (in Paul) and Eve (in Justin) are tied to disobedience and death. The parallel is far from perfect, but it is at least visible.

The upshot of this analysis is that Justin was far from simply expanding Paul's Adam/Christ typology. Assuming Justin was aware of Paul's work, Justin has either set Paul's typology aside to produce an alternative or he has replaced Paul's typology with the Eve/Mary typology. Why would an early Christian apologist who is looking for links between the Hebrew Scriptures and the gospel make such a move? Unfortunately, all answers to this question must be speculative.

As with the *Protoevangelium*, it may be that Justin is here following a popular Christian tradition of his own day. If this is the case, it is another instance where we witness a potential reaction against the exclusivity of masculine images of salvation in the early church—this time articulated by a male theologian.

One need not, however, appeal to gendered politics to produce a reason Justin would have avoided Paul's typology. I have noted above the case in which Justin may be *implicitly* rejecting or clarifying Paul's theology on the question of the resurrection of the flesh. This, perhaps not coincidently, concerns a claim that Paul makes in 1 Corinthians 15 where he is first developing the Adam/Christ typology. There Paul focuses on the opposing natures of Adam's created flesh and Christ's spiritual, resurrected body. In the context of fights against Marcionism and gnostic versions of Christianity, perhaps Justin found that Paul's typology was more trouble than it was worth. With the framing device of the "prophecy" in Genesis 3:15, he could create a narrative of continuity and progress using Eve and Mary without having to deal with Paul's rhetorical dualisms. Such an account of Justin's motivation has the benefit of putting Justin's judgment in historical context and maintaining continuity with what appears to have been his general approach to Paul.

Irenaeus

What we have found so far is that while early Christianity was likely developing the Eve/Mary typology in relation to Paul's Adam/Christ typology, the relationship between the two was complex and Paul's typology was not received with universal acceptance. This mirrors the more general fortunes of Paul's writings in the early second century. But by the end of the century, Paul would emerge more clearly as an authoritative voice, and his works would start to take on the aura of scripture.

The task of coordinating the Adam/Christ typology with the Eve/Mary typology then fell to later theologians. Central both to this chapter's argument and to this coordinating effort was the work of Irenaeus. While not a systematic theologian in a modern sense, Irenaeus's thought was more systematic than most of his near contemporaries.[50] Further, he was especially concerned with the beauty and elegance of God's plan for creation and salvation.[51] As such, it is not surprising that he, more than the other theologians treated here, saw the need to coordinate these two typologies, and that in doing so he took seriously the need to solve the problem of Eve's being left out of Paul's soteriological formula.

Recapitulation

Before turning to the question of the Eve/Mary typology, it is helpful to start with the general location of Mary in Irenaeus's argument. Like Tertullian after him, Irenaeus deploys Mary primarily to establish Christ's divinity and humanity (5.21.1). Against docetists, who deny Christ's humanity, he focuses on Mary's role as the true human mother of Christ. Against adoptionists, who deny Jesus ontological divinity, he focuses on Mary as the prophesied virgin mother.[52] The dual natures of Christ are central to Irenaeus' theology in a more explicit way than they had been for Justin or would be for Tertullian.[53] This is because, while Justin and Tertullian may assume some doctrine of recapitulation, this doctrine is most explicitly and systematically worked out in the thought of Irenaeus.

So, what is the doctrine of recapitulation?[54] Ephesians 1:8–10 speaks of the economy of salvation in terms of God's work in "bringing together" (ἀνακεφαλαιώσασθαι) all things in Christ. Irenaeus took this idea seriously,

50. Mary Ann Donovan, *One Right Reading? A Guide to Irenaeus* (Collegeville, MN: Liturgical Press, 1997), 7–17.

51. Dunning, *Specters of Paul*, 136.

52. M.C. Steenberg, "The Role of Mary as Co-Recapitulator in St Irenaeus of Lyons," *Vigiliae Christianae* 58, no. 2 (2004): 119.

53. In *Adversus Heresies* 3.22.1 Irenaeus speaks of Christ receiving "the substance of flesh from a human being" (ab homine substantiam carnis). To connect this to the Nicene tradition, I use the language of "human nature" in what follows to refer to this "substance." As M.C. Steenberg notes, this is not Irenaeus' language, though he does "speak of the 'two generations' of Christ to largely the same effect." Steenberg, 125.

54. For a comprehensive treatment of the doctrine, see Eric Osborn, *Irenaeus of Lyons* (New York: Cambridge University Press, 2001), 97–116.

indeed at times literally, seeing Christ as reliving the story of creation from its beginning and setting it right where it had gone wrong. This was a story of action. As in Paul, Christ's obedience corrects for the disobedience of those who had come before. But in Irenaeus, this was expanded to also be a story of substantial transformation brought about through reenactment.

The preexistent Christ existed from all eternity, and humanity was created in the image of Christ. But, being a creation and not the original perfection, humanity could only be good and not perfect (5.16.2).[55] Where Christ was incorruptible, humanity was corruptible (3.19.1). Where Christ was eternal, humanity was contingent. And so on. Being less than perfect, humanity had the possibility of going wrong. But humanity also had the possibility of improvement. Humanity could learn, grow, and mature.[56] From the beginning the divine plan had been for humanity to mature and then, in God's good time, for humanity to be elevated through an infusion of divinity. This was always to be achieved via the incarnation. By God becoming human, the way would be open for humanity to become divine. What was required was that Christ take on all the particularity of humanity and in the process transform humanity from the corruptible to the incorruptible, from the contingent to the eternal (3.19.1). Sin complicated this picture in that it required Christ to correct those errors in the creation that had been committed by imperfect humans. In this effort, Christ relived humanity's failures without failing, and took onto himself the sins of humanity and put them to death in his death.[57] The divine Christ became human and retook the test that all of humanity had failed. He passed that test and transferred his passing grade to the rest of humanity. But even without sin, the incarnation would have been necessary for the perfection of humanity.[58] Humanity could only be perfected by a God-man. Had God not taken on humanity, humanity could not be infused with divinity. If humanity had not been taken on by God, there would be no divinity to inject into the human. The God-man was necessary for the perfection of imperfection.

The point is worth laboring because of its centrality for Irenaeus. The incarnation of Christ was necessary for salvation, for no simple human could achieve this and God could not have achieved it without humanity.

> For it was incumbent upon the mediator between God and humanity, by his relationship to both, to bring both to friendship and concord, and

55. Rhee, "Irenaeus and Paul: Sexuality, Virginity, and Women," 203.

56. Donovan, *One Right Reading?*, 132–33.

57. Osborn, *Irenaeus of Lyons*, 100.

58. John Behr, *Asceticism and Anthropology in Irenaeus and Clement*, Oxford Early Christian Studies (New York: Oxford University Press, 2000), 60.

> present man to God, while he revealed God to man. For, in what way could we be partaken of the adoption of sons, unless we had received from him through the Son that fellowship which refers to himself, unless his Word, having been made flesh, had entered into communion with us? (3.18.7)

How "can they be saved unless it was God who wrought out their salvation upon earth? Or how shall humans pass into God, unless God has [first] passed into humanity?" (4.33.4). Clearly, they cannot. As Mary Ann Donovan writes: "Christ had to be both [human and divine]; God needed to come close to humanity and humanity to God for saving work to be accomplished."[59] And as Eric Osborn summarizes: "Recapitulation means incarnation, where the word, who was in the beginning and always present with mankind has, in the last days and at the appointed time, united himself to his workmanship, that is, to passible man."[60] Christ's "priority is exclusive and his universality is inclusive."[61] In addition to being necessary, the incarnation is also sufficient. "The totality of humanity and the universe is recapitulated in Christ."[62]

If true, the doctrine of recapitulation should be, to some extent at least, observable. The recapitulation should look, discernibly, like what has come before. In developing the picture of this recapitulation, Irenaeus was far more concerned than Justin with maintaining parallels, making sure that even the details of human life were recapitulated. Behr notes what he calls the "literalism of Irenaeus's understanding of τύπος, as an imprint or impression."[63] At one point, Irenaeus goes as far as to argue that Christ lived through all the distinct stages of human life, so as to redeem each stage.

> Being a master, therefore, he also possessed the age of a master, not despising or evading any condition of humanity, nor setting aside in himself that law which he had appointed for the human race, but sanctifying every age, by that period corresponding to it which belonged to himself. For he came to save all through means of himself—all, I say, who through him are born again to God—infants, and children, and boys, and youths, and old men. He therefore passed through every age, becoming an infant for infants, thus sanctifying infants; a child for

59. See Donovan, *One Right Reading?*, 84.

60. Osborn, *Irenaeus of Lyons*, 107.

61. Osborn, 105.

62. Osborn, 116.

63. Behr, *Asceticism and Anthropology in Irenaeus and Clement*, 58, n. 81.

> children, thus sanctifying those who are of this age, being at the same time made to them an example of piety, righteousness, and submission; a youth for youths, becoming an example to youths, and thus sanctifying them for the Lord. So likewise he was an old man for old men, that he might be a perfect master for all, not merely as respects the setting forth of the truth, but also as regards age, sanctifying at the same time the aged also, and becoming an example to them likewise (2.22.4).

But just as Christ recapitulated every moment of individual human lives, he was required also to recapitulate the drama of humanity writ large. This is where the story of Adam, as a story of humanity, becomes crucial.[64] The new beginning should look like the beginning. This is the drama that must be replayed in the life of Christ. The "end is connected to the beginning within the fabric of salvation history."[65] Thus, for Irenaeus, "Theological hermeneutics must at least bring together (though not necessarily fuse) the points of departure in Old and New Testaments in order to demonstrate that together they articulate a single economy."[66]

Christ must become the new Adam so that the substance of humanity, which began in Adam, could be saved and transformed (5.1.3; 5.14.1). This aim accounts for both the continuity and difference in the narratives of Christ and Adam. On the one hand, unlike Adam, Christ's birth must be from a human woman so that Christ maintains continuity with Adam's human substance (3.21.10). On the other, Christ must reverse the curse that Adam brought upon that substance. The parallel must be "worked out with great elaboration in an endeavor to show that every circumstance in the career of Adam was duplicated in the career of Christ, and that every point where the former made a wrong choice the latter made the counter-balancing right choice."[67] It is to hold together this tension that Irenaeus develops the idea that Adam is born from virgin earth while Christ is born to a virgin woman (3.18.6–7).[68]

---

64. Presley, *The Intertextual Reception of Genesis 1–3 in Irenaeus of Lyons*, 103–9.

65. D. Jeffery Bingham, "Irenaeus and Hebrews," in Parvis and Foster, *Irenaeus*, 72. See *Adversus Heresies* 3.22.3.

66. Thomas Holsinger-Friesen, *Irenaeus and Genesis: A Study of Competition in Early Christian Hermeneutics*, Journal of Theological Interpretation Supplements 1 (Winona Lake, IN: Eisenbrauns, 2009), 223; See also Presley, *The Intertextual Reception of Genesis 1–3 in Irenaeus of Lyons*, 110.

67. John Lawson, *The Biblical Theology of Saint Irenaeus* (Eugene, OR: Wipf & Stock, 2006), 150.

68. Robert M. Grant, *Irenaeus of Lyons*, The Early Church Fathers (New York: Routledge, 1997), 139.

The *and Eve* Problem

But what about Eve? In developing the Adam/Christ parallel, Irenaeus has followed Paul. In some ways this works better in Irenaeus's theology than it does in Paul's because Irenaeus locates the parallel in the context of a discussion of substance or nature. Adam is the origin of human nature, and Christ's existence must be continuous with this nature to transform it. But we run into the same problem we have seen before when we switch from the order of creation to the order of sin. Handy as it may be to hang the corruption of human nature on the same peg as the origin of that nature, the narrative of Genesis complicates things. "For it was by means of a woman that [our enemy] got the advantage over man at first. . ." (5.21.1). Irenaeus suggests Eve's disobedience formed a "knot" (*nodus*) that needed to be unsnarled and even goes as far as to attribute the "cause of death" (*causa . . . mortis*) to *Eve's* disobedience (3.22.4).[69]

As it will be for Tertullian, the distinction between Adam and Eve is an important one for Irenaeus. The distinction between male and female is original to God's creation and will not be erased even in the eschaton. In Eden, Adam and Eve did not participate in sex, but they were loving beings, and their love was expressed physically, "kissing [and] embracing one another in holiness as children."[70] Sex and reproduction were envisioned from the beginning as a part of God's good creation, even if in the fullness of time humanity was to return to an original sexed, but sexless, innocence.[71] Thus sexual difference is a permanent facet of human existence. Benjamin Dunning argues that sexual difference is also soteriologically significant to Irenaeus. The penetrable female form is ontologically different from the male. "The difference of the feminine therefore emerges as a kind of excess in Irenaeus's theological project—a remainder in his recapitulative equation."[72]

---

69. Presley, *The Intertextual Reception of Genesis 1–3 in Irenaeus of Lyons*, 110, 112.

70. *Epid* 14. Translation: Irenaeus, *On the Apostolic Preaching*, trans. John Behr (Crestwood, NY: St. Vladimir's Seminary Press, 1997).

71. Behr, *Asceticism and Anthropology in Irenaeus and Clement*, 112–13, 118–19; Rhee, "Irenaeus and Paul: Sexuality, Virginity, and Women."

72. Dunning, *Specters of Paul*, 103. Presley critiques Dunning's conclusion, though it is not clear whether the critique has taken the full measure of Dunning's position. He correctly notes that there is nothing about Eve's sin that is gendered in Irenaeus, but at issue is not just the character of the sin, but the significance of sexual and gender difference in Irenaus' thought. Presley, *The Intertextual Reception of Genesis 1–3 in Irenaeus of Lyons*, 111 n.75; Both Helen Rhee and Tina Beattie appear to agree with Dunning that these distinctions are significant to Irenaus. Rhee, "Irenaeus and Paul: Sexuality, Virginity, and Women," 212; Beattie, *God's Mother, Eve's Advocate*, 166.

In the light of these considerations, Irenaeus needed some soteriological mechanism to reach back to Eve. Intertwining the Adam/Christ typology with the Eve/Mary typology presented a tempting solution. As Helen Rhee writes: "Irenaeus complements the Pauline contrast of the Adam-mortality and Christ-immortality with the Eve-death and Mary-life contrast; more precisely, he puts the latter parallel into the former so as to tighten up a single pattern of God's economy of salvation that encompasses sexuality, virginity, and generation."[73]

> [Eve] having indeed a husband, Adam, but being nevertheless as yet a virgin . . . having become disobedient, was made the cause of death, both to herself and to the entire human race (*inobediens facta, et sibi, et universo generi humano causa facta est mortis*); so also did Mary, having a man betrothed [to her], and being nevertheless a virgin, by yielding obedience, become the cause of salvation, both to herself and the whole human race (*obediens, et sibi et universo generi humano causea facta est salutis*). And on this account does the law term a woman betrothed to a man, the wife of him who had betrothed her, although she was as yet a virgin; thus indicating the back-reference from Mary to Eve (*a Maria in Evam recirculationem significans*), because what is joined together could not otherwise be put asunder than by inversion of the process by which these bonds of union had arisen; so that the former ties be cancelled by the latter, that the latter may set the former again at liberty (3.22.4).

What Irenaeus has articulated here appears to be an independent act of recapitulation undertaken by Mary on behalf of Eve, one that itself can be said to be the cause of salvation for all of humanity. Later, Irenaeus again engages the typology:

> If the former did disobey God, yet the latter was persuaded to be obedient to God, in order that the Virgin Mary might become the patroness (*advocata*) of the virgin Eve. And thus, as the human race fell into bondage to death by means of a virgin (*adstrictum est morti genus humanum per virginem*), so is it rescued by a virgin (*salvatur per virginem*); virginal disobedience having been balanced in the opposite scale by virginal obedience. For in the same way the sin of the first created man receives amendment by the correction of the First-begotten (*adhuc enim protoplati peccatum per correptionem primogeniti emendationem acceipiens*), and the coming of the serpent is conquered by the harmlessness of the dove, those bonds being unloosed by which we had

73. Rhee, "Irenaeus and Paul: Sexuality, Virginity, and Women," 212.

> been fast bound to death (*vinculis autem illis resolutis, per quae alligati eramus morti*) (5.19.1).

Not only does Irenaeus claim here that the human race is saved by Mary, but he suggests that Eve's sin is corrected by Mary in the same way that Adam's sin is corrected by Christ.

Determinations

Surely something has gone wrong here. Was Christ's action sufficient for salvation? Was it necessary to salvation? Irenaeus's general disposition is to answer both questions with a resounding "Yes." But the way he has located Mary raises significant problems for this answer. As M.C. Steenberg has argued, Irenaeus presents Mary's recapitulation of Eve alternately as both necessary and redundant. "If Adam is characterized as the type of human nature itself, then it will logically follow that the recapitulation of Adam equates to the recapitulation of humanity."[74] And yet, Irenaeus clearly sees something necessary about Mary's activity in undoing the knot tied by Eve. As such, "it seems that Irenaeus' claims of the necessity of Eve's recapitulation in Mary and the latter's status as *advocata* and source of freedom stand on questionable theological ground, if they do not in fact contradict outright his own claims of salvation as offered uniquely in and by Christ."[75]

Approached from a different angle, this problem reproduces itself as a conundrum regarding the nature of Christ's incarnation itself. "Recapitulation," as Eric Osborn has argued "means incarnation."[76] Christ is capable of transforming humanity through recapitulation because of his unique place as the divine-human. This is why Irenaeus needed to spend so much time refuting docetists and adoptionists. How then could Mary recapitulate Eve in the same way as Christ recapitulates Adam without fulfilling this ontological role? Was the incarnation not necessary? Irenaeus would certainly want to hold to the necessity of Jesus' divine/human natures. But if he does so, the choices left are theologically unappetizing. Should Mary be honored as another savior, like Jesus? Or shall we say that Eve was recapitulated in a secondary, less adequate way?

Perhaps it is notable here that Osborn, who has rightly emphasized Irenaeus's view of the uniqueness of Christ, avoids calling what Mary does an act of recapitulation. The "disobedience of Adam and Eve," he writes, "was 'amended by

---

74. Steenberg, "The Role of Mary as Co-Recapitulator in St Irenaeus of Lyons," 131.

75. Steenberg, 129.

76. Osborn, *Irenaeus of Lyons*, 107. See above section on recapitulation.

correction' in Christ (5.19.1)."[77] But we cannot avoid attributing recapitulation to Mary's action.[78] Nor can we find refuge in an account that grants Mary special status because of her role as the mother of Christ. Her definitive act in recapitulating Eve is found in her agreement to conceive, and thus necessarily precedes Christ's incarnation, even in fetal form.

How have we gotten here? Various accounts can be offered concerning how Irenaeus worked himself into this cul-de-sac. Francis Hitchcock suggested that in treating Eve and Mary, Irenaeus "allows the antithesis to get the better of his doctrine."[79] Eric Osborn notes Irenaeus sense of "beauty and proportion," which he likens to a spiritual vision, grasping truth from the perceived aesthetic value of parallels in the biblical text.[80] Dunning suggests that the problem might lie in Irenaeus's doctrine of recapitulation itself.[81] Sara Parvis suggests that it may have been Irenaeus's effort to be positive about women that got him into "theological hot water, at least in some traditions."[82]

Steenberg, focusing on the problem of redundancy in Irenaeus's soteriology, posits that "there must exist some kind of distinction in the human roles of Adam and Eve that warrants a co-ordinate recapitulation of each."[83] He goes on to propose a reading in which Adam is representative of individual sin and Eve is representative of the social dimension of sin. This, he suggests, solves his problem. The two acts of recapitulation are not redundant inasmuch as they address different facets of sin. This proposal offers a more internally coherent account of Irenaeus' thought than one finds without the distinction, but it is not without problems. It sits uneasily with what Behr has called Irenaeus's

77. Osborn, 101.

78. Andrew Louth, "Mary in Patristics," in *The Oxford Handbook of Mary*, ed. Chris Maunder, Oxford Handbooks (New York: Oxford University Press, 2019), 57; Brian Reynolds, "Marian Typological and Symbolic Imagery in Patristic Christianity," in *The Oxford Handbook of Mary*, ed. Chris Maunder, Oxford Handbooks (New York: Oxford University Press, 2019), 83; Steenberg, "The Role of Mary as Co-Recapitulator in St Irenaeus of Lyons," 128; Lawson, *The Biblical Theology of Saint Irenaeus*, 151–152.

79. Francis Hitchcock, *The Treatise of Irenaeus of Lugdunum against the Heresies* (London: Society for promoting Christian Knowledge, 1916), Comment on 5.19.1.

80. Osborn, *Irenaeus of Lyons*, 18. See also Steenberg, "The Role of Mary as Co-Recapitulator in St Irenaeus of Lyons"; Presley, *The Intertextual Reception of Genesis 1–3 in Irenaeus of Lyons*, 107.

81. Dunning, *Specters of Paul*, 53.

82. Sara Parvis, "Irenaeus, Women, and Tradition," in Parvis and Foster, *Irenaeus*, 161.

83. Steenberg, "The Role of Mary as Co-Recapitulator in St Irenaeus of Lyons," 131.

"literalism" concerning the use of τύπος (typology).[84] It also does not address the theological question of how to locate the incarnation in relation to both Christ's and Mary's separate acts of recapitulation.

I have been arguing something closer to Dunning's position: that Eve represents a kind of "excess," or a "remainder" in Irenaeus'/Paul's original formula for the recapitulation of Adam that needs to be addressed.[85] Dunning locates this remainder in Eve's status as a female. I find his and other's arguments for this conclusion to be correct, but not complete. To the importance of gender/sexual distinction in Irenaeus' thought I add the basic structural patterns of narrative order, which leaves Eve as an outlier in the Adam/Christ soteriological typology. First, if Eve is, as the narrative of Genesis suggests, the first, independent, active agent in the narrative of sin, Mary as her parallel must be the first, independent, active agent in bringing salvation.[86] Steenberg is right: if we focus on Adam as the origin of human nature, it is entirely possible to produce a soteriology that covers everyone by constructing an inclusive bridge between Adam and Christ. But the order of sin deviates from the order of creation. Eve sins first, and she is a distinctive person who cannot be submerged into Adam. As such, if Adam is the type of Christ, one needs something more to cover Eve. This is why Irenaeus needs a back-reference (*recirculationem*) to Eve to finish his soteriological picture. The lifeline to Eve is necessitated by her falling outside the narrative of sin and salvation encompassed by Adam and Christ.

What I am proposing is that, far from being a side effect of overzealous concern for style, Irenaeus's theological problems were built into the tradition that he inherited and that he was trying to work out. His rigor in working out these problems made these problems starkly visible, but it did not create them. Adding the Eve/Mary typology seemed necessary when starting with Paul's Adam/Christ typology. But it was inevitably going to lead here. If one were to attempt to solve the problems created by the Adam/Christ typology, at least one of the premises with which Irenaeus started would need to be abandoned.

Tertullian

Irenaeus was not alone in championing Paul, neither in attempting to coordinate Paul's typology with the Mary/Eve typology nor in falling into the trap that this created. Tertullian is often located as the father of Latin theology. He is purposefully less of a systematic thinker than Irenaeus. And he showed "somewhat more

84. Behr, *Asceticism and Anthropology in Irenaeus and Clement*, 58 n.81.

85. Dunning, *Specters of Paul*, 103.

86. Lanne, "Marian Doctrine and Piety up to the Council of Chalcedon," 41.

restraint" than Irenaeus in his Mariological statements.[87] But none of this saves him entirely from the problems we have witnessed in Irenaeus' scheme. Indeed, at points he is likely dependent on Irenaeus for some concepts,[88] and I have left some of these points of dependency to be discussed here rather than in the section on Irenaeus simply because Irenaeus gives us such a clear picture of the theological problems at stake. Tertullian's treatment includes the theological problems we saw in Irenaeus's work, but it also highlights even more the structural problems of coordinating the two typologies.

Like Irenaeus before him, Tertullian's use of Mary first concerns the nature of Christ.[89] Tilting against a variety of docetists who denied the full humanity of Christ, Tertullian found in the story of Mary a way to shore up Christ's claim to fleshly human existence. But also like Irenaeus before him, Tertullian was interested in reclaiming Paul's Adam/Christ typology.[90]

Thus, in *De Carne Christi* 17.15–30, just before proposing his Eve/Mary typology, Tertullian cites the authority of "the apostle" in claiming that Christ was called Adam. But Tertullian does not stop at rearticulating Paul's typology. To show that the newness of Christ "in all its bearings, was prefigured of old," Tertullian presents the claim that both Adam and Christ were produced by virgin generation. Christ from the virgin Mary. Adam from the earth "still virgin, not yet deflowered by husbandry, not yet subdued to seedtime."

This extraordinary effort produced rhetorical fruit in that it allows Tertullian to tie the new birth (*nativitas nova*) to the last (*novissimus*) Adam.[91] But the payoff is not simply alliterative. It also begins to weave together the Adam/Christ typology with the Eve/Mary typology. Perhaps Tertullian (as Irenaeus before him) saw this as justifying what is, at best, a "contrived" analogy between field and womb.[92]

But why work so hard to put these two together rather than simply returning to Paul's typology? Again as in Irenaeus, it seems likely that gender plays a significant role in Tertullian's efforts to maintain both typologies. As Peter Brown

87. Shoemaker, *Mary in Early Christian Faith and Devotion*, 66.

88. Eric Osborn, *Tertullian, First Theologian of the West* (New York: Cambridge University Press, 2003), 193.

89. Beattie, *God's Mother, Eve's Advocate*, 89.

90. See *Adversus Marcionem* 5.9–10

91. Willemien Otten, "Christ's Birth of a Virgin Who Became a Wife: Flesh and Speech in Tertullian's De Carne Christi," *Vigiliae Christanae* 51, no. 3 (1997): 254.

92. Rhee, "Irenaeus and Paul: Sexuality, Virginity, and Women," 209; George H Tavard, *Woman in Christian Tradition* (Notre Dame; London: University of Notre Dame Press, 1975), 70.

states, Tertullian "sunk sexuality deep into the human body."[93] And it was the body that Tertullian maintained must survive to the eschaton. This did not mean that sexual desire would make the leap to eternity. According to Tertullian, the Christian's future was, to borrow Carly Daniel-Huges phrase, "sexed, but sexless."[94] But we should not narrow gender and sex down to sexual desire. Tertullian did not. For him, there were fundamental ontological differences between the sexes.[95] Dunning argues that the distinctions are so important that they influenced Tertullian's views on the economy of salvation.[96] In this context, one can see why it would be important to treat both the sin of Adam and the sin of Eve explicitly in some way. And if one wishes to maintain Paul's Adam/Christ typology, then the Eve/Mary typology seems to present an opportunity, even if this gave rise to problems.

To see how deep these problems go, we need to move a few verses along in *De Carne Christi* to see Tertullian's explicit treatment of the Eve/Mary typology:

> Into Eve, while still a virgin, had crept the word (*verbum*), constructive of death: into a virgin no less needed to be introduced the Word of God (*dei verbum*), constructive of life, so that that which through that sex had gone astray into perdition should through the same sex be led back again into salvation. Eve had believed the serpent: Mary believed Gabriel. The sin which the former committed by believing, the latter by believing blotted out. "But Eve on that occasion conceived nothing in her womb by the devil's word." Yes, she did. For the Devil's word was to her a seed (*verbum diaboli semen illi fuit*), so that thenceforth she should be abject and obedient, and should bring forth in sorrows: and in fact she did give birth to the devil, the murderer of his brother. Mary, on the other hand, brought forth him who should sometime bring to salvation his brother according to the flesh, Israel, by whom he himself

93. Brown, *The Body and Society*, 81.

94. Carly Daniel-Huges, "'We Are Called to Monogamy': Marriage, Virginity, and the Resurrection of the Fleshly Body in Tertullian of Carthage," in *Coming Back to Life: The Permeability of Past and Present, Mortality and Immortality, Death and Life in the Ancient Mediterranean*, ed. Carly Daniel-Hughes and Frederick S. Tappenden (Montréal, QC: McGill University Library and Archives, 2017), 241. See De Resurrectione Carnis 60–61.

95. F. Forrester Church, "Sex and Salvation in Tertullian," *Harvard Theological Review* 68, no. 2 (April 1975): 83–101; Elizabeth Clark, "Status Feminae: Tertullian and the Uses of Paul," in *Tertullian and Paul*, ed. Todd D Still and David E Wilhite, 2019, 127–155; Barbara Finlay, "Was Tertullian a Misogynist? A Reconsideration," *Journal of The Historical Society* 3, no. 3–4 (June 2003): 503–525.

96. Dunning, *Specters of Paul*, 124–50.

> was slain. So then, God brought down into the womb his own Word, the good brother, that he might erase the memory of the evil brother for the salvation of man Christ must needs come forth from that organ to into which man already under condemnation had entered (*De Carne Christi*. 17.30–40).[97]

Determinations

Tertullian's self-voiced objection in the middle of the typology stands as at least a partial acknowledgement of the trouble he was getting himself into. Despite his protest to the contrary, he was quite aware that Eve did not conceive by the devil's word. "Indeed, to rescue [the typology] he had to ignore the lack of connection between the devil and Eve's pregnancy."[98] But more than that, the Adam/Christ typology, presented only a few sentences before, has collapsed as Tertullian is forced to "introduce a contrast between Cain and Jesus in a 'new brother' typology."[99] All of this is representative of the structural problem we have noted in coordinating the two typologies. There is no way to square the mother/son relationship of Mary and Jesus with the marriage relationship of Eve and Adam.

Tertullian may, however, have one last go. In what follows, Tertullian returns to the Adam/Christ typology in 22.30 before continuing to discuss Mary's virginity. Here it is noteworthy that unlike most of the Marion tradition from the *Protoevangelium* on, Tertullian rejects the doctrine of Mary's virginity in partu. She is "a virgin as regards her husband, not a virgin as regards child baring. She who began the night as a virgin, ended the night as a wife" (23.5–25). It may sound offensive to ask, "Who violated Mary's virginity?" but *Tertullian* is not shying away from the risqué here. "For she became a wife by the same law of the opened body, in which it made no difference whether the violence was of the male let in or let out: the same sex performed that unsealing (*nam nupsit ipsa patefacti corporis lege, in quo nihil interfuit de vi masculi admissi an emissi: idem illud sexus resignavit*)." Tertullian's primary concern here is to establish, against docetic understandings, that Christ's birth was a fleshly birth.[100] But one cannot

97. Latin and translation from Tertullian, *Tertullian's Treatise on the Incarnation*, trans. Ernest Evans (London: S.P.C.K., 1956).

98. Geoffrey Dunn, "Mary's Virginity 'in Partu' and Tertullian's Anti-Docetism in 'De Carne Christi' Reconsidered," *The Journal of Theological Studies* 58, no. 2 (October 2007): 478.

99. Dunn, 478.

100. Otten, "Christ's Birth of a Virgin," 248; Gambero and Buffer, *Mary and the Fathers of the Church*, 65; Dunn, "Mary's Virginity," 467–484.

avoid the conclusion that it was Christ who took his mother's virginity. It is not impossible that Tertullian sees this as at least a partial fix for the problem of the Adam/Christ parallel. As Adam took Eve's virginity, so Christ took Mary's.

With this we may leave behind the structural problem of coordinating the Adam/Christ and Eve/Mary typologies. But we are still left with the primary theological problem. Tertullian was not, in general, a theologian who held a high Mariology.[101] He was perfectly capable of criticizing Mary.[102] And yet, in the middle of his Eve/Mary typology he is able to claim "that which through that sex had gone astray into perdition should through the same sex be led back again into salvation (*ut quod per eiusmodi sexum abierat in perditionem per eundem sexum redigeretur in salute*)." This is a significant claim. Do women need a savior of their own sex? It seems in some sense so, for Mary does not just open the opportunity for salvation through Jesus Christ, but also by herself leads (or drives) her sex back to salvation. Further, she does so by means of her own belief (*crediderat*) prior to the incarnation, or indeed even the conception of Christ.

What is suggested in this sentence is more than a high Mariology, it is an independent soteriological act on behalf of women. How did we get here? As I have suggested above, two pressures are pushing in this direction. One is internal to the Eve/Mary typology. Namely, if Eve is the active cause of sin and death, then Mary, by parallel, must be the active cause of salvation and life. The second arises from the attempt to coordinate and supplement the Adam/Christ typology with the Mary/Eve typology. The Adam/Christ typology leaves Eve's sin exposed because in the order of sin, Eve precedes Adam. As such, there is a need for a second savior figure, one suited to Eve rather than Adam.

Those familiar with Tertullian may rightly argue that such tensions in his theology should not be surprising. Tertullian was a master of paradox and reveled in shocking and even offending his audience for a theological point.[103] In this tradition "a tolerance for inconsistency does seem to undergird the various typological maneuvers that Tertullian makes in *De carne Christi* 17, particularly in terms of how he portrays Mary."[104] While this may alleviate concerns about Tertullian's loose typology, however, it cannot resolve the problem of idolizing Mary. In this way, Tertullian is truly haunted by the specter of Paul, whose Adam/Christ typology must be corrected and yet whose typology resists adequate correction by following this trajectory.

---

101. Otten, "Christ's Birth of a Virgin," 248.

102. See *Adversus Marcionem* 4.19.11

103. Virginia Burrus, *Saving Shame: Martyrs, Saints, and Other Abject Subjects*, Divinations (Philadelphia: University of Pennsylvania Press, 2008), 52–53.

104. Dunning, *Specters of Paul*, 138.

Gregory of Nazianzus

We conclude our exploration of the Mary solution in early Christianity with a consideration of the treatment of these themes in the works of Gregory of Nazianzus. Gregory was born more than a hundred years after Tertullian and is usually located on the other side of an East/West, Latin/Greek divide from the earlier theologian. He also is properly located among the Cappadocian theologians who are associated with a vision of Christ transcending sexual difference in the work of salvation. In a later chapter, I will treat approaches that emphasize the "transcendsexualism" of Christ in the narrative of salvation more directly. But here I wish to focus on the extent to which some of the problems noted in the above theologians continue to manifest even in the works of someone like Gregory. This highlights the depth of the problems even across other significant differences in Christian theology.

We can start our inquiry at an apparent point of overlap with earlier theologians: the doctrine of recapitulation.

Recapitulation

Gregory is at points able to talk in terms that sound quite like those Irenaeus was deploying, but the content of his thought about the doctrine is significantly shifted from that earlier theology.[105] Here we can take up Gregory's most famous statement on soteriology: "that which he has not assumed he has not healed; but that which is united to his Godhead is also saved (Το γάρ απρόσληπτον, αθεράπευτον, ο δέ ήνωτται τω Θεώ τούτο και σώζεται)" (*Ep.* 101.5).[106] This could be taken as an endorsement of the idea from Irenaeus that Christ incarnation must reenact the full drama of sinful humanity, correcting it as Christ goes. Gregory can write of Christ "who has borne *our* infirmities" (*Or.* 14.15), he can contrast Christ's sinlessness with Adam's disobedience (*Or.* 2.23), and he can see Christ reversing the effects of Adam's sin (*Or.* 39.16).[107]

---

105. Christopher A. Beeley, *Gregory of Nazianzus on the Trinity and the Knowledge of God: In Your Light We Shall See Light*, Oxford Studies in Historical Theology (New York: Oxford University Press, 2008), 147.

106. For this translation and a note on the history of the phrase, see Brian E. Daley, *God Visible: Patristic Christology Reconsidered*, Changing Paradigms in Historical and Systematic Theology (Oxford, United Kingdom: Oxford University Press, 2018), 134; For a full translation of the letter, see Gregory of Nazianzus, *On God and Christ: The Five Theological Orations and Two Letters to Cledonius*, ed. Frederick Williams, trans. Lionel R. Wickham (Crestwood, NY: St. Vladimir's Seminary Press, 2002).

107. Translations of Gregory's Orations are taken with slight variations from Gregory of Nazianzus and Cyril of Jerusalem, *Cyril of Jerusalem and Gregory Nazianzen*, ed. Philip Schaff

But Gregory's focus is never on Christ's reenactment of what came before. Where Irenaeus had balanced emphasis on the mixing of divine and human natures with an emphasis on reenactment, Gregory's emphasis falls consistently on the commerce of substance between divinity and humanity. As such, what is key is Christ's divine "assumption" of the fullness of humanity. Christ "humbled himself so as to assume the lump of which we consist" (*Or.* 14.15). As Susanna Elm writes, for Gregory "Christ incarnate was the supreme *paradoxon*, signifying salvation, by mixing ontologically distinct, even contradictory, essences, divine and human, heaven and earth, God and man."[108] The mechanism of salvation is not the reenactment and correction of former disobedience so much as it is the leavening of human substance with divine substance, which leads the whole of humanity to rise.[109] Christ "came forth then as God with that which He had assumed, one person in two natures, flesh and spirit, of which the latter deified the former" (*Or.* 38.13–14).[110]

Such a scheme can easily lead to a soteriology that imagines the space between Adam and Christ as all-inclusive of humanity, because it focuses on human substance, which originates with the creation of Adam. If the problem is human substance, then the focus in the Genesis narrative falls on the order of creation. Many theologians following such a scheme hold that the incarnation would have been necessary to deify human nature even if sin had never entered the world.

Transcending Sex

Several scholars have read Gregory as emphasizing the ways in which Christ and human nature transcend sex and gender.[111] There is some significant truth to this approach. Some of Gregory's comments on Christology and anthropology fit well with this reading.

---

and Henry Wace, trans. Charles Browne and Swallow, Nicene and Post-Nicene Fathers: Second Series 7 (Buffalo, NY: Christian Literature Publishing Co., 1894), and Gregory of Nazianzus, *Select Orations*, trans. Martha Vinson, Fathers of the Church 107 (Washington, DC: Catholic University of America Press, 2017).

108. Susanna Elm, *Sons of Hellenism, Fathers of the Church: Emperor Julian, Gregory of Nazianzus, and the Vision of Rome*, Transformation of the Classical Heritage 49 (Berkeley, CA: University of California press, 2014).

109. Verna Harrison, "Eve, the Mother of God, and Other Women," *The Ecumenical Review* 60, no. 1–2 (January 4, 2008): 80.

110. Beeley, *Gregory of Nazianzus on the Trinity and the Knowledge of God.*

111. Verna Harrison, "Male and Female in Cappadocian Theology," *The Journal of Theological Studies* 41, no. 2 (1990): 456–465; Gabrielle Thomas, *The Image of God in the Theology of Gregory of Nazianzus* (New York: Cambridge University Press, 2019), 77–86.

Anticipating the Chalcedonian definition, Gregory emphasizes the extent to which the two natures of Christ, while joined together, are yet not confused with one another. The incarnation is clearly a paradox. Christ was simultaneously "impassible in his godhead, passible in that which he assumed" (*Or.* 40.45). Emphasizing the extent to which Christ holds together the divine and the human without qualifying either allows Gregory at times to marginalize the importance of sex and gender in Christ. God is not gendered. Christ is God. The nongendered nature of God is not lost in the incarnation. As such, the divination offered by Christ is available to both men and women. As Gabrielle Thomas writes: "women are able to image Christ because Christ is God, and . . . Gregory does not appropriate gender to God."[112]

It must also be said that Gregory's anthropology does not locate sex and gender as centrally in human identity as Irenaeus's and Tertullian's do. Gregory of Nyssa, Nazianzus's close friend, explicitly claimed that human nature was first created in a non-gendered, spiritual form. Gregory of Nazianzus does not explicitly endorse this reading of Genesis, but he does at points marginalize gendered and sexual differences in the light of deeper spiritual similarity between men and women: "the distinction between male and female is one of body not of soul" (*Or* 8.14).

In the light of these emphases, it is possible for Gregory to locate both divine and human nature as relating only marginally to sex and gender. "There is," he writes, "one maker of man and woman; one debt is owed by children to both their parents" (*Or.* 37.6–7). And this transcendence of sex and gender can carry over into his interpretation of the narrative of sin and salvation.

> The woman sinned, and so did Adam. The serpent deceived them both; and one was not found to be the stronger and the other the weaker. But do you consider the better? Christ saves both by his passion. Was he made flesh for the man? So he was also for the woman. Did he die for the man? The woman also is saved by his death. He is called of the seed of David; and so perhaps you think the man is honored; but he is born of a virgin, and this is on the woman's side (*Or.* 37.6–7).[113]

In a later chapter, I will have the opportunity to engage more rigorously with theologies that attempt to transcend sex and gender in their anthropology and thus soteriology. Here, I mean only to draw attention to the fact that Gregory can be interpreted as deploying this kind of solution to the problems I have been

---

112. Thomas, *The Image of God in the Theology of Gregory of Nazianzus*, 82.

113. Andrew Hofer, *Christ in the Life and Teaching of Gregory of Nazianzus*, Oxford Early Christian Studies (New York: Oxford University Press, 2013), 215.

highlighting before going on to show that he does not consistently embrace this solution. There are two reasons for this. First, he is too tied to Paul's new Adam formulation, and ends up at points accepting the gendering that comes along with it. Second, while his focus is upon human substance, he also wants to claim that originating sin plays a significant role in the drama of salvation. In developing that theme, he must acknowledge the order of sin, which places Eve outside of the salvation offered to all those between Adam and Christ.

The New Adam and the Restoration of Adam's Glory

While some of Gregory's exploration of the image of God can be taken as pointing to the way in which the image is found in both male and female, it can hardly be contested that when Gregory thinks of the image of God, he thinks paradigmatically of Adam. This seems to follow from two points. First Gregory is aware of the pre-Christian tradition of the glorification of Adam. As Gabrielle Thomas argues, Gregory was familiar with the pseudepigraphic tradition in which, after the initial creation, the angels were commanded by God to worship Adam as the image of God.[114] If, after baptism, one is tempted by Satan, Gregory suggests that they respond by citing the reality of their restored glory.

> If [Satan] wrestle against you to a fall through avarice, showing you all the kingdoms at one instant and in the twinkling of an eye, as belonging to himself, and demand your worship, despise him as a beggar. Say to him relying on the seal, "I am myself the image of God; I have not yet been cast down from the heavenly glory, as you were through your pride; I have put on Christ; I have been transformed into Christ by baptism; worship me" (*Or.* 40.10).

The tradition that relays the story of the commanded worship of Adam is one part of the broader tradition of seeing Adam glorified and Eve blamed. Gregory does not frequently emphasize the second part of this tradition, which sees Eve as specially responsible for the originating sin, but this does not erode the primary place that Adam plays as a symbol of the original untarnished image of God.

But a second tradition also pushes Gregory in this direction: the tradition of seeing Christ as the new Adam. He often writes of the old Adam being set aside and replaced by the new (*Or.* 30.5, *Or.* 39.5, *Or.* 45.1) And he consistently sees the upshot of Christ's activity in terms of the restoration of Adam's glory. Thus, he speaks of Christ "restoring the old Adam to the place whence he fell" (*Or.* 2.25), receiving "again the first Adam" (*Or.* 39.2), Christ's work to "redeem Adam and

114. Thomas, *The Image of God in the Theology of Gregory of Nazianzus*, 147–153.

restore our fallen image" (24.4), and Christ bringing about "my perfection and return to the first condition of Adam" (*Or.* 38.16).[115] In such passages the name "Adam" becomes synonymous with "the image of God."

Such references obscure Eve's place as created in the image of God, but do not deny this place. The closest Gregory comes to undermining the claim that the image is represented in Eve is in his treatment of her creation as a "fragment" of Adam. "What was Adam?" Gregory writes, "A creature of God (Πλάσμα θεοῦ). What then was Eve? A fragment of the creature (Τμῆμα τοῦ πλάσματος)" (*Or.* 31.11).[116]

But more than this, Gregory's writings run the danger of erasing Eve when he takes up the formula of Romans 5. Gregory is not unique here; as Verna Harrison writes, the Greek fathers "usually speak of Adam and his sin without mentioning [Eve] at all."[117] As such, Gregory claims that the new Adam came because of "Adam who fell under sin" (*Or.* 41.4). At his baptism, Jesus "sees the heaven opened which Adam had shut against himself and all his posterity" (*Or.* 39.16). Gregory contrasts Adam's glorification with his fall: "Adam was honored by the hand of God, and the delights of Paradise, and the first legislation: but, unless I slander the reputation of our first parent, he kept not the command." (*Or.* 43.70) It was Adam who was "led to believe that it was through denial of access to the tree of knowledge up to then that his claim to be a god was begrudged him" (*Or.* 36.5). In these passages, Adam displaces Eve's role in Genesis, even becoming the recipient of the temptation to godlikeness which was explicitly offered by the serpent to Eve.

It is here that Gregory comes closest to the kind of reenactment soteriology that Irenaeus had posited. Gregory shapes the story of the incarnation itself as a retelling of the original creation of Adam.[118] But Christ's incarnation is a trap for Satan, where Satan's temptation had been a trap for Adam. Just as Satan had tempted and taken Adam, Satan now believes he will be able to trap Christ, the new Adam. Jesus, however, is not simply Adam, he is the divine with the appearance of the old Adam (*Or.* 24.9, 39.1).

> *It is as though another, new Adam, appearing to those on earth,*
> *And cloaked round with a shawl, should heal the former one*
> *(For I could not draw close, because of my passions),*

---

115. Thomas, 98.

116. Greek for Gregory's orations is taken from Jacques Paul Migne, ed., *Patrologiae Cursus Completus*, Series Graeca 35–36 (Paris: Imprimerie Catholique, 1857).

117. Harrison, "Eve, the Mother of God, and Other Women," 73.

118. Ben Fulford, "Gregory of Nazianzus and Biblical Interpretation," in *Re-Reading Gregory of Nazianzus: Essays on History, Theology, and Culture*, ed. Christopher A. Beeley, CUA Studies in Early Christianity (Washington, DC: Catholic University of America Press, 2012), 45.

And trip up unexpectedly the seeming-wise snake
Who, approaching this Adam, met up with God,
Thinking to carry him off through the force of his wickedness,
Like the ocean that breaks on a hard and jagged rock.
(Carmen *1.1.9.53–59)*[119]

It is here, with Adam as the paradigm of the image of God and the appearance of the old Adam as the cloak for the new Adam, that Gregory makes his most explicitly sexed and gendered statements about the incarnation. Christ was undoubtedly male.

> A male, because offered for Adam; or rather the stronger for the strong, when the first man had fallen under sin; and chiefly because there is in him nothing feminine, nothing unmanly (Ἄῤῥεν δὲ, ὡς ὑπὲρ τοῦ Ἀδὰμ προσαγόμενον, μᾶλλον δὲ τοῦ στεῤῥοῦ τὸ στεῤῥότερον, τοῦ πρώτου πεσόντος ὑπὸ τὴν ἁμαρτίαν, χαὶ ὅτι μάλιστα μηδὲν θῆλυ, μηδὲ ἄνανδρον ἐν ἑαυτῷ φέρον); but he burst from the bonds of the virgin-mother's womb with much power, and a male was brought forth by the prophetess, as Isaiah declares the good tidings (*Or.* 45.13).

Unfortunately, this clearly throws a spanner in the works of salvation. Whether we conceive of the commerce between the divine and the human happening through reenactment or through assumption, with this picture of the incarnation we have clearly left women outside of the scope of Christ's gift. As Verna Harrison concludes: "Nazianzen's central soteriological axiom . . . is that 'what is not assumed is not healed, but what is united to God, that also is saved.' In other words, Christ brings salvation to every aspect of the human condition by uniting it to God within himself in the incarnation. It follows from this that if Christ saves *as male*, half of the human race is excluded from salvation."[120]

Can Eve Be Saved?

Eve is, of course, in need of saving. While Gregory's approach to the narrative of originating sin is more egalitarian than the approaches of other theologians, he does acknowledge the distinct place of Eve in the order of sin. Eve is the

119. Translation, Gregory of Nazianzus, *On God and Man: The Theological Poetry of St. Gregory of Nazianzus*, trans. Peter Gilbert, Popular Patristics Series (Crestwood, NY: St. Vladimir's Seminary Press, 2001), 73; Christopher A. Beeley and Andrew Hofer, eds., "The Stoning of Christ and Gregory Nazianzus," in *Re-Reading Gregory of Nazianzus: Essays on History, Theology, and Culture*, CUA Studies in Early Christianity (Washington, DC: Catholic University of America Press, 2012), 151.

120. Harrison, "Male and Female in Cappadocian Theology," 458.

"mother of our race and of our sin" (*Or* 8.14). "She indeed who was given to Adam as a help meet for him, because it was not good for man to be alone, instead of an assistant became an enemy, and instead of a yoke-fellow, an opponent, and beguiling the man by means of pleasure, estranged him through the tree of knowledge from the tree of life" (*Or.* 18.8). By Eve, the man was "consigned to perdition" (*Or.* 44.6).

But how can Eve be saved if she is not assumed by Christ? Like those before him, Gregory finds Mary to be useful here. But he diverges from the earlier theologians we have treated in significant ways. As we have seen, in comparison to Irenaeus and Tertullian, the theme of reenactment is suppressed in Gregory's understanding of recapitulation. For Irenaeus and Tertullian, because recapitulation required reenactment, they posited that Mary, before Christ's conception, reenacted Eve's disobedience and replaced it with obedience to the call of God. Gregory can draw enacted parallels between Mary and Eve: "the virgin on behalf of the woman, Bethlehem because of Eden, the manger because of the garden" (*Or.* 2.24). But Gregory does not locate Mary as reenacting and reversing the temptation of Eve. This saves him from some of the troubles to which Irenaeus and Tertullian fell. Mary is not, for Gregory, an independent savior figure.

Typical of his own theological emphases, Gregory replaces the problem of the reenactment of Eve's activity with the problem of divine assumption to cover Eve. Mary, the representative of Eve (and of female substance) again stands in as Eve's proxy. Gregory just must figure out how it might be that Mary in any sense is "assumed" in the incarnation. His answer is that the assumption must have happened in utero. Mary was "assumed" by the Christ child before birth.

> *But when Christ came by way of a holy Virgin Mother,*
> *being himself unyoked, divine in form, spotless*
> *(since it was needful that he should come to be apart from*
> *marriage and a father),*
> *he hallowed womankind, and shook off bitter Eve (*Carmen *1.2.1.197–200)*[121]

Verna Harrison offers a helpful exegesis of the passage:

> Gregory sees Christ's birth from a virgin mother as releasing Eve from the consequences of her fall and sanctifying the feminine as such. This was a crucial theological point. Since as Gregory says elsewhere 'what is not assumed' [by Christ in the incarnation] 'is not healed', how can whatever is distinctively female in the human condition be saved, since he assumes a male humanity? Since all human persons are of one gender or

121. Translation Gregory of Nazianzus, *On God and Man*, 96.

> the other, he cannot become fully human while assuming both at once. The answer to this potential difficulty is that he dwelt within a woman's body and thus purified and sanctified the female reproductive process by his presence within it, thereby uniting feminine existence in himself with the divine. This enables the salvation of Eve and all her daughters.[122]

Determinations

Gregory has avoided the dangers of idolatry to which the Eve/Mary typology tended to lead. It is clear in his treatment that salvation comes only through Christ. But is his solution satisfactory? It seems not, on his own account. The premise to which we have returned repeatedly in Gregory's thought is "that which he has not assumed he has not healed; but that which is united to his Godhead is also saved" (*Ep.* 101.5). He thus must claim that Mary was assumed by the Son, and assumed in a way that was sufficient to salvation. This is a deeply problematic claim.

Can we say that Mary was assumed in the same way that Christ was? Shall we say that Christ was incarnate in the body of Mary during her pregnancy? It hardly seems so. In classical theology the Son fully assumes humanity in Jesus. The Son becomes fully human, united to soul and body. Whatever we want to claim about the union that occurs in pregnancy between child and mother, we surely do not want to claim that it is tantamount to the mother being the baby incarnate.

We also face a problem concerning the necessity of Christ. If salvation could be achieved through a relation that does not unite the divine and human in one person, say through the relation between a fetus and a woman carrying the fetus, why did we need the full incarnation of Christ? Or did we?

Thus, while assumption soteriology avoids some of the problems of recapitulation by reenactment, it produces a parallel set of problems concerning what is sufficient for assumption, again with undesirable alternatives. Either the hypostatic union was not necessary for salvation, or we are left with a second-best route of salvation for the female; assumption one step removed. Such hardly seems an adequate resolution to the problem of Eve.

As our treatment of Gregory has suggested, he and those around him could more consistently have attempted to offer the suggestion that Christ transcends sex and gender, truly incarnating only human substance. I will take up and critique this kind of solution in a later chapter. Intriguingly, however, Harrison's interpretation of Gregory just rehearsed accidentally points in an alternative direction. "Since all human persons are of one gender or the other," she writes, Christ "cannot become fully human while assuming both at once." The question is whether we should accept the first part of her claim, which entails her

---

122. Verna Harrison, "Gender, Generation, and Virginity in Cappadocian Theology," *The Journal of Theological Studies* 47 (April 1, 1996): 50.

conclusion. What if we rejected the claim that Christ could only incarnate "one gender or the other"? What if we took seriously the possibility that Christ is not so limited? Here, we approach our goal—but I get ahead of myself.

Conclusion

Before turning to my own proposal for resolving this theological problem, I should stop for a moment to say something more about Mariology. It is easy enough for a non-Catholic like myself to launch an attack upon perceived idolatry within the doctrines of Mariology. The history of Protestantism is filled with unsympathetic attacks on idols projected upon Catholicism. I do not wish to locate myself as a Biblicist, attempting to reject Mariological doctrine because it is a development of church tradition. I recognize myself as a participant in the Christian tradition, which stretches back to before the Bible was collected and which continues to develop today. Nor do I wish to be seen as launching a broadside against Mariology as a whole.

Nothing in the critique offered in this chapter undermines the doctrine of Mary as *Theotokas,* guarantor of Christ's humanity, fulfiller of prophecy, exemplar of the faith, handmaid of the Lord, or woman of valor.[123] Untouched here are claims about the immaculate conception, the virgin conception and birth of Jesus, and Mary's assumption.[124] I find the concept of Mary, and Mary's faith as the contingent condition for the incarnation of the necessary savior, to be theologically quite fruitful. And nothing here has undermined Mary's role as mediatrix of grace and mother of all believers. Such claims, as Yves Congar suggests, present "a proper role for Mary," locating her "between Christ and the Church" as "the neck between the head and the body."[125]

What Congar thought should be avoided was a "direct association of Mary with the Savior."[126] Congar's concern is a consistent theme in modern Mariology, where most authors and contemporary Catholic church documents emphasize the need for Mary to be subordinated to Jesus in the economy of salvation.[127] Thus, these sources seek to avoid the troubles in which Irenaeus

123. See Pelikan, *Mary through the Centuries.*

124. This is not to say that I endorse all these doctrines, but they are not relevant to my current argument.

125. Yves Congar, "Marie et l'Église: Perspective Médiévale," *Revue Des Sciences Philosophiques et Théologiques* 39, no. 3 (1955): 409, 411. Translation mine.

126. Yves Congar, "Marie et l'Église Dans La Pensée Patristique," *Revue Des Sciences Philosophiques et Théologiques* 38, no. 1 (1954): 3 n.1. Translation mine.

127. Fastiggi, "Mary in the Work of Redemption," 306; Mark I. Miravalle, *"With Jesus": The Story of Mary Co-Redemptrix* (Goleta, CA: Queenship Publ, 2003), 11, 13; Austin Flannery, ed., "Dogmatic Constitution on the Church, Lumen Gentium, 21 November, 1964," in *Vatican*

landed. Contemporary Catholic doctrine rejects an idolizing of Mary. In being concerned about the potential for idolizing of Mary, I then stand in the main line of those doing Mariology.

I differ from many who advocate for Mariology in pointing out that such idolizing is a necessary correlate of the kind of Eve/Mary parallel that some Mariologists pursue, and have pursued since Irenaeus.[128] If one is going to toss a soteriological life line to Eve through Mary, they will be reduced to either idolizing Mary, subordinating the role and thus salvation of Eve and Mary, or failing to carry through their scheme to its logical conclusion. Take, for instance, Mark Miravalle, who attempts to both embrace the Eve/Mary typology and avoid idolatry by subordinating Mary to Christ. As a correlate, he is required to assert that Eve was subordinated to Adam in her act of sin, a claim that does explicit harm to the Genesis narrative.[129]

Yet, it would be wrong to simply reject this whole line of theological development wholesale. Tina Beattie has made a compelling case that something like the Eve/Mary parallel can play a significant role in addressing gender inequalities within contemporary theology.[130] There is value in recognizing gendered diversity represented by the distinct persons of Adam and Eve and in taking that gendered diversity up in the economy of salvation. In this, I see significant value in the work by early Christians who attempted to address the problem of women in relation to the male savior. Reclaiming what is good in their intentions, and indeed in Paul's intentions before them, requires reworking the tradition that Paul and those early Christians left to us. It is to this work that I turn in the next chapter.

Council II: The Conciliar and Post Conciliar Documents, Vatican Collection (Vatican Council, Collegeville, MN: Liturgical Press, 1974), paras. 60, 62; Vatican Council, "Schema of the Dogmatic Constitution on the Blessed Virgin Mary, Mother of God and Mother of Men," trans. James T. O'Connor, *Marian Studies* 37, no. 1 (1986): 201.

128. On Bernard of Clairvaux and Bonaventure's later expansion of Irenaeus' recapitulation scheme, see Thomas Weinandy, "The Annunciation and Nativity: Undoing the Sinful Act of Eve: The Annunciation," *International Journal of Systematic Theology* 14, no. 2 (April 2012): 217–232.

129. Miravalle, *With Jesus*, 83.

130. Beattie, *God's Mother, Eve's Advocate*; Though, how to locate Mary has been an ongoing dispute in Christian feminism. See, for instance, Elizabeth A. Johnson, *Truly Our Sister: A Theology of Mary in the Communion of Saints* (New York: Continuum, 2006); Anne E. Carr, *Transforming Grace: Christian Tradition and Women's Experience* (San Francisco, CA: Harper & Row, 1988), 189–94; Marina Warner, *Alone of All Her Sex: The Myth and the Cult of the Virgin Mary* (New York: Vintage Books, 1983); Ruether, *Mary, the Feminine Face of the Church.*

CHAPTER FOUR

Theological Reflections on Sex and Gender

> While, we were still with the prosecutors, my father, because of his love for me, wanted to change my mind and shake my resolve. 'Father,' I said, 'do you see this vase lying here, for example, this small water pitcher or what-ever?' 'I see it,' he said. And I said to him: 'Can it be called by another name other than what it is?' And he said: 'No.' 'In the same way, I am unable to call myself other than what I am . . .'
>
> —Perpetua

IN EARLY CHRISTIANITY, soteriology largely drove Christological arguments. Christ offered salvation to all of humanity. That was agreed. The question was: What kind of being must Christ be to make such salvation possible?[1] It was in response to this question that the Chalcedonian definition was eventually offered as an answer. Christ's full divinity and full humanity was necessary to facilitate the commerce between humanity and divinity. Therefore, theologically this had to be an accurate statement of Christ's nature, regardless of whatever apparent logical problems it might produce.

What I have been doing thus far is highlighting a soteriological problem that was recognized but never adequately resolved in the early church. At this point, it is worth articulating a few sets of premises that schematize this problem. Later in the chapter I shall have the opportunity to provide some supporting arguments for my articulation of premises, but here we need only present the premises that are in tension with one another.

- First, that sexual/gender diversity is a significant element in God's creation. It is a significant element in the story of the fall. And it will be taken up in redemption without being destroyed in the process.
- Second, that redemption depends upon Christ's recapitulation of human life and inversion of the narrative of sin in a way that

1. See Jaroslav Pelikan, *The Emergence of the Catholic Tradition: 100–600*, The Christian Tradition: A History of the Development of Doctrine 1 (Chicago, IL: University of Chicago Press, 2007), 172–256.

embodies (incarnates, assumes) the significant elements of that story.

- Third, (correlative to the first premise) that in the narrative of salvation we should honor the gender/sexed distinction internal to the narrative of sin. The narrative of sin, as opposed to the story of creation, begins with Eve and then continues to Adam. These two represent sex/gender diversity. While their sins are not gendered/sexed, the two are gendered/sexed and neither should be reduced to the other or erased from this narrative as their distinctive gendered/sexed selves.

We can read part of what was happening in early Christian theology as an effort to correct the Pauline formula of the Adam/Christ typology, which failed to deliver on the third premise. In part to honor gendered/sexed diversity and make the typology adequate to be inclusive of Eve in the narrative of sin, theologians sought to augment the Adam/Christ typology, harmonizing it with an Eve/Mary typology. Unfortunately for this proposed solution, carrying the solution to its logical conclusion required violating the second premise above. The harmonization either led to a second-rate path to salvation for Eve, or it idolized Mary to make her a second savior, in some way equal with Christ. In either case, Christ fails to be what Christ needs to be to open redemption to the whole of humanity inclusively.

As I have suggested at several points in this work, there is a viable solution to this problem that maintains all the above premises. It does cause logical problems, which will partly need to be addressed with the note that Christ's existence is inevitably mysterious to us and as such we should not be expected to understand all the details. But, in both the form of argument and the need to appeal to mystery, this solution follows the pattern of early Christian conclusions about Christology.

The answer is to recognize Christ as the new Adam *and* the new Eve; assuming not only their abstract humanity, but the diversity of their sexed/gendered existences. Just as Irenaeus saw it as essential that Jesus incarnated every life stage of the human, we can see Jesus as incarnating gendered/sexed diversity.

But this move, required by the theological premises on which I have been drawing, may seem problematic to some. Verna Harrison's comment when interpreting Gregory of Nazianzus is illustrative: "Since all human persons are of one gender or the other," she writes, Christ "cannot become fully human while assuming both at once." If sex and gender exist only in binary opposite alternatives, then it may be impossible to solve the problem previous chapters have pointed out. In contrast, other theologians will suggest that sex and gender are ephemeral social constructions, representing nothing true about the person who identifies with them. If this view is correct, then it is hardly worthwhile to construct a theological argument about Christ's sex and gender at all.

The argument that we have followed so far leads to the conclusion that Christ is trans*, but is there a Christian understanding of sex and gender that can make sense of this claim—one that both acknowledges the diversity of sex and gender and takes these categories to be significant enough to admit them as constitutive of Christ's identity? If not, our conclusion would require us to create one. But our situation is not that dire.

There is no doubt that secular scholarship has outpaced theology in charting the nature of sex and gender in recent decades. But this is not to say that we are left without resources. Debates about sexuality (sexual orientation) have received a significant amount of attention in theology, and today developed theologies of sex and gender that include trans*, intersex, and gender queer people are starting to emerge.[2] In service to the overall argument of this work, this chapter both draws upon and hopefully contributes to this developing literature. In it, I locate sex and gender within the moral theological framework provided by "contexts of responsibility" and "calling." Drawing on these ideas, I suggest that it is possible to build bridges both to more deconstructionist queer theologies and more conservative, modernist/anti-modernist theologies. Building these bridges requires producing a more positive account of sex and gender than many queer theologians have and providing a more adequate account of the diversity of sex and gender than most modernists/anti-modernist theologians have.

Sex and Gender as Context of Responsibility

Humans are composite creatures: compounds of culture(s), nature, and will.[3] Though we can draw these sources of identity apart to some extent, none exist

2. See, for instance Justin Edward Tanis, *Trans-Gendered: Theology, Ministry, and Communities of Faith* (Cleveland, OH: Pilgrim Press, 2003); Virginia R. Mollenkott, *Omnigender: A Trans-Religious Approach*, Revised and expanded edition (Cleveland: Pilgrim Press, 2007); Lisa Isherwood and Marcella Althaus-Reid, eds., *Trans/Formations* (London: SCM Press, 2009); Marcella Althaus-Reid, *Indecent Theology*; Pamela R. Lightsey, *Our Lives Matter: A Womanist Queer Theology* (Eugene, Oregon: Pickwick Publications, 2015); Christina Beardsley and Michelle O'Brien, eds., *This Is My Body: Hearing the Theology of Transgender Christians* (London: Darton, Longman and Todd, 2016); Scott Bader-Saye, "The Transgender Body's Grace," *Journal of the Society of Christian Ethics* 39, no. 1 (2019): 75–92; Craig Ford, "Born That Way? The Challenge of Trans/Gender Identity for Catholic Theology," in *Sex, Love, and Families: Catholic Perspectives*, ed. Julie Hanlon Rubio and Jason E. King (Collegeville, MN: Liturgical Press Academic, 2020), 91–102.

3. The theological anthropology presented here draws deeply on Christian realism. See Reinhold Niebuhr, *The Nature and Destiny of Man*, 2 vols. (London, UK: Nisbet & Co., 1941);

innocent of implication in the activity of the others. There is no one foundation for the self. There is no way to access human nature independent of social construction, and there is no social construction not influenced by human nature. Further, the human partially transcends what it has received from nature and society using comparison, memory, reason, and imagination.[4] The human is always capable of limited transcendence, reflecting critically on its current state of natural and social givenness, and acting to change its, and its society's, current state.

Theologically considered, these sources of identity are always already corrupted gifts from God. They are gifts inasmuch as existence itself is the unmerited gift of the triune God; the effect of the unboundable love that is God's being. As such, culture(s), nature, and will are all divine gifts. But these gifts are always received by sinful individuals in a world stained by sin. In our freedom, in myriad ways, we refuse to accept the gifts of God as gifts. We pretend that we have created ourselves *ex nihilo*. We reject the sufficiency of God's gifts and seek our own fulfillment at the expense of other beings. We embrace pretensions to be able to know with unjustified certainty what gifts we need and pretend to be self-sufficient in gaining these gifts.[5] We reject the continual and ever new outpouring of the gifts of God, attempting to find solace in established structures of society and established theories of nature without participating in the ongoing reformation of those structures and theories.[6]

Below, we will return to look more deeply at the development of individuals in terms of calling. But here, we need to stop and look at the ways in which nature and society give rise to social institutions and norms in which individuals live. Social institutions and norms are caught up in the churning of giftedness and sin. They provide frameworks of life and action in which individuals are formed and against which they strain. Theologians have previously analyzed these in terms of powers, *sittlichkeit*, natural laws, orders of creation, orders of preservation, subsidiary institutions, and divine mandates.[7] Robin Lovin has recently written

---

Robin W. Lovin, *Reinhold Niebuhr and Christian Realism* (New York: Cambridge University Press, 1995).

4. Lovin, *Reinhold Niebuhr and Christian Realism*, 119–157.

5. Niebuhr, *The Nature and Destiny of Man*, 1:198–215; Lovin, *Reinhold Niebuhr and Christian Realism*, 142.

6. Niebuhr, *The Nature and Destiny of Man*, 1: 242–255; Lovin, *Reinhold Niebuhr and Christian Realism*, 143–151.

7. Robin W. Lovin, *Christian Faith and Public Choices: The Social Ethics of Barth, Brunner, and Bonhoeffer* (Philadelphia: Fortress Press, 1984); Emil Brunner, *The Divine Imperative: a Study in Christian Ethics*, trans. Olive Wyon (Cambridge, UK: Lutterworth, 2003); Dietrich Bonhoeffer, *Ethics*, ed. Clifford J. Green, trans. Reinhard Krauss, Charles C. West, and Douglas W. Stott, Dietrich Bonhoeffer Works 6 (Minneapolis, MN: Fortress Press, 2005).

about them as the "contexts of responsibility" in which we live.[8] Among the contexts, he highlights institutions like jobs, families, governments, and churches.

These are, on the one hand, divine providential gifts. The contexts allow for social coordination, enhancing human freedom and making possible goods that would be otherwise unrealizable. They also can serve to hem in our sinful inclinations, drawing us out of the self and into relationships and placing limits on our sinful dispositions that might harm ourselves and others.

But Lovin reminds us that we should not "say that the contexts are themselves the human good. Families, governments, jobs, and churches can be horrible evils, which do great harm to the people involved in them and to others."[9] In our sinfulness, we can distort the contexts and make idols of them. As such, no context should be treated as innocently natural, immutable, or ultimately authoritative. There is, in human society, no context that provides a divine view or ideology that could be used as the measuring stick for all others. "The only possible unity is the ultimate unity in Christ, which preserves for the duration of history the diversity" of the contexts.[10] The Christian is called to live responsibly amid these different contexts, working within them, offering critical analysis of them, and working to bring them to approximate the fullness of justice as much as possible under the limitations of a society stained by sin at each moment. I propose that sex and gender should be taken as a particular context of responsibility in which we live today.

As deconstructionists have suggested, sex and gender are social constructs (we might also say "social institutions") in multiple senses. The distinction between sex and gender is itself a distinction that is not available in every culture or time. The number of genders and sexes, and the sets of biological traits, virtues, goods, and rules associated with the sexes and genders, vary across time and culture. And configurations of sex and gender are not just constructed by societies, they also construct the societies in which they become established. The people in a society are shaped in part by how sex and gender are conceived and embedded in the society. Perceptions, emotions, and desires are influenced by the possibilities and limitations that are presented in these institutions.[11]

But if sex and gender are contexts of responsibility, this is not all there is to say about them. It should be expected that they can function to orient us toward

8. Robin W. Lovin, *Christian Realism and the New Realities* (New York: Cambridge University Press, 2008), 84–116.

9. Lovin, 101.

10. Lovin, 106–7.

11. Martha Nussbaum, "Constructing Love, Desire, and Care," in *Sex, Preference, and Family: Essays on Law and Nature*, ed. Martha Nussbaum and David Estlund (New York: Oxford University Press, 1997).

and coordinate, or even create access to, a set of true human goods. While not themselves "natural," they should provide conditions that can be used to serve human nature. One can see these facets of the categories of sex and gender even as we acknowledge their imperfection. They have been used to put forward ideals to shame violent and aggressive tendencies among men. Medical treatment can be made more efficient and effective with functioning categories of sex that provide shorthand summaries of relevant biological information. Sex and gender have long been used to establish greater levels of fairness, for instance in sports, where organizing people by their tendencies toward physical traits can make sport more accessible and enjoyable for a range of people. As Patricia Jung and Joan Roughgarden point out, gender distinctions can help in facilitating "intimacy and communion."[12] Government protections based on gender and sex categorization can be crucial in realizing greater approximate justice in society. And, sex and gender have provided categories of identity formation that have been used, and continue to be used, to empower and fulfill those who are able to identify within provided gender categories. As with all contexts, sex and gender are not "natural" in the sense that they exist from time immemorial or are immutable. But they do channel and order humans toward goods that are very real in any society.

While no one construction of sex and gender is necessary, it is probably impossible for human society to exist without some such construction. Doing without such a construction would render a whole set of genuinely human goods unattainable. Indeed, even more than other contexts of responsibility, sex and gender are immediately linked with fundamental human goods because sex and gender relate so intimately to embodied differences. And while sex and gender constructions will never be subtle enough to capture the full plenitude of such differences, such constructions, even more than the constructions of other contexts of responsibility, are intimately linked with human nature.

This, of course, is not to say that sex and gender should be uncritically accepted in any particular form. It is clear enough that modern sex and gender constructions have been reductive, overly simple, inhibiting to human creativity, and harmful, even deadly, to some who could not find fulfillment within the available categories. This is why Western society has been in the business of reforming the context provided by sex and gender. This is exactly what we should expect from a context of responsibility. Within the dynamic tension of divine gift and sinful reception, they are sites of perpetual reformation.

---

12. Patricia Beattie Jung and Joan Roughgarden, "Gender in Heaven: The Story of the Ethiopian Eunuch in Light of Evolutionary Biology," in *God, Science, Sex, Gender: An Interdisciplinary Approach to Christian Ethics*, ed. Patricia Beattie Jung and Aana Marie Vigen (Urbana, IL: University of Illinois Press, 2010), 230.

Sex and Gender from the Classical to the Modern

Sex and gender are probably always in "crisis." At the very least, so long as theories of sex have existed, the meaning and significance of sex and gender have regularly been contested. As we shall see, modernity was marked by a reductive naturalism that has endured into postmodernity, while postmodernity witnessed the rise of varieties of deconstructive sex and gender voluntarism. Moving beyond these options, toward a nonreductive naturalism, is one of the primary goals of this chapter.[13]

The ancient world witnessed multiple theories relating to what we would call sex.[14] The Hippocratic tradition posited that sex came in clearly distinguished kinds. These kinds differed not only in genitalia but also in other bodily conditions. Males had different flesh and circulatory systems from females. Diseases experienced by women should not be diagnosed or treated as if they were the same as diseases afflicting men.[15] But the Hippocratic tradition did not limit these kinds to male and female. The sex of a fetus was determined by the "seed" contributed by the mother, the "seed" contributed by the father, and the location of the implantation in the womb. This matrix allowed for various possibilities including manly males, effeminate males, virile females, and feminine females. In the middle of this classification was the possibility of the "hermaphrodite" — a being with fully functional "male" and "female" genitalia.[16]

Aristotelian medicine rejected the plurality of potential sexes pictured in the Hippocratic corpus. In one sense, the true goal of nature was the male alone. The

---

13. On nonreductive naturalism, see Lovin, *Reinhold Niebuhr and Christian Realism*, 105–118; Kevin Carnahan, "Moral Realism," in *The Oxford Handbook of Reinhold Niebuhr*, ed. Robin Lovin and Joshua Mauldin (New York: Oxford University Press, 2021), 328–46.

14. In what follows, I draw upon the wealth of recent research in ancient medicine, sex, and gender. See especially Leah DeVun, *The Shape of Sex: Nonbinary Gender from Genesis to the Renaissance* (New York: Columbia University Press, 2021); Helen King, "The Body beyond Laqueur: Hippocratic Sex and Its Rediscovery," in *Natur—Geschlecht—Politik*, ed. Andreas Höfele and Beate Kellner (Brill | Fink, 2020), 199–216; Helen King, *The One-Sex Body on Trial: The Classical and Early Modern Evidence*, The History of Medicine in Context (Burlington, VT: Ashgate, 2013); Rebecca Flemming, *Medicine and the Making of Roman Women: Gender, Nature, and Authority from Celsus to Galen* (New York: Oxford University Press, 2000); Anne Fausto-Sterling, *Sexing the Body: Gender Politics and the Construction of Sexuality* (New York: Basic Books, 2000); Thomas Laqueur, *Making Sex: Body and Gender from the Greeks to Freud* (Cambridge, MA: Harvard University Press, 2003).

15. King, "The Body beyond Laqueur," 212.

16. DeVun, *The Shape of Sex*, 105; Lorraine Daston and Katharine Park, "The Hermaphrodite and the Orders of Nature: Sexual Ambiguity in Early Modern France," in *Premodern Sexualities*, ed. Louise Fradenburg and Carla Freccero (New York: Routledge, 1996), 119.

female was a male with malformed genitalia. Thus, the male and female were two instances (perfect and imperfect) of a singular kind: humanity. But in another sense, since procreation was part of the natural telos of humanity, both male and female were proper natural kinds. Sex on this account was primarily a matter of the proper reproductive organs. In contrast to the totalizing tendencies of Hippocratic thought, the male and female remained similar in their more basic biological humanity. In conception, the male provided the seed, while the female provided the crass matter for the fetus. If the female's body provided too much matter, a monstrosity could occur, a fetus with an extra limb or even conjoined twins. Intersex people in this scheme were monstrosities created with extra and superfluous genitalia. Regardless, these people were always "truly" either male or female, depending on the part they could play in reproduction.

Galenic medicine posited the greatest continuity between male and female. This has been called the "one-sex" model because it can be read as positing a single sex that existed on a continuum from perfection (male) to imperfection (female).[17] The female and male on this model shared genitalia and each contributed "seed" in the process of conception. The female's genitalia were inversions of the male's. The male, associated with heat and activity, projected its genitalia outside the body. Galenic humeral theory was also significant. The testicles were especially important for the male because they heated and converted blood into male seed.[18] Women, in contrast, were cool and processed blood less efficiently, thus their bodies had to expel this humor on a regular schedule through menstruation. Intersex possibilities were not separate in kind but were people who had been formed at different locations on the continuum between male and female. Individuals also moved along the continuum across their lives. As females got older, they became dryer, and thus more male. As men got older, they cooled and thus became more female.[19]

Partially related to these theories, and partly existing as an independent tradition, were narratives of gender transition. Stories traced to figures like Diodorus Siculus (first century BCE), Aulus Gellius (c. 125–180 CE), Phlegon of Tralles (second century CE), and, most influentially, Pliny the Elder (c. 23–79 CE) told of women who had by various routes transformed into men.[20] Though in

---

17. This language was proposed by Laqueur as a way of talking about all pre-modern views. His view has been critiqued as overly simple, but as an ideal type, even some critics of Laqueur continue to find it useful in talking about Galenic medicine. See Laqueur, *Making Sex*; King, *The One-Sex Body on Trial*; King, "The Body beyond Laqueur."

18. Flemming, *Medicine and the Making of Roman Women*; Patricia Simons, *The Sex of Men in Premodern Europe: A Cultural History*, Cambridge Social and Cultural Histories (New York: Cambridge University Press, 2011).

19. Flemming, *Medicine and the Making of Roman Women*, 154.

20. King, *The One-Sex Body on Trial*, 99–104.

Galenic medical theory sex change was theoretically possible in both directions, these stories were universally in the direction of female to male transitions. This made sense in the ancient world as nature's telos moved from imperfection to perfection, and it was taken for granted that male sex was the more perfect of the options.[21] The causes of such transitions were variously located. Some were due to fever (excessive heat). Some were associated with loneliness or the absence of a husband. The transitions could be brought about with the help of medical intervention, but this was not necessary. And at least in some cases, such transitions were located as evidence of the power of "imagination and the desire to be a man."[22]

Important to note here is the way in which "sex" could be influenced by "gender." Across much of the premodern world, whether one enacted masculine or feminine behavior could influence one's biology. Those who acted typically male could harden, dry, and heat their bodies to make themselves more male. Those who acted more typically female could do the opposite. In some extraordinary cases, the causal power of thought and enactment could even take one across the threshold from one sex to another. There was thus, at least in some models, the potential for a commerce between biological sex and enacted gender.[23]

It is also noteworthy that in pre-modern society, sex determinations in complicated cases relied primarily on self-testimony. "Prior to [early modernity] it had been widely assumed that the mature hermaphrodite could be depended on to know and choose which sex predominated, for it was one's 'nature' that spoke in the urgent tones of attraction to the 'opposite' sex, and what possible motive could there be to dissimulate?"[24] The self could be counted upon to know its own nature through its own desires.

The different models of sex competed with one another and were mixed together across the Latin Middle Ages. Male and female could be regularly distinguished well enough to establish a "patriarchal equilibrium," maintaining male dominance in society.[25] But whether to conceive of that distinction as existing on a continuum, a plurality of distinct kinds, or a binary accompanied by malformed

---

21. King, 13, 115; Flemming, *Medicine and the Making of Roman Women*, 154.

22. Katharine Park, "Rethinking the 'One-Sex' Body" (Lecture, The Lionel Trilling Seminar, Columbia University, November 24, 2014), 100, https://www.youtube.com/watch?v=AyC5J9riUWM.

23. Laqueur, *Making Sex*, 7.

24. Daston and Park, "The Hermaphrodite and the Orders of Nature," 124.

25. Judith M. Bennett, *History Matters: Patriarchy and the Challenge of Feminism*, Gender in History (Philadelphia: University of Pennsylvania Press, 2006), 54–81; Sari Katajala-Peltomaa and Raisa Maria Toivo, *Lived Religion and Gender in Late Medieval and Early Modern Europe*, Themes in Medieval and Early Modern History (New York: Routledge, 2021), 7.

alternatives varied depending on time and place. The early medieval period suffered from a paucity of medical source texts, but generally was influenced by a mixture of Galenic and Hippocratic ideas that admitted sexual continuum. The Aristotelian renaissance in the scholastic period led to an emphasis on binarity, but Aristotelian ideas were mixed with Hippocratic in ways that complicated the claim that alternative sex/genders were "unnatural."[26] By the early sixteenth century, the one-sex model saw a resurgence. Then translation of the Hippocratic corpus into Latin in the mid-1500s contributed to an emphasis on classification of sex that reinforced binary theorizing.[27] But throughout, no one approach to sex managed to completely banish the alternatives.

Read in this context, the modern emphasis on sexual binarity can be located as a short period of dominance of one discourse for understanding human sex; a period that favored a mix of Aristotle's picture of binarity with a Hippocratic picture of the totalizing scope of biological sex. Some of this modern rage for order was built upon developments in scientific inquiry. The discovery of the clitoris and fallopian tubes, problems finding a parallel to the womb in male anatomy, decline of humor theory, and developments in embryology all contributed to the exclusivity of sexual binarity in modernity.[28] Certainly, many of those participating in the crafting of modern binary sex thought of themselves as simply following science. These contributed to the "objectifying" of sex determinations. No longer were individuals the best sources for knowledge about their own sex/gender. As is modernity's wont, it undermined the "subjective" perspectives of selves in favor of the "objective," empirically perceivable world. But one should not think that this development was driven by "impartial" observations. The problems of finding exact parallels between male and female anatomy had long been known in the ancient world. And it is still possible to point to general homologies between male and female genitalia. As Helen King writes: "denials of the 'one-sex' body were not due to an increased focus on what could actually be seen, in anatomy, what was seen depended on what the viewer expected to see."[29]

Underneath this shift were a set of contingent and culturally shaped changes.[30] In the premodern West, priests, monks, and nuns lived lives aimed

---

26. DeVun, *The Shape of Sex*; Daston and Park, "The Hermaphrodite and the Orders of Nature."

27. King, *The One-Sex Body on Trial.*

28. Flemming, *Medicine and the Making of Roman Women*, 154; King, *The One-Sex Body on Trial*, 63.

29. King, *The One-Sex Body on Trial*, 223.

30. In the following narrative I draw upon Charles Taylor, *A Secular Age* (Cambridge, MA: Belknap Press, 2018).

at perfection and represented the height of human telos in the pursuit of holiness. Thus, the emphasis fell upon one form of perfection for all of humanity. This class practiced religious vocations. Lay people were held to much lower standards of behavior, and while they participated in divisions of labor, these were not seen as being imbued with religious importance. This fit well with an emphasis on the relative continuity between genders.

The Reformation in the 1500s challenged this social order from multiple directions. Luther's doctrine of the priesthood of all believers undermined the separation of lay and priestly classes. The Lutheran doctrine of vocations expanded religious importance to all divisions of labor in society. At the same time, the rise of the bourgeois class was deconstructing the feudal orders of society, destabilizing distinctions between groups that had been cemented into life for generations. Society needed new ordering principles, and these principles would have to focus on common life. The upshot was a set of reform movements intent on providing more structure to the life of commoners and inculcating the senses of duty necessary for these commoners to live up to these structures.

At the same time, the decline of emphasis on the celibate priestly class brought about shifts in thought about sex and gender in marital relations. While marriage and gendered differentiation in marriage had been a part of the medieval landscape, it was a secondary concern to the ultimate telos of humanity realized in saintly life. This was compatible with an emphasis upon the unified telos of humanity. There was one perfection, found in relationship to God. After the Reformation, as marriage became a kind of religious calling unto itself, weight fell more upon the division of labor within the marriage.[31] As the scholastics had taught, the telos of marriage was procreation, and procreation depended on a sexed division of labor. Recognition of this called not for a single form of human perfection, but a particular perfection for the husband and a separate perfection for the wife.[32] Thus, the Reformation ironically contributed to an intensification of Aristotelian thinking about sex identification. The telos of men and women subtly shifted apart.

The continued erosion of class and guild-based distinctions in society gave rise to the need to organize society around other poles. Anxiety about sexual ambiguity loomed large. As Lorraine Daston and Katharine Park have noted, the "objectification" of hermaphrodite sex determinations predates most of the developments in modern anatomy.[33] At the beginning of modernity, hermaphrodism came to be associated with sexual ambiguity and, thus, with immorality.

---

31. Katajala-Peltomaa and Toivo, *Lived Religion and Gender in Late Medieval and Early Modern Europe*, 10.

32. King, *The One-Sex Body on Trial*, 70.

33. Daston and Park, "The Hermaphrodite and the Orders of Nature," 124–125.

Modern notions of volunteerism raised questions about whether the testimony of the hermaphrodite might be a willful defiance of their nature. Because of such developments, trust in the self-assessment of hermaphrodites was already undermined when "modern science" articulated what it took to be the objective basis of sex. As modernity developed, both race and gender science served to provide new bases for categories of living that could transcend class boundaries or reestablish such boundaries on new foundations. Again, this was a slow shift. But the trend is well reflected in Anne Fausto-Sterling's statement that claims that "all men are created equal" paradoxically made it all the more important to scientifically distinguish men from non-men.[34]

As George Mosse writes, throughout the eighteenth century, thought about masculinity and femininity came increasingly to focus on "sciences," such as physiognomy, and gender differences became "ever more clearly defined."[35] "Masculine and feminine beauty were usually by mid-eighteenth century no longer perceived as complementary but as distinct and separate without any connection between them, narrowing the ideal of human beauty."[36]

Freud's "scientific" approach to psychology was further put forward as mapping the different inward lives of women and men—lives that developed distinctively based on the presence or absence of the penis itself.[37] In Galenic medicine, the penis had been relatively insignificant: the outward extension of the female sheath, a mechanism for the delivery of the male seed. It was the gonads that were essential to the constitution of the male. After Freud it became practically impossible to imagine that sexual difference was not a perpetual matter of anxiety about the phallus as the greatest sign of sexual identity.

Over time, "hermaphrodites" were classified into smaller and smaller groupings. In Hippocratic thought intersex people once had their own location in the uterus, but by the modern period "scientific literature tried to deconstruct the category of 'hermaphrodite' to classify it out of existence."[38] The development of modern science gave humans not only new ability to observe human anatomy but new possibilities to mold it. These powers were used to make the bodies of intersex people fit to the binarity that had become the only option in scientific thought. On the basis of "science," doctors claimed "the authority to declare that

34. Fausto-Sterling, *Sexing the Body*, 2000, 39.

35. George L. Mosse, *The Image of Man: The Creation of Modern Masculinity* (New York: Oxford University Press, 2010), 28.

36. Mosse, 28.

37. Simons, *The Sex of Men in Premodern Europe*.

38. King, *The One-Sex Body on Trial*, 81.

certain bodies were abnormal and in need of correction."[39] This correction was always to make those bodies align with the categories that the doctors themselves were imposing. "Under the mantle of scientific advancement, the ideological work of science was imperceptible to turn-of-the-century scientists."[40]

In the works of figures as recent as the sociologist Patrick Geddes and the theologian Hans Urs von Balthasar, one can find the idea that males and females are distinguished from one another as far down as the cellular level.[41] Sex was seen as foundational, with gender growing out of sex. In Geddes thought, for instance, male cells produced energy, female cells absorbed energy. Thus, gendered differences (feminine passivity vs. masculine activity) were seen as arising directly from sexed cells.[42]

Modern feminism (in both theological and secular forms) contested the "naturalness" of gender roles that justified the subjugation of women and tied women to activities outside of the public sphere. Discursively, this proceeded in various forms. Some accepted the modern scheme of "masculine" virtues but argued that women were capable of higher levels of rationality and, indeed, "manliness" than they had been given credit for.[43] Women differed from men in that society had not allowed them to develop these virtues. Alternatively, modern feminism could claim that women should gain equal recognition for their (in some ways superior) difference from men.[44] Throughout the articulation of these alternatives, however, feminism tended to draw upon modern notions of binary sex to provide a category of identity in need of proper recognition and to provide a marker for the development of solidarity. "Women" were called to work together for the greater rights of "women." It was "women" who needed recognition while transgressing or embodying traditional feminine gender standards. One outcome was a tendency to police the category of "woman" (either

---

39. Fausto-Sterling, *Sexing the Body*, 2000, 36.

40. Fausto-Sterling, 39.

41. Laqueur, *Making Sex*, 6; Hans Urs von Balthasar, *Theo-Drama: Theological Dramatic Theory: Volume 2: The Dramatis Personae: Man in God*, trans. Graham Henderson (San Francisco: Ignatius, 1992), 365–366; Gerard Loughlin, "Omphalos," in *Queer Theology: Rethinking the Western Body*, ed. Gerard Loughlin (Malden, MA: Blackwell Pub, 2007), 119.

42. Laqueur, *Making Sex*, 6.

43. See, for instance, Mary Wollstonecraft, *A Vindication of the Rights of Woman: An Authoritative Text, Backgrounds, the Wollstonecraft Debate, Criticism*, ed. Carol Poston, 2nd ed, A Norton Critical Edition (New York: Norton, 1988), 8.

44. Paradigmatically, Carol Gilligan, *In a Different Voice: Psychological Theory and Women's Development* (Cambridge, MA: Harvard University Press, 2003).

as sex or as gender) as a means of gaining greater political recognition for those within the category.[45]

Towards a Dialogue on Sex and Gender

In the late twentieth and early twenty-first centuries, disputes about homosexuality and lesbianism pushed this debate further, giving rise to queer theory and queer theology. More consistently deconstructionist in its bent, queer theory challenged the "naturalness" of all sex and gender categories. In her most famous work, Judith Butler developed the concept of gender "performativity." This concept was meant to banish the claim that gender arose from an interior essence of the individual. Gendered actions "are *performative* in the sense that the essence or identity that they otherwise purport to express are *fabrications* manufactured and sustained through corporeal signs and other discursive means."[46] Butler's position has frequently been (mis)read as locating gender as if it were "a theatrical role that could be chosen."[47] Such a "voluntarist" approach to gender has deeply influenced some manifestations of queer theory and theology. Take, for instance, queer theologian Robert Goss's claim that "All gender is a form of 'drag,' for there is no 'essential' core for gender to signify. Gender is thus a fantasy construct."[48]

Partially in reaction to this kind of voluntarism, which they view as all too modern, some more communitarian, often anti-modernist theologians have come to the defense of the binary conception of sex and gender. John Milbank, deploying "overwrought, apocalyptic rhetoric,"[49] sees in transgender voluntarism "a deadly earnest attempt to abolish gender altogether." With the demise of gender, he believes, will go "eros," "relationality," and the order necessary for self-government and religion.[50]

---

45. Janice G. Raymond, *The Transsexual Empire: The Making of the She-Male* (Boston: Beacon Press, 1979); Sandy Stone, "The Empire Strikes Back: A Posttransexual Manifesto," in *The Transgender Studies Reader*, ed. Susan Stryker and Stephen Whittle (New York: Routledge, 2006), 221–235.

46. Judith Butler, *Gender Trouble: Feminism and the Subversion of Identity*, Thinking Gender (New York: Routledge, 1990), 136.

47. Jay Prosser, "Judith Butler: Queer Feminism, Transgender, and the Transubstantiation of Sex," in *The Transgender Studies Reader*, ed. Susan Stryker (New York: Routledge, 2006), 262.

48. Robert Goss, ed., *Queering Christ: Beyond Jesus Acted Up* (Cleveland, OH: Pilgrim Press, 2002), 177.

49. Bader-Saye, "The Transgender Body's Grace," 81.

50. John Milbank, "What Liberal Intellectuals Get Wrong about Transgenderism," *Catholic Herald*, January 13, 2017, https://catholicherald.co.uk/long-read-what-liberal-intellectuals-get-wrong-about-transgenderism/.

Many of the theologians who critique transgender voluntarism also end up embracing a reductive naturalism similar to that which marked earlier modern approaches to gender. When discussing the phenomenon of transgenderism, David Cloutier and Luke Timothy Johnson, for instance, interpret "assigned sex and gender" as "the gender you were born into," as if sex and gender were reducible to one's observable physiological state at birth.[51]

Similarly, critiques of transgenderism as "gnostic" presuppose a reductive naturalism. The charge brought against the transgender person is that they posit a dualism of body and soul, then identify themselves with the soul in opposition to the body. Thus, they reject the gift of their given sex and gender. The origins of the problems here can be traced to early expressions of transgenderism, which attempted to articulate the experience of being transgender in rebellion against the framework of modern reductive naturalism. From 1864 to 1865, Karl Heinrich Ultichs published a set of booklets in which he described his own male to female transgenderism in terms of being *anima muliebris virile corpore inculsa* ("a female soul enclosed within a male body").[52] Positing a kind of dualism provided a means of talking about the ways in which the self defies reductive identification with the "scientifically" observable body. As such, similarly dualistic formulas became shorthand for many transgender people who were attempting to articulate their experiences within, and rejection of, reductively naturalistic frameworks. Christians must reject such a dualism. Unfortunately, those who critique transgender persons for Gnosticism have tended to do so in favor of a reassertion of a reductively naturalistic account of sex and gender. The scientifically observed morphology of the body (presumed always to fit within a gender binary) becomes the only mediator for God's gift of sex and gender.[53] Thus, ironically, many of these anti-modernists end up remarkably close to a paradigmatically modern position, projecting modern binary understandings of sex back upon the whole of the Christian tradition.[54]

In such forms, some queer theory and theology ends up being the mirror image of modern, and some anti-modern, gender theory and theology. One asserts a natural or God-given, essential, binary ordering of sex and gender. The

---

51. David Cloutier and Luke Timothy Johnson, "The Church & Transgender Identity," *Commonweal*, February 27, 2017, https://www.commonwealmagazine.org/church-transgender-identity.

52. Susan Stryker, *Transgender History: The Roots of Today's Revolution*, revised edition (Berkeley, CA: Seal Press, 2017), 53.

53. Oliver O'Donovan, "Transsexualism and Christian Marriage," *The Journal of Religious Ethics* 11, no. 1 (1983): 147; Cloutier and Johnson, "The Church & Transgender Identity."

54. For a much more developed account of this trend, see Adrian Thatcher, *Redeeming Gender* (New York: Oxford University Press, 2016), 84–114.

other offers an anti-realist, voluntarist approach to sex and gender. The result is an increasingly unbridgeable gap between the two sides. Many theologians today seek an alternative to either of these options.[55]

Must Postmodernity Be Voluntarist?

The good news is that potential bridges can be built, if not between these two options, then at least to some third alternative. Judith Butler's position, for instance, can be better read as significantly more nuanced than the voluntarist interpretation suggests. As Butler clarified in her later *Bodies That Matter*, "performativity" should not be confused with "performance." Drawing on J. L. Austin's theory of performative speech acts, she distinguishes between speech that is meant to convey information and speech that creates a reality by its utterance.[56] Take, for example the presider's utterance "I pronounce you . . ." at the end of a wedding ceremony. The statement has communicated no preexistent content. Rather it does something with language. It proclaims, and in the proclaiming makes so, a new relationship, the relationship of being married.

This is a socially constructed possibility. History has been home to many socially sanctioned types of relationships between men and women, not all of which would qualify as "marriage" today. Witness polygamy, for instance, or the Hebrew patriarch's relationships with both wives and concubines or servants. And marriage has existed in many cultures without such a performative utterance. In some cultures, for instance, it is the consummation of the marriage or cohabitation rather than a ceremony that is determinative in making one married.[57] But even while the pronouncement (and indeed the whole wedding ceremony) is socially constructed, the significance of the utterance is not voluntarist. It is embedded in a set of embodied social and discursive practices that give it its power. The relationship it enacts even changes the married couple's relationship to the law. As such, while socially constructed, one cannot accurately say that the ceremony or the marriage is not real. For Butler, gender performativity happens

55. Taylor, *A Secular Age*, 767; Bader-Saye, "The Transgender Body's Grace," 77; Rowan Williams, "The Body's Grace," in *Theology and Sexuality: Classic and Contemporary Readings*, ed. Eugene F. Rogers, Blackwell Readings in Modern Theology (Malden, MA: Blackwell Publishers, 2002), 314.

56. Judith Butler, *Bodies That Matter: On the Discursive Limits of "Sex,"* Routledge Classics (New York: Routledge, 2011), 224–226; Prosser, "Judith Butler: Queer Feminism, Transgender, and the Transubstantiation of Sex," 262.

57. Carol Braun Pasternack, "Negotiating Gender in Anglo-Saxon England," in *Gender and Difference in the Middle Ages*, ed. Sharon A. Farmer and Carol Braun Pasternack, Medieval Cultures 32 (Minneapolis, MN: University of Minnesota Press, 2003), 108; Troy D Allen, *The Ancient Egyptian Family: Kinship and Social Structure* (New York: Routledge, 2012), 29.

in a related nexus of embodied social and discursive practices. These practices channel and limit human possibilities.

Accounting for social institutions and norms in terms of performativity and discursive practices lacks several of the qualities that I have identified with the "contexts of responsibility" above. Butler is more likely to say that gender constructs form a kind of prison than that they could be a divine gift.[58] And, one might be concerned that her account of essence-less gender combined with her emphasis on the bounds of discursive practice leaves too little room and motivation for large-scale reform movements.[59] Still, this nuanced picture of Butler's position has many points of contact with the kind of theological sociology I was suggesting above. In our transcendence of the context of sex and gender, we can recognize the ways in which the norms of this context have been harmful, and could be experienced by many, not the least women and members of LGBTQAI+ communities as prison-like. This does not mean that we can, or should, abandon the context altogether. But we should be open to reform of the context, and open to seeing the extent to which, in the light of God's constant activity, it has been and is already being transformed.

Must Christianity Be Reductively Naturalist?

On the other side of the divide are those modern/anti-modern theologians who already appreciate the ways in which gender constitutes a gift from God, but who fail to appreciate the full diversity of gender and sex and who underestimate the extent to which this context of responsibility has been warped by sinful human abuse. As Scott Bader-Saye has noted, many of these theologians offer significant qualifications in their analysis, suggesting that their concerns may be more about voluntarist constructions of gender than about all alternatives to the binary model of sex and gender.[60] If Bader-Saye's analysis is correct on this point, then what is needed is a more robust theological account of sex, gender, and transgenderism. Bader-Saye himself begins to provide such an account that I build on below. I hope that the location of gender and sex as providing a context of responsibility adds to this account.

It is worthwhile here to say something about how to conceive of God and the world in relation to contexts of responsibility. There is a tradition at least

58. For a "queer" theory that emphasizes the ambiguity of gender categories (in both oppressing and liberating people) see Teresa De Lauretis, *Technologies of Gender: Essays on Theory, Film, and Fiction*, Theories of Representation and Difference (Bloomington, IN: Indiana University Press, 1987).

59. Martha Nussbaum, "The Professor of Parody," *The New Republic*, February 22, 1999.

60. Bader-Saye, "The Transgender Body's Grace," 83.

as old as Plato that conceives of God primarily in terms of being. God in this tradition is the One, source of all being and all order in creation, and yet always aloof from the creation because of its imperfection. The creation only exists in relation to God, and God is not in need of relations. God is the source of perfect forms, which appear only in shoddy copies in the creation, which is always becoming something else, and thus failing to be in the eternal and unchanging sense that God is.

Christianity, much as it has made use of platonic philosophy, can only stand in tense relationship with this tradition. The God of Christianity is triune, and thus constituted by relation rather than solitary being. The God of Christianity is not aloof from the world but is filled with love for the world in all its messy becoming. The Christian God exists in perichoresis, the inter-existence and perpetual motion of the triune persons within the Godhead.[61] God is ordered as the trinity inasmuch as God is always becoming the trinity. As such, the Christian God is not only the source of form, but also of vitality in the world; God of form and reform.[62] This truth is only heightened when God comes to deal with sin.

It is in the light of such a conception of God that we should see the contexts of responsibility. The contexts as they exist are gifts from God inasmuch as they allow humanity to attain goods that would not be possible without them. They provide for us ideals and structure within a broader system of human life at a particular time. But every broader system of human life in a sinful world is a unique mix of possibilities and limitations created by God's grace in the face of human sinfulness, where neither the shape of grace nor the shape of sinfulness is stable. The shape of one generation's sinfulness may be overcome by God's grace in the next, and each generation finds its own ways to rebel against the grace of God. As such, God is never done with the contexts.

In some ways, gender voluntarists and those insisting on immutable gender categories fail while recognizing God's activity in the contexts in opposite ways. The voluntarist would have us eliminate the context, thus failing to accept God's gift of order. The defender of immutable categories would have us idolize a particular form of the context, thus failing to accept God's gift of new opportunities. Acknowledging the good gifts of God requires not only giving thanks for the forms that God has provided, but also being open to God's grace when it calls us to move beyond those forms toward new possibilities.

Interestingly, an upshot of this analysis is that trans advocates and scholars of trans studies may represent promising dialogue partners for the discussion of

61. Sarah Coakley, *God, Sexuality and the Self: An Essay "on the Trinity"* (New York: Cambridge University Press, 2013), 252; Jürgen Moltmann, *The Trinity and the Kingdom: The Doctrine of God* (Minneapolis, MN: Fortress Press, 1993), 174.

62. Niebuhr, *The Nature and Destiny of Man*, 1: 27–56.

moral theology in this area. Enmeshed in activities of gender transgression, trans advocates often have a deep appreciation for the extent to which the construction of gender extends deep into the self and can be oppressive and harmful. At the same time, in contrast with some queer theorists, trans advocates tend to celebrate the extent to which gender is experienced as something given to the person, even if this given gender conflicts with contemporary social expectations and norms.[63] As I will suggest below, theologians could learn a great deal from trans advocates and trans studies scholars about the extent to which gender and sex can be conceived in terms of a "calling." For present, it is enough to look at the claim of Christina Beardsley, an advocate for trans inclusion in the church: "The assumption . . . that a transsexual person 'chooses' his or her gender identity is ill-conceived. As far as the person is concerned their gender identity is perceived as given (even God given . . .)"[64]

Gender and Sex

With the above context in place, we can now put forward some working definitions of sex and gender for this project.[65] I offer the below accounts in the context of the rich recent history of arguments about defining these terms in secular scholarship.[66] And I do so in the light of previous excellent theological treatments of related topics.[67] But, my account is shaped especially by the above-mentioned framework and the desire to produce accounts of sex and gender that fit within this framework. As such, it highlights the relation between sex and gender, the formation of human identity (a particularly central human good), and the realization of other human goods.

---

63. Genny Beemyn and Susan Rankin, *The Lives of Transgender People* (New York: Columbia University Press, 2011), 42–68; Cáel Keegan, "Transgender Studies, or How to Do Things with Trans*," in *The Cambridge Companion to Queer Studies*, ed. Siobhan B. Somerville (New York: Cambridge University Press, 2020), 70; Sally Hines, "Introduction," in *Transgender Identities: Towards a Social Analysis of Gender Diversity*, ed. Sally Hines and Tam Sanger, Routledge Research in Gender and Society 24 (New York: Routledge, 2012), 5.

64. Christina Beardsley, "Taking Issue: The Transsexual Hiatus in 'Some Issues in Human Sexuality,'" in *This Is My Body: Hearing the Theology of Transgender Christians*, ed. Christina Beardsley and Michelle O'Brien (London: Darton, Longman and Todd Ltd, 2016).

65. I do not offer this as an account that is sufficient for all situations. As Edward Schiappa argues, we need multiple conceptions and definitions of such terms to fit the varied goods at stake in different situations. Edward Schiappa, *The Transgender Exigency: Defining Sex and Gender in the 21st Century* (New York: Routledge, 2022).

66. For a short history, see Schiappa, 15–31. For a longer treatment, see Mary Holmes, *What Is Gender? Sociological Approaches* (Los Angeles, CA: Sage, 2007).

67. See especially Williams, "The Body's Grace"; Rogers, *Sexuality and the Christian Body*.

- Sex and gender concern how identities are realized in relation to particular sets of goods (e.g., standards of beauty, fashion, etc.), virtues and vices (e.g. assertiveness, caring, etc.), and social rules (e.g. "gender roles") in the light of patterns of embodied differences (esp. genital formation, chromosomal patterns, hormones, the development of breasts, facial hair, relative physical strength, and so on).
- Sexes and genders (e.g., male/masculine, female/feminine) name identity types associated (in a paradigmatic/ideal way) with patterns of embodiment, sets of goods, virtues and vices, and rules like those noted above.

In many discussions, sex is taken to refer to embodied differences while gender is taken to refer to social differences. This distinction is obviously overly simple, and it plays into a modern picture of the world where "biology" is foundational and "culture" epiphenomenal. Since biology (and the other hard sciences) are themselves socially constructed and culture is always a way of making sense of our life in a material world, such a view will not do.

Still, I maintain the two terms, sex and gender, to mark the messiness of relating relatively public or private morphology and gender expectations in the process of identity formation. Most people who are born intersex do not consider themselves to be "intergender" or "transgender." Many transgender persons do not undergo sex reassignment. Distinguishing when an issue is one of "sex" as opposed to "gender" is an activity that itself is essentially contested within the sex/gender context of responsibility. Philosophically it seems to me that anything like "sorting this out" will require a fundamental shift in the categories themselves. It is sufficient for current purposes to say that the two are intimately related to one another because they both concern the ways our identities are formed. I shall assume wide latitude in relating the two in my own theoretical analysis, highlighting that this is a different activity from recognizing a person's identity in the terms that they accept.

The Diversity of Sex and Gender

Just as scientific observation contributed to the collapse of Galenic and Aristotelian medicine, so today it should contribute to the collapse of modern sex/gender binarity.[68] Even when focused exclusively on biologically observable

68. Megan K. DeFranza, *Sex Difference in Christian Theology: Male, Female, and Intersex in the Image of God* (Grand Rapids, MI: Eerdmans, 2015); Christine Gudorf, "The Erosion of Sexual Dimorphism: Challenges to Religion and Religious Ethics," *Journal of the American Academy of Religion* 69, no. 4 (December 1, 2001): 863–892.

traits, sex and gender can be alternatively conceived as related primarily to the presence or absence of reproductive organs, to one's chromosomal makeup, or to the presence or absence of certain "secondary," often hormonally triggered, traits, such as facial hair, musculature, and facial structure. Today it is known that there is no necessary connection between these diverse kinds of sexual traits.

In part as a send-up of the absurd reductivism of the project, the biologist Anne Fausto-Sterling has written that "scientifically" one could categorize at least five different sexes even if one looks just at the configurations of reproductive organs.[69] To the traditional categories of "male" and "female" she adds a category (Herm) to cover persons born with one testis and one ovary, another (Merm) for those with one testis and some "female" genitalia but no ovaries, and a final (Ferm) for those with ovaries and some "male" genitalia but no testes. To be more accurate, one would have to further distinguish between intersex people depending on what typically male or female genitalia they do have. And all of this is before we get to discussing chromosomal makeup or secondary sex traits (which are the ones that the public actually sees).

Recognition of this diversity in the creation is not new within Christianity.[70] In Matthew 19:12, Jesus refers to "eunuchs who have been so from birth." This is probably a reference to some form of intersex person.[71] In *De Civitate Dei*, Augustine discusses people who are bi-sex (*utriusque sexus esse naturam*), having both "male" and "female" secondary sex qualities (breasts in this case), and intersex, those he calls the "*Androgyni*" or "*Hermaphroditos*," having both "male" and "female" genitalia.[72]

On theological grounds, he refuses to de-humanize such people.

> Anyone who is born anywhere as a human being, that is, as a rational and mortal being, derives from the original, first created man—no matter how strange he may appear to our senses in his bodily form, his color, his mode of movement, his voice, or in any power, part, or quality of his nature whatsoever.

---

69. Anne Fausto-Sterling, "The Five Sexes," *The Sciences* 33, no. 2 (March 4, 1993): 20–24; Anne Fausto-Sterling, "The Five Sexes Revisited," *The Sciences* 40, no. 4 (July 8, 2000): 18–23.

70. DeVun, *The Shape of Sex*, 16–39.

71. Michelle O'Brien, "Intersex, Medicine, Diversity, Identity and Spirituality," in *This Is My Body: Hearing the Theology of Transgender Christians*, ed. Christina Beardsley and Michelle O'Brien (London: Darton, Longman and Todd, 2016); Jung and Roughgarden, "Gender in Heaven," 232.

72. The term hermaphrodite is taken today as a derogatory term. I use Augustine's terminology here for purposes of historical accuracy but leave them in Latin for the same reason.

He also includes within this section praise for the God given diversity of the creation.

> For God is the creator of all things; and he himself knows where and when it is right or was right for anything to be created. He knows how to weave together the beauty of the whole in the similarity and diversity of its parts. But the person who is unable to see the whole is offended at what appears to be the deformity of a part, for he does not know how it fits in or how it is connected with the whole.[73]

After all, he quips, "no one should be so foolish as to imagine that God made a mistake."

Unfortunately, following his own parochialism rather than his theological insight, Augustine quickly takes his place among those "who are unable to see the whole." He could have allowed his belief in the goodness of creation to lead him toward a grace-filled reading of the creation of humanity that would have recognized the diversity that he knew the world witnesses, but instead he allowed a reductive reading of the creation to drive him to the conclusion that intersex people, along with pygmies (*Pygmaeos*), conjoined twins, and people born with more or less than five fingers per hand, were "monstrous" (*monstrosis*).[74]

Today the globe hosts somewhere between one million and six million intersex people.[75] Intersex traits are, no doubt, statistically rare (as Augustine himself notes). But the point here is that even a reductive naturalism, which looks only at empirically observable characteristics, must abandon the idea that humans fit within a simple binary picture of sex and gender. How much more should a full Christian anthropology, which takes humans as "cultural," spiritual, and willful beings, and which recognizes "callings" that are nowhere inscribed in the flesh, be open to greater diversity?[76] Nothing here suggests that Christians are obligated to accept all constructions of sex and gender, but at the very least

---

73. De Civitate Dei 16.8. Translations taken from Augustine, *The City of God: 11–22.*

74. See De Civitate Dei, 16.8, De Trin 12.6.8; De Genesi ad litteram, 89–90.

75. A great deal depends on how intersex is defined. This is, of course, a question of social construction. On broader definitions, 1.7% of people born may be intersex. Anne Fausto-Sterling, *Sexing the Body*, 55. More limited definitions produce the claim that .018% are born intersex. Leonard Sax, "How Common Is Intersex? A Response to Anne Fausto-Sterling," *The Journal of Sex Research* 39, no. 3 (August 1, 2002): 174–178; Here I follow a middle ground definition that finds intersex births to occur in between 0.05% and 0.02% of cases. Selma Feldman Witchel, "Disorders of Sex Development," *Best Practice & Research Clinical Obstetrics & Gynaecology* 48 (April 2018): 90–102.

76. Williams, "The Body's Grace," 312.

before labeling an expression of the creation to be corrupt, there should be an onus of justification on the one suggesting to toss stones.

Study of the shape of the sex/gender contexts of responsibility in diverse cultures points in the same direction.[77] As should be expected, non-Western cultures frequently construct gender/sex much differently than Western cultures. As such, it is overly simple to imagine that they would share the same framework but recognize more sexes/genders. Yet, it is fair to say that many non-Western cultures have contexts of responsibility that recognize greater diversity than what is available in the Western binary system. To take a small sample, the Lakota category of *winkte*, the Navajo category of *nádleehí*, and the Bugis categories of *calabi*, *calalai*, and *bisu* all resist simple translation into Western terms and challenge the notion of a binary picture of sex and gender.[78]

One need not, however, depart from Western, Christian societies to find cultures recognizing a greater plurality of gender and sex than has been imagined since modernity or even the possibility of gender transitions. Again, we should not expect these to look the same as they do in our culture. They exist in different contexts of responsibility. But we can find analogies throughout Christian history.

Roman conceptions of gender and sex, which profoundly influenced early Christianity, worked significantly differently from modern categories. This is not to say that there were not differentiations in gender status. There were many. But in a significant sense, all individuals fell somewhere on a sliding scale of masculinity. The question of gender status concerned how perfectly one manifested masculinity. Masculinity was identified with relative autonomy (lack of dependence on others), power, and activity.[79] As such, the "male" Roman citizen was more a man then the "male" noncitizen, who had less power and ability to protect his bodily integrity under the law. Similarly, it was manlier to penetrate

77. Classically, *ius gentium* refers to the natural law as that law can be found in the variety of human cultures. Here I am drawing on this as an epistemological frame. But I am interpreting the "natural law" as worked out through contexts of responsibility.

78. Sabine Lang, *Men as Women, Women as Men: Changing Gender in Native American Cultures* (Austin, TX: University of Texas Press, 1998); Sue-Ellen Jacobs, Wesley Thomas, and Sabine Lang, eds., *Two-Spirit People: Native American Gender Identity, Sexuality, and Spirituality* (Urbana, IL: University of Illinois Press, 1997); Daniel Stables. "Asia's isle of five separate genders." BBC, April 12, 2021, https://www.bbc.com/travel/article/20210411-asias-isle-of-five-separate-genders; Michael G. Peletz, *Gender Pluralism: Southeast Asia since Early Modern Times* (New York: Routledge, 2009); Gilbert H. Herdt, ed., *Third Sex, Third Gender: Beyond Sexual Dimorphism in Culture and History* (New York: Zone Books, 1996).

79. Jonathan Walters, "Invading the Roman Body: Manliness and Impenetrability in Roman Thought," in *Roman Sexualities*, ed. Judith P. Hallett and Marilyn B. Skinner (Princeton, NJ: Princeton University Press, 1997), 29–43.

one's sexual partner than to be penetrated, regardless of the partner's sex or gender.[80] To penetrate was a sign of activity and power. To be penetrated was a sign of passivity and openness to having one's bodily integrity violated. One could lose their legal status as a male if they "played the part of a passive female."[81] In this context, females could be conceived as people who manifested maleness particularly badly—"failed males" as Peter Brown puts it.[82]

From the perspective of this ancient model, the modern relation of "gender" and "sex" (seeing gender performance as deriving from biological sex) is wrongly unidirectional. In the premodern world it was often taken that physiological characteristics were dependent on one acting manly or effeminately, not the other way around. If one acted effeminate, one's body would take on effeminate qualities, and vice versa for masculinity.

This Roman model of gender had to exist in tension with Jewish conceptions of sex and gender. The dominant gender constructs in Jewish history are often viewed as "rigidly bipolar" and having "little tolerance for intermediate gender categories."[83] There is a great deal of truth to this picture. Unlike the Roman conceptualization that saw sex and gender on a gradient scale, much of the Jewish tradition appears to have posited a metaphysical chasm between male and female.

This distinction was especially important as one came to consider issues of purity, which were often so important in Jewish culture. As Daniel Boyarin has argued, this concern appears to lie behind prohibitions of penetrative anal intercourse between males, which was seen as violating purity standards, much like sowing two different kinds of seed in a single field or mixing different kinds of fabric in a single piece of clothing.[84] This was different from the Roman concern about penetration, which focused on the potential of being lowered on the scale of masculinity.

The Jewish context was also quite different from the modern binary conception of sex and gender. As Boyarin points out, "sexual orientation" appears not to

---

80. Holt Parker, "The Teratogenic Grid," in *Roman Sexualities*, ed. Judith P. Hallett and Marilyn B. Skinner (Princeton, NJ: Princeton University Press, 1997), 47–65.

81. Colleen M. Conway, *Behold the Man: Jesus and Greco-Roman Masculinity* (New York: Oxford University Press, 2008), 21.

82. Peter Brown, *The Body and Society*, 10.

83. Kathryn Ringrose, "Reconfiguring the Prophet Daniel: Gender, Sanctity, and Castration in Byzantium," in *Gender and Difference in the Middle Ages*, ed. Sharon A. Farmer and Carol Braun Pasternack, Medieval Cultures 32 (Minneapolis, MN: University of Minnesota Press, 2003), 78.

84. Daniel Boyarin, "Against Rabbinic Sexuality: Textual Reasoning and the Jewish Theology of Sex," in *Queer Theology: Rethinking the Western Body*, ed. Gerard Loughlin (Malden, MA: Blackwell Pub, 2007), 136.

have been a category that existed in the Jewish conception of sex and gender. To gain sexual release via friction with a member of the same sex did not fall into the same category as penetrative anal sex acts, and since women could not penetrate another person in the relevant way to violate purity standards, what we might consider "sex" between women also fell outside of the concern of purity codes. Thus, we can say that the context of responsibility for sex and gender within much of Jewish society did posit a strict binary, but it was quite different from the one known in modernity.

Given this emphasis on binarity, it is even more intriguing that early Jews and Christians found themselves in some ways obligated to transgress the pictures of male and female as posited in the dominant Roman system. As an oppressed, minority class, most Jews were excluded from the possibility of being "true" men. Though Zealots could aspire to revolutionary activity that would manifest significant masculine virtue, the Pharisaic/Rabbinic life, focused on study of the Torah, was less amenable to the dominant Roman conception of masculinity. Christian identification with a crucified savior, embrace of asceticism, and servitude also challenged at least part of the dominant gender constructions of the period. As Boyarin writes: "Both early rabbinic Jews and early Christians performed resistance to the Roman imperial power-structure through 'gender-bending,' thereby marking their own understanding that gender itself is implicated in the maintenance of political power."[85]

Rabbis eventually came to cast the dominant Roman construction of manliness as violent and cruel (something like what is achieved today with the category of "toxic masculinity"). This allowed the Rabbis to construct a Jewish, alternative form of masculinity that rejected aggressiveness and activity as paradigmatic symbols of manliness. Such a movement can be seen in terms of a proposal for a minority conception of masculinity, but they constructed this alternative against what they saw as the dominant gender framework of the time. The Rabbis were advocating for a life that they believed would be seen as "effeminate" by the Roman standard.[86]

---

85. Daniel Boyarin, "Homotopia: The Feminized Jewish Man and the Lives of Women in Late Antiquity," *Differences* 7, no. 2 (July 1, 1995): 42.

86. Boyarin, "Homotopia"; Daniel Boyarin, *Unheroic Conduct: The Rise of Heterosexuality and the Invention of the Jewish Man*, Contraversions 8 (Berkeley: University of California Press, 1997), 99–107. The Roman conception of masculinity was more diverse than the caricature that the Rabbis offered of it. By the first century there were multiple imperial conceptions of masculinity, the more philosophical of which could make room for scholarship and contemplation as "manly" arts. See Angela Hobbs, *Plato and the Hero: Courage, Manliness, and the Impersonal Good* (New York: Cambridge University Press, 2006); Conway, *Behold the Man*; Susanna Asikainen, *Jesus and Other Men: Ideal Masculinities in the Synoptic Gospels*, Biblical Interpretation Series 159 (Boston: Brill, 2018). Here, with Boyarin, I am focusing on how the Rabbis conceived of their gender construction and how it shaped the perception of Jewish men more broadly.

Emerging from the Judaism of the first century, Christian identity similarly required transgression against Roman gender norms. More on this in the next chapter, as we explore the ways in which Jesus should be considered as sex and gender transgressive. But here it is more relevant to trace out one way in which early Christianity's constructions of gender drew from possibilities within the Roman model. Given the paradigmatic status of the male in the Roman system, a male becoming more like a female entailed some level of dishonor. But there were significant senses in which a woman becoming manly (or even, at least symbolically, a man) could be seen as highly praiseworthy.

The theme of women "becoming men" was frequent in early Christianity. Ephesians 14:12–13 pictures a process of spiritual maturing. God has given Christians gifts to aid them in this process until they all become "perfect man" (ἄνδρα τέλειον). Clement of Alexandria would speculate about this theme in terms of eschatology, positing that the woman might become "the perfect, manly, woman" in life after death.[87] In the Odes of Solomon, when considering Mary giving birth without pain, the author lauds her, stating that she must have given birth "like a strong man" (19.10). Gregory Nazianzus could complement a woman for having "the soul of a man in the body of a woman (ῶ ψυχῆς ἀνδρείας ἐν γυναικείῳ τῷ σώματι)."[88] One wonders if anyone ever charged him with Gnosticism for the comment.

The positive transitioning of women was especially associated with martyrdom. In The Acts of Paul and Thecla, after God delivers her from efforts to martyr her, Thecla dons the cloak of a man (2.40). In The Passion of Perpetua and Felicitas, Perpetua's last vision before being martyred provides a symbolic preview of her struggle against the powers of the devil in her last moments. In the vision she is led to an amphitheater where she is to partake in combat with her opponent. Her supporters come to her, and she reports: "I was stripped naked, and I became a man" (καὶ ἐγενήθην ἄρρην/*et facta sum masculus*) (10.7).[89] In this moment, as Candida Moss writes, Perpetua emerges as a "transgendered gladiator" marked by the glory of masculinity in the Roman gender construct.[90]

87. Kari Vogt, "'Becoming Male': One Aspect of an Early Christian Anthropology," in *Feminism and Theology*, ed. Janet Martin Soskice and Diana Lipton, Oxford Readings in Feminism (New York: Oxford University Press, 2003), 50.

88. Quoted in Gabrielle Thomas, *The Image of God in the Theology of Gregory of Nazianzus*, 79.

89. Translation and original languages taken from Thomas J. Heffernan, ed., *The Passion of Perpetua and Felicity* (New York: Oxford University Press, 2012).

90. Candida Moss, "Heavenly Healing: Eschatological Cleansing and the Resurrection of the Dead in the Early Church," *Journal of the American Academy of Religion* 79, no. 4 (December 1, 2011): 992.

Another example of positive Christian views of gender options beyond the modern binary conception can be found in the treatment of eunuchs at different periods in Christian history. The term *eunuch* was used to refer to people with either underdeveloped or removed "male" genitalia.[91] In the Roman gender construct, they presented a problematic form of existence. Not only were they effeminated. Their effemination was visible, not just in their lack of genitalia but often in the many secondary sexual characteristics that related to this lack. As such, they stood as a sign of the contingency of masculinity. The "physical appearance and reputed character of eunuchs," writes Peter Brown, "acted as constant reminders that the male body was a fearsomely plastic thing."[92] If "there is a figure in the ancient world that embodied a challenge to hegemonic masculinity, it was the eunuch."[93]

Within this context, it was part of the transgressiveness of Christianity that it could transform the eunuch into a symbol of faith. In Matthew, after teaching against divorce, Jesus faces skepticism from his disciples, who suggest, "If such is the case of a man with his wife, it is better not to marry" (19:10). In response, Jesus suggests that his followers should make "themselves eunuchs for the sake of the kingdom of heaven" (19:12). As Colleen Conway notes, the transgressiveness of Jesus suggestion is qualified by the fact that the suggestion appears to be symbolic, referring to self-control (a masculine trait).[94] But Jesus's immediately following statement, "Let anyone accept this who can," suggests how controversial even a symbolic invocation of a command to become eunuchs must have been.

The biblical embrace of the eunuch did not, however, limit itself to symbolism. In Acts 8:26–40, Philip converts and baptizes an Ethiopian eunuch who then continues on his way back to his homeland. This unlikely hero becomes one who will fulfill the last words of Jesus before the ascension, taking the good news "to the ends of the earth" (Acts 1:8). In making a eunuch such a key figure in the mission of the early church, Christianity raised significant questions about the Roman construction of sex and gender.

In time, however, Christians would go even further. Following the Matthean use of the term, by the time of Eusebius in the late third to early fourth century, it could be an honor in the Christian church to be labeled a "eunuch" for one's

---

91. Jung and Roughgarden, "Gender in Heaven," 232.

92. Brown, *The Body and Society*, 10–11.

93. Conway, *Behold the Man*, 123; See also, Karen L. King, "Jesus," in *The Oxford Handbook of New Testament, Gender, and Sexuality*, ed. Benjamin H. Dunning (New York: Oxford University Press, 2019), 416.

94. Conway, *Behold the Man*, 123–124.

sexual continence.[95] But again, it was not such a great leap from this to the praise of actual eunuchs. While the practice was controversial, some early Christians (perhaps including Origen) appear to have castrated themselves to secure their own chastity.[96] As Kathryn Ringrose has shown, by the twelfth century in Byzantium, literal eunuchs held high church positions, including several archbishoprics.[97] Even the biblical prophet Daniel had been reconceived as a court eunuch. This is not to say that the distinction between eunuchs and others had been erased. Indeed, in terms of what we would call gender, Byzantine society by this point had several more categories than the ones recognized in modernity. Uncastrated men could be divided into aristocratic and ecclesial genders, each with their own set of cultural norms and expectations. Beyond this, eunuchs represented at least one further possibility. Eunuchs "represent a distinct gender category, one that is defined by dress, assumed sexual behavior, work, physical appearance, quality of voice, and, for some eunuchs, personal affect."[98] The eunuch was not capable of all the virtue attained by, say, the non-eunuch ecclesial man, because the eunuch did not need to overcome the same sexual desires. But their own apparently necessitated virginity made them a potential symbol of desirable continence within the church.

The point here is not to suggest that the historical church once recognized "transexuals" in the modern sense. It could not have, as that sense did not exist.[99] The point is to establish that (1) there is no *one* structure for the context of responsibility that moderns recognize as sex and gender that has been universal in Christian history; (2) Christian constructions of gender have at points included alternatives beyond the binary picture that modernity offers; and (3) Christian constructions have recognized the potential of significant forms of transgressions against, and indeed transitions between, what moderns would see as the binary options available in sex/gender categories.

As should be expected, the context of responsibility that we call sex and gender is not a stable framework. Sex and gender (at times conceived quite differently from our present categories) have provided structures in which Christians have lived. These structures made sense of the contemporary landscape and

95. Brown, *The Body and Society*, 67–68; For a full study of the role of the eunuch in the context of gender constructs in early Christianity, see Mathew Kuefler, *The Manly Eunuch: Masculinity, Gender Ambiguity, and Christian Ideology in Late Antiquity*, The Chicago Series on Sexuality, History, and Society (Chicago: University of Chicago Press, 2001).

96. Jung and Roughgarden, "Gender in Heaven," 235–236.

97. Ringrose, "Reconfiguring the Prophet Daniel," 74.

98. Ringrose, 77.

99. O'Brien, "Intersex, Medicine, Diversity, Identity and Spirituality."

provided for the realization of significant goods in that landscape. At the same time, these structures were always received by sinful humanity. They were abused and were tied to patriarchy, to the degradation of the divine dignity of some persons, and to unjust hierarchies. Not only can we not return to these earlier forms of the context, we should not want to return, as we have hopefully learned about the ways in which they were problematically structured. No doubt, every effort to reform the context in our own time will give rise to further ironic reversals of justice. That has certainly been the case as feminism occasionally caused problems for gay rights activists, and feminism and the gay rights movement occasionally gave birth to trans-denialism. But this is not a reason to stop reforming. God is always doing something new, and we are called to participate in this gift.

What about Genesis?

Perhaps the most frequent appeal from those who wish to retain a binary model of sex and gender comes from a reading of the early chapters of Genesis. This is a particularly critical point for the argument of this book, because I have been arguing for a doctrinal shift in Christology based on problems with consistently connecting Genesis to an adequate soteriology. In previous chapters I have left uncriticized the picture of a gender binary arising from the creation of Adam and Eve. The careful reader will have noticed a shift in the first section of this chapter. In the first premise of my argument laid out there, I wrote that "sexual/gender diversity is a significant element in God's creation." This is clearly different from the statements of those who would claim that "a sexual/gender binary is a significant element in God's creation." And doubtless some of the figures that I have drawn upon to make my case up to the present chapter would endorse only the latter claim. So, what warrants this shift?

The need for recognition of greater sex/gender diversity follows from my theological argument. I have proposed a solution to the problem of locating Eve in the drama of salvation. In this solution Christ is the new Adam *and the new Eve*. This solution fits all the premises that I laid out at the beginning of the chapter. But accepting it requires accepting more sex/gender diversity than the binary model admits. At the very least, it requires acknowledging the reality of transsexual and transgender identities. If Christ is trans*, then Christianity must accept trans* identity as a legitimate possibility. However, some will properly push me to show that it is possible to read scripture in a way that is coherent with the theological conclusion to which I am pointing. Historically, the discovery of scriptural readings that allow for a more consistent and harmonious parallel among scriptures and between scripture and proposed doctrine has played a significant role in Christian arguments. This is a process of discovery, as the reading finds the expression of a divine authorial intent in the text.[100] As such, it is important here to show that a reading of Genesis as concerned with gender diversity (as opposed to gender binary) is possible.

In Genesis 1 we find a short statement on the creation of sex and gender diversity: "So God created humankind in his image, in the image of God he created them; male and female he created them. God blessed them, and God said to them, 'Be fruitful and multiply, and fill the earth and subdue it." Clearly this is a location where gender diversity is at stake in relation to procreation. God has produced males and females. The following command suggests what is important about this diversity, God has produced a diversity that makes procreation possible. And, by God's command, humans are obligated to procreate. The important question is how comprehensive we are to take this statement to be in describing the full diversity of sex, gender, and human obligation? Are these the *only* kinds of humans that God has created, or are they simply the kinds most immediately relevant to the following command? Is everyone obligated to have children, or are only some so obligated?

Christianity has never found the narrative to be comprehensive regarding the last question. Rather, it has recognized different callings for different people. Some are called to marriage and procreation. But some are not. Exactly how Christians have drawn the lines between these groups depends on denomination, location, and time. This too concerns contexts of responsibility. But Christians from the beginning have recognized that, though God tells humans in Genesis to "be fruitful and multiply," this is not intended as a comprehensive statement of God's will for all individuals.

Implicitly, Christianity has also recognized that some of the people God created are not the kinds of people that can procreate. Inasmuch as the comprehensiveness of the command to multiply is tied to the comprehensiveness of the claim that God created males and females (a diversity capable of multiplying), the statement that God created males and females should also not be taken as comprehensive of the kinds of people God created.

The idea that the full plenitude of God's creation is presented in one chapter of the Bible is absurd. Rather, as many scholars have recognized, Genesis uses a series of merisms (Latin: *merismus*, Greek: μερισμός) to schematize the creation. Merisms occur when a word pair or selective listing of representatives from a set stand for a full set.[101] Genesis 1 is shot through with merisms. God creates

100. Nicholas Wolterstorff, *Divine Discourse: Philosophical Reflections on the Claim That God Speaks* (New York: Cambridge University Press, 1995).

101. Wilfred G. E. Watson, *Classical Hebrew Poetry: A Guide to Its Techniques*, Journal for the Study of the Old Testament 26 (Sheffield, England: JSOT Press, 1984), 321–323. Thanks to Daryl Jefferies for pointing me in this direction.

"heavens and earth" (1:1; 2:1), separates "light from darkness" (1:4), "day from night" (1:5, 14), and "earth from sea" (1:10). God creates animals of "water," "air," and "land" (1:20, 24). And each day passes with an "evening" and a "morning" (1:5, 8, 13, 19, 23, 31). In none of these cases should the reader take it that the listing of these constituents rules out a greater diversity in the set. The fact that God creates animals of "water" and "land" should not lead to the denial of the existence of platypuses or frogs. The creation of "day and night" should not lead to the denial of twilight.

In the middle of this section filled with merisms comes the creation of "male and female" (1:27). There is nothing special that sets this act of creation apart from the formula used for the others. Nothing suggests that this is any less a merism.[102] The ancient world could acknowledge that not all people fit a binary reading of this passage. See above Jesus's comment on those who were born as eunuchs. As such, there is no necessity in seeing what is articulated here as a limit.

A more promising approach is to take the passage as a positive statement about a particular part of the sex/gender diversity God has created. God did create males and females, meaning people who are sexually diversified in ways that allow for procreation. This categorization clearly does not cover the full diversity of the humans God created. Some humans are born without the ability to participate in procreation. Similarly, we should not (in denial of the reality of intersexed persons) claim that God's creation only admitted of the dimorphism represented in paradigmatically "male" and "female" physiology.

Even more clearly, Genesis 2 need not be read as requiring binary sex and gender. In verse 7, God creates *adam* from the ground. At this point the text leaves unsaid anything more specific about the sexing or gendering of this created being. As we shall see in a later chapter, many Christians have read this creation as having given rise to either an unsexed or a multiply sexed being. For present purposes, I will pass over this issue as what interests us primarily is the question of the relation between Adam and Eve in the creation. However, we should not jump straight to the creation of Eve. There is quite a bit between the creation of Adam and the creation of Eve that can tell us about the intent behind the creation of Eve. First, it is important to note God's given reason for the second act of creation. After observing *adam* in the garden, God concludes "It is not good that *adam* should be alone; I will make him a helper as his partner" (2.18). What is at stake here is companionship and mutual aid. God suggests that what is needed is someone other than *adam* with whom *adam* can have relationship. This requires the creation of diversity and entails the rejection of any picture of any human as properly an island unto themselves. But nowhere in view is the

102. Margaret A. Farley, *Just Love: A Framework for Christian Sexual Ethics* (New York: Continuum, 2012), 142–143.

idea that *adam* needs a specifically dimorphic pairing, or even that God's goal here is the creation of a pair immediately suited to the production of offspring.

This point is confirmed in the immediately following section, where God, having announced that *adam* needs a companion, now creates "every animal of the field and every bird of the air." These beings are clearly not dimorphic alternatives for *adam*, nor are they suitable reproductive partners. But they are God's first creations in the search for an adequate pairing for Adam. One wonders if God looked at *adam* with the dog or the cat and thought for a moment that the goal of finding a partner might have been achieved. This brings to the fore another element of the story. As in Genesis 1, there is no effort here to present a comprehensive account of the diversity of creation. We do not gain a view of every animal that God created. Indeed, the options provided here are much more schematic even than the account provided in Genesis 1. The point here is not to explore all the options given in God's plenitude, but instead to find the key component necessary to an adequate companion.

Eventually, it is clear that this effort has not been fully fruitful: "there was not found a helper as his partner" (2:20). It is at this point that God puts *adam* in a deep sleep and, from his own body, creates Eve. But those who are looking for an indication that it is the binary relation between the two that makes Eve a suitable pairing for Adam will be disappointed. When articulating what it is that makes the two fit with one another, Adam focuses on similarity rather than distinction: "This at last is bone of my bones and flesh of my flesh." It is their common humanity that makes these two suitable. In contrast to all those non-human animals that God had previously created, it is the sameness of their flesh that makes Eve and Adam fit. Note, that their descendants will all also be of the same bone and flesh, whether male or female. Eventually, in Christian theology, this is key to the idea that Christ, through Mary, is born of the same substance as Adam. Like Eve, Jesus too is "bone of my bones."

Clearly *some* diversity is presupposed here. The idea of having a pairing entails the existence of difference. But is there any reason to assume that, simply because there are two beings created, that the diversity should be limited to a binary? As we have noted above, the story does not aim at comprehensiveness in its account of the creation. Why should we any more think that the fact that only two humans were created should limit us to two kinds of human? In many ways we know Adam and Eve represent a diversity greater than any binary. In their creation is the creation of every race, height, body type, and so on. Again, as Augustine observes, "whoever is anywhere born a human . . . no matter what unusual appearance he presents in color, movement, sound, nor how peculiar he is in some power, part, or quality of his nature, no Christian can doubt that he springs from that one protoplast." Why should we, in the midst of the creation of such diversity, decide that the creation of sex and gender must be limited to a literal binary when these other characteristics are not? Doing so seems much more a reflection of our fixations than something necessitated by the narrative itself.

But do not the next lines set up the model of the binary marriage? "Therefore a man leaves his father and his mother and clings to his wife, and they become one flesh" (2.24). The verse is a later gloss on the preceding story. But in context, there is no reason to read it as indicative of a set binary. The point in the creation of Adam and Eve was the need for sociality, not dimorphism or sexual reproduction. This verse tells of how humans move from one social set of relations to another. The man moves from his relationship with his birth family to the creation of his own family. He moves from relatedness to relatedness. Again, why should we treat this token as if it is a limit? Not every man has a father and mother at the time when he marries. Not every man marries. Nor should this be a message only for men. Thus, no Christian can assume that this presents a strict normative limitation to God's meaning in the text. Rather, it should be taken to represent a truth about our sociality. Does the human not emerge from many of the social institutions of youth to find its way into more mature institutions? How much healthier would we be if we recognized this as a part of the created order, maintaining the great diversity of our activities and relationships in adulthood as well as we did when we were required to participate in sport and social organizations as children? To limit the point here to a reductive picture of marriage is to undercut a divine message in the text.

As such, there is nothing in the first two chapters of Genesis that requires a Christian to cling to a binary model of sex and gender. When read in the light of God's purpose in creating *adam*'s partner and the ensuing search for this partner, it is clear that what is needed is common humanity embodied in a diversity of individuals. Sex/gender diversity is a part of this diversity, perhaps a particularly important part given the embodiment of this diversity in Adam and Eve. But there is no reason to see male and female as the only options, or as options so separated as not to admit of transition between the two. There are certainly limits and norms here. The human is called to relationship with others in full recognition of the common dignity of each in their humanness. And this happens inside contexts of responsibility, such as family, work, and so forth. But there is nothing here to justify our thinking that these institutions or the human identities that they enable will be unchanging or that they should be limited by the exact expression that they take on in this schematized summary of human engagement. To read the story in such a way is to deny the full plenitude of God.

Calling

The concept of "contexts of responsibility" is helpful in making sense of sex and gender, but it is not sufficient. This is because individuals both live in and transcend the contexts. People invest their identities in contexts, partially choosing their locations in the contexts and partially being chosen by locations in the contexts. Thus, in addition to an account of the contexts, we need an account of how individuals come to find themselves in the contexts or at their margins.

In Irenaeus, we find an image of the created human as a good but unstable and unfinished self. God does not create the human as perfect. God creates the human in need of a process of maturing into who they are called to be. It is this state that makes possible the failure of humanity, but it is also this state that allows the human to move beyond the simply human toward sanctification or *theosis*. Maturing in this way is a path that must be found, a path from one state of being to another. It is always a transitioning. But it is never a transitioning untethered from a truth to which one is called.

Further, it is a transitioning that never happens alone. Rather, this process is always antiphonal.[103] God's grace calls the individual away from being who they were to being who they could be. The individual responds. We should not imagine this process as one of unmediated divine command and response. God's grace comes through many streams. Augustine's *Confessions* is a brilliant presentation of this process. Through engagement with family, friends, education, his own internal senses, and a variety of vocations, Augustine finds his way to becoming who he is called to be. God works through and around the contexts of responsibility in which the individual is enmeshed. It is only at the end that Augustine can begin to catch a glimpse of what God has been doing throughout his life. It is only in the arc of God's storytelling that Augustine's story begins to make sense. To gloss Søren Kierkegaard's famous claim: "Life can only be understood backwards; but it must be lived forwards."[104]

Today calling is found at the intersection of what can be called the ethics of authenticity and the ethics of recognition.[105] Authenticity is, as Charles Taylor has suggested, a recently discovered moral ideal. Roughly stated, it is an ideal of "being true to oneself."[106] While this can be expressed in voluntarist terms of reductive individualism, Taylor recognizes that it is also possible to make sense

103. See Scott Bader Saye's treatment of Catherine Pickstock on identity. Scott Bader-Saye, "Gender Identity, Redemption, and Sanctification," in *Routledge Companion to Christian Ethics*, ed. Rebekah Miles and D. Stephen Long (New York: Routledge, Forthcoming).

104. "Livet maa forstaaes baglaends. Men derover glemmer man den anden Saetning Bader-Saye, at det maa leves forlaends." Søren Kierkegaard, *Journalen JJ:167 (1843)*, Søren Kierkegaards Skrifter 18 (Søren Kierkegaard Research Center, 1997), 306.

105. Charles Taylor, *The Ethics of Authenticity* (Cambridge, MA: Harvard University Press, 2018); Charles Taylor, "The Politics of Recognition," in *Multiculturalism: Examining the Politics of Recognition*, ed. Amy Gutmann (Princeton, NJ: Princeton University Press, 1994), 25–73.

106. Taylor, *The Ethics of Authenticity*, 15.

of this ideal with a richer conception of the self. The self in Taylor's model is fundamentally "dialogical." It is always already shaped by exchange between the self and society. The self always seeks recognition of its embodiment and expression from others. But this self cannot ever be simply reduced to its society. The self always exists as a unique point at the intersection of cultures, subcultures, institutions, roles, and relationships—we might also say at the intersection of multiple contexts of responsibility. It is from this point that the self, drawing upon the contradictions, redundancies, and pluralism around it, must come to imagine itself and where the self is called to. In this sense we can speak of a unique self, with its own moral senses, that often chafes against the available categories of the systems in which it lives. "There is a certain way of being human that is *my* way. I am called upon to live my life in this way, and not in imitation of anyone else's life. But this notion gives a new importance to being true to myself."[107] In this way, one is *called* into being an individual.

As Christians, we can talk about this ideal more explicitly theologically. Taylor notes that the concept of authenticity "can be seen as just a continuation and intensification of the development inaugurated by Saint Augustine, who saw the road to God as passing through our own self-awareness."[108] Rowan Williams has written of the way in which we can conceive of finding "the grace of the body" internal to such a framework, recognizing the work of God in the dialectic: in our desiring, and our desire to be desired.[109]

> The whole story of creation, incarnation, and our incorporation into the fellowship of Christ's body tells us that God desires us, *as if we were God*, as if we were that unconditional response to God's giving that God's self makes in the life of the Trinity. We are created so that we may be caught up in this, so that we may grow into the wholehearted love of God by learning that God loves us as God loves God.[110]

For most of us, this experience of divine grace is mediated through love of neighbor and recognition from our neighbor(s). We express ourselves and seek the recognition of the other.

It is in this dialogue of grace and response that the Christian finds freedom: the freedom to transcend one's own current social location and ultimately one's

---

107. Taylor, "The Politics of Recognition," 30.

108. Taylor, 29.

109. Williams, "The Body's Grace."

110. Williams, 311–12.

own current self in a process of becoming.[111] Calling is always calling to somewhere that is not here. Robin Lovin writes: "Freedom that transcends given circumstances must soon include transcendence of the self, for I cannot get very far toward imagining a different world to live in without imagining myself as in some sense a different person."[112] This is not the freedom of the voluntarist. The self is not self-made. Nor can it create its own meaning by a superior act of will. But it is the freedom of a person on a journey, or a quest: the freedom of one who must make decisions in the process of finding their way, discerning the signs of the landscape around them, and attempting to keep moving in the right direction, even while discerning what that direction is.[113]

As such, it is a freedom that entails risk.[114] One can choose to go in different directions. One can choose the wrong direction. And the directions in which one goes may create or limit possibilities for the future. Further, recognition can fail, even if one is properly responding to the calling of God. The contexts into which we are called are, as we have said, always already corrupted. And the people within these contexts are always making their own way through the tumultuous world marked by grace and sin. The grace of God responds to each decision made in this process, aiming ultimately for the bliss of fulfillment in the kingdom, but also calling the individual to whatever approximation of this fulfillment is available in the sin-stained world at any given time. It is because of the imperfection of the recognitions we receive from the contexts that we must ultimately find our calling in relation to recognition from God: God who graces us with the contexts, but also transcends the contexts. This is also what allows us to find callings in reforming the contexts.

Calling and Embodiment

It is important to note that calling is not something that can be discerned by scientific observation. Calling is not separate from one's observable embodied state at any given time. The body provides us with opportunities and limitations. But neither is calling reducible to one's observable embodied state at any given time. Morphology is certainly relevant to being called to play professional basketball, but this is no reason to count Spud Webb out.

---

111. Elizabeth Sweeny Block, "Christian Moral Freedom and the Transgender Person," *Journal of the Society of Christian Ethics* 41, no. 2 (2021): 331–347.

112. Lovin, *Reinhold Niebuhr and Christian Realism*, 124.

113. Charles Taylor, *Sources of the Self: The Making of the Modern Identity* (Cambridge, MA: Harvard University Press, 1989), 3–110.

114. Williams, "The Body's Grace," 312; Taylor, "The Politics of Recognition," 35.

Bodily modification is often an expression of one's calling to a particular identity. Māori identity is embodied in tattoos. Kayah women extend their necks with the use of brass rings. In the Kayapó tribe, lip piercings are eventually widened to allow for the insertion of disks. These might seem quite strange practices to some Christians, but they should remember that the Jewish practice of circumcision was employed for quite similar reasons. It was a sign of one's identity, of belonging, and of one's set-apartness. Such bodily modification is usually a signal of one's tribal or religious origin, but it is also possible for one to choose to transition into such an identity. According to Acts, Paul, for instance, saw it as important to Timothy's calling in reaching out to Jewish populations that Timothy be circumcised (16:3).

Modern Western society has, of course, made the choice of body modifications more individual as it has discovered the value of demanding autonomy in the making of such choices. But this has not eliminated the importance of body modification for the embodiment of calling. Various piercings and tattoos allow one to embody their calling in ways that locate them within the broader social fabric of culture and subculture.[115] Body modification can also be much more extreme. For a Christian, for example, the decision to have bariatric surgery, which might significantly change one's digestive system, not only can but should be intimately related to one's sense of being called to be a particular kind of person—a kind of person that might not be possible without such surgical intervention.

Extreme as such transitions might be, they are all accepted today as relatively mainstream options. But Christians also recognize special callings. Some are called to celibacy. Some are called to the priesthood or to religious orders. And some are called to versions of ascetic life. Each one of these leads one to approach the margins of the contexts of responsibility that we might expect of the majority.

Discussing the ascetic life, Kallistos Ware distinguishes between "natural" and "unnatural" asceticism. The two are differentiated by their attitude toward the body. Unnatural asceticism seeks to transform the body out of a motive of hatred for the body. But natural asceticism seeks bodily transformation out of a love for the body. Natural asceticism, Ware writes, "has a positive objective: it seeks not to undermine but to transform the body, rendering it a willing instrument of the spirit, a partner instead of an opponent."[116] But this does require bodily transformation. And transformation that might, if

115. Nadia Bolz-Weber, *Pastrix: The Cranky, Beautiful Faith of a Sinner & Saint* (New York: Jericho Books, 2013).

116. Kallistos Ware, "The Way of the Ascetics: Negative or Affirmative?," in *Asceticism*, ed. Vincent L. Wimbush and Gay L. Byron, 1. issued as paperback (Oxford: Oxford University Press, 2002), 10.

viewed from a reductive perspective, look as if it were mortification. In *On Hermits and Desert Dwellers*, Ware finds what he takes to be a description of those who practice natural asceticism: "They greatly afflict their bodies, not because they do not love their bodies, rather, they want to bring their bodies to Eden in glory."[117]

However peculiar, special callings are not private callings, at least not in the sense that they call people away from service to the community. In many ways, special callings are the most public of callings, even if they exist on the margins of contexts of responsibility. Indeed, part of the publicity of these callings is constituted by their countercultural status. By stepping beyond standard roles in the contexts of responsibility, they remind us of the instability of the contexts.[118] These callings remind us of the gap that always exists between the order achieved in this world and the ultimate order of the kingdom of God. Those in special callings do not live in the kingdom; no one within history does. But they can become purer symbols of particular goods, virtues, or rules than are enabled through the contexts of responsibility. This always comes with a cost, a sacrificing of some of those goods that the contexts make available. The celibate cannot know the joys of parenthood. But they can know the joy of a life uniquely devoted to God. And by living that life, they become a symbol not only of that devotion, but of the ways in which the context of marriage (however that context is arranged at the time) fails in realizing the fullness of what is available in the kingdom. As such, the special calling reminds us of the unfinished nature of the context, and calls those in the context to perpetually reform it.

Sex and Gender as Calling

For our purposes, what is notable here is the extent to which this discussion of calling, without yet explicitly engaging issues of sex and gender, has already come to overlap with the treatment of these issues. Witness a few samples from recent nonreligious treatments of sex and gender.[119]

Writing in 1987, Candace West and Don Zimmerman suggested that gender is something that is achieved in dialogical social space:

---

117. Ware, 11.

118. Lisa Sowle Cahill, *Sex, Gender, and Christian Ethics*, New Studies in Christian Ethics (New York: Cambridge University Press, 1996), 182; Elizabeth Stuart, "Sacramental Flesh," in *Queer Theology: Rethinking the Western Body*, ed. Gerard Loughlin (Malden, MA: Blackwell, 2007), 69–70.

119. The relation between gender and calling has been helpfully elaborated in Tanis, *Trans-Gendered*, 146–161.

> When we view gender as an accomplishment, an achievement property of situated conduct, our attention shifts from matters internal to the individual and focuses on interactional, and ultimately, institutional arenas. In one sense, of course, it is individuals who "do" gender. But it is a situated doing, carried out in the virtual or real presence of others who are presumed to be oriented toward its production. Rather than as a property of individuals, we conceive of gender as an emergent feature of social situations: both as an outcome of and rationale for various social arrangements and as means of legitimating one of the most fundamental divisions of society.[120]

Engaging with the problematic of recognition for transgender persons, Wendy Davidson writes:

> Gender is an interactive process. While a person may identify beyond the categories of "female" or "male," and project this in the public domain, if the widely held belief in society is that there are only "females" and "males," and "women" and "men," then in practice an observer is likely to "read" the person's gender as falling within one or the other of the binary categories.[121]

Describing Judith Butler's position, Sara Salih writes that "one is not born, but rather one is called a woman, and it is discourse that does the metaphorical 'calling.'"[122] This is, of course, quite far from the Christian notion of calling. Butler imagines this calling as coming more as an external imposition from the surrounding culture than from a caring God. Still, phenomenologically, it is not clear that the experience she refers to is that distinct. To be called a woman is not just to be labeled as such; this calling will manifest in certain feelings tied to obligations, goals, and identity formation. Further, it is not enough to be "called" a woman in Butler's scheme. One must respond to that call. One could resist the call. One could subvert the call. The discourse may

---

120. Candace West and Don Zimmerman, "Doing Gender," *Gender and Society* 1, no. 2 (1987): 126.

121. Sara Davidmann, "Beyond Borders: Lived Experiences of Atypically Gendered Transsexual People," in *Transgender Identities: Towards a Social Analysis of Gender Diversity*, ed. Sally Hines and Tam Sanger, Routledge Research in Gender and Society 24 (New York: Routledge, 2012), 187.

122. Sara Salih, "Introduction to 'The Lesbian Phallus and the Morphological Imaginary,'" in *The Judith Butler Reader*, ed. Judith Butler and Sara Salih (Malden, MA: Blackwell Pub, 2003), 193.

even have alternative "callings" that are left open for the individual. Butler's call for causing gender trouble presupposes a level, or some kind, of freedom within the discourse.

The disagreement in how to make sense of these experiences of calling is significant, but the Christian who views sex and gender as a calling does not imagine an entirely separate set of experiences from those posited by Butler. The Christian sees God at work in the calling, though cultural discourse is doubtless one of the mediators of this work. And the Christian sees in this calling both gift and frustration. God calls us all to fulfillment as that is available in a sinful world. But this is never the realization of our *summum bonum*. It is always a state of fulfillment that is realizable within the particular, always partially corrupted, contexts of responsibility into which we are born.

It is within, and at times in tension with, these contexts that we find the kind of maturity that is available to us. For many this will be a relatively friction-free process, in which we find our place in established categories and are provided with scripts and norms. Within the mix of dominant and minority versions of gender constructions, we will find a place to identify. And we will be well suited to these. Some will work to grow into the gender construction. But just as some are called to cross boundaries in other contexts, including work, family, and even religion, some will be called to cross boundaries within the context provided by sex and gender. Some will require body modifications. Others will transition only through the way that they present themselves to the world. As with people crossing other boundaries, some of these transitions will be right, healthy, and fulfilling. Some will not. Some transitions will go easily, and some will proceed only with significant effort and hardship.

It is here where we must return to the idea of special callings. In general, transitioning across boundaries is no threat to the boundaries. If one can cross the boundary and find a new identity on the other side, the person may even be seen as supporting the boundary and its usefulness in forming identity. But there will always be examples where people are called not to cross the boundary but to live lives on the margins of the context, reminding the world of the imperfection and instability of the context in its current formation. Here we can see a special role for gender queer individuals, people who reject gender boundaries and purposefully embrace identities that not only cross gender and sex boundaries but efface those boundaries. We need not see this as an appeal to reductive or voluntarist individualism. Rather, like celibates and other ascetics, these people can serve a useful, public, theological role. They can remind us that every construction of gender and sex in our sinful world falls short of the glory of God.[123] They will call us perpetually towards that transformation of gender and sex that

123. See the concept of "denaturalization" in Tonstad, *Queer Theology*, 55.

will occur in the eschaton, and that should perpetually inform the reformation of the context even now.

Here it is useful to hear the voice of Michelle O'Brien as s/he reflects upon her own journey as an intersex, non-binary person. We find here both the idea of traveling to her identity and the idea that, in retrospect at least, like Augustine, she has found herself called to what she truly was to be the entire time.

> I have come to see walking a middle way between the sexes as my path. It is a path between the two compulsory genders, another way, a narrow way, a difficult place, but the only place I can genuinely be. It is like living in a crack in the world from which comes a specific type of knowledge and power. But, as a realization, it is not about what I have become, but the way I am, the way I always was. It is how it has always been for me, physically, mentally, and emotionally, and reflects things about me from when I was born, before somebody decided to correct the ambiguities in me. Finding and being myself is like a religious calling, because this is how it was meant to be.[124]

A calling lived forward, understood backward.

Conclusion

In this chapter I have argued for a reconceptualization of sex and gender using the concepts of contexts of responsibility and calling. I have sought to locate my position on these issues in relation to more deconstructionist positions and more "conservative" proposals that uphold modern binary visions of sex and gender. On the one hand, I have advocated for a more positive view of sex and gender than deconstructionists often offer, locating sex and gender as related to the divine gift of contexts of responsibility and calling within these contexts that make possible genuine human goods (even if they are always already corrupted by sin). On the other hand, I have also advocated for a greater appreciation of the diversity of sex and gender than the modern binary picture allows. I have argued that the binary vision is incompatible with the plenitude we witness in the creation. I have offered a reading of Genesis 1 and 2 that does not require a binary vision of sex and gender. And I have suggested maintaining the binary view requires turning away from the continual gift of reformation of the contexts that is made available by the perichoretic God of Christianity amid a sinful world.

There is much that remains to be done in considering sex and gender. I certainly do not pretend to have plumbed the depth of the morality of particular

124. O'Brien, "Intersex, Medicine, Diversity, Identity and Spirituality," 54.

contemporary proposals for sex and gender construction, much less particular sex and gender identities. And I have not engaged at all the ways in which sex and gender are related to sexual orientation. If some wish to critique the present chapter for being insufficiently detailed or comprehensive for a Christian ethics of sex and gender, I must agree.

But my goal here was not to produce such an ethics. It was only to sketch a theology of sex and gender sufficient to make sense of my claim that Christians should accept a solution to the problems I have highlighted concerning soteriology with a Christology that admits Christ's trans* existence. What we have achieved in this chapter is enough to provide the backdrop for an investigation of Christ's special calling within the sex/gender contexts of his own time, and of our own. It is to fill out this picture that we must now turn.

CHAPTER FIVE

Toward the Trans* Christ

> We cannot nourish others unless we nourish ourselves at the breasts of divine charity . . . We must attach ourselves to the breast of Christ crucified, which is the source of charity, and by means of that flesh we draw milk. The means is Christ's humanity which suffered pain, and we cannot without pain get that milk that comes from charity.
>
> —Catherine of Sienna, Quoted in Caroline Walker Bynum, *Holy Feast and Holy Fast*, 173.

IF WE ARE going to accept (1) the significance of gendered diversity (from Adam to Eve and everything in between), and (2) that Christ incarnates the significant differences of humanity in his work of recapitulation, then we need to be able to claim that Christ is the new Adam and the new Eve. Having explored sex and gender in a theological context in the last chapter, we are now able to say a bit more about how this last claim should be understood.

It is an understatement to say that Christ's messianic calling was a special calling. According to the Christian narrative, Christ was called to a life that constantly challenged, undermined, destabilized, and even inverted the contexts of responsibility of his own time.[1] He was an unemployed, homeless, celibate holy man who cavorted with sinners, criticized familial loyalties, violated the letter of the law, and gained glorious victory by dying in ignominy on a cross. He also challenged and destabilized the dominant sex and gender constructs of his own time. Given the countercultural nature of the rest of his activities, this was inevitable. But upon analysis, it plays what might at first seem to be a surprisingly vital role in Christ's mission. As we shall see, the crucifixion itself and Christ's willingness to accept the *passionem* was the height of sex and gender transgression. Later Christians understood Christ as symbolically both male

1. For the historian, such claims will always need to be nuanced. Culture is not a monolith, and Christ's actions took place within particular historical milieus and precedents. Historians are called by the norms of their own context of responsibility to focus on the ways in which Jesus must have fit into this cultural web. But the theological self-understanding of Christianity has tended in the opposite direction, to emphasize what was unique in Christ, thus understanding Christ more in terms of a message sent from beyond culture than one that was created from within.

and female, picturing Christ as mother. Some even had mystical experiences of suckling at Jesus's breast. What I propose is to take the step of formalizing the recognition of Christ's complex gender to make the doctrinal claim that Christ is trans*.

I am not the first theologian to argue (or just report) that Christ transgressed or transgresses sex and gender boundaries. As I will explore later, there is significant theological movement that locates Christ as transcending sex and/or gender. Like myself, most of the scholars who hold this position are driven to it by theological concerns. Though I shall have to dissent from many of these scholars' conclusions, I shall also find much to admire in their positions. There are also substantial historical studies of the way Jesus and his movement transgressed gender norms of the first century and how Christ was seen (both literally and symbolically) as both male and female later in the Christian tradition. I shall draw upon these studies to show that the claim that Christ is trans* is not so novel as it may at first appear.[2]

Prior to the present age, the articulation of the doctrine I am proposing would have been problematic due to the lack of adequate concepts and language concerning sex and gender. As was necessary with the language of *ousia* (*substantia*) and *hypostasis* (*personae*) in articulating the doctrine of the trinity, we need new language to express this doctrine.[3] Today we have an emerging language that addresses gendered/sexed diversity. Drawing on that language, I am using the term trans*.

Trans* combines "transgender," an umbrella term used to talk about sex and gender diversity, with the asterisk, which functions both symbolically and in reference to the multidirectionality of trans identities. Transgender was originally a term referring to individuals who wished to transition gender categories but did not wish to undergo medical body modifications. This distinguished the transgender person from the transsexual, who did seek medical body modifications, and the transvestite or crossdresser, who took on only the outward appearance of an alternative gender category in specific contexts. Since the 1990s, however, transgender has emerged as an umbrella term for multiple forms of transgressing and transitioning between gender categories. This can include transsexualism, crossdressing, the rejection of gender categorization expressed by gender queer individuals, and multiple other forms of sex and gender embodiment and expression.[4] The category has become so broad

2. Marcella Althaus-Reid, *Indecent Theology*, 80–82, 117–119`; Goss, *Queering Christ*, 176–182.

3. Pelikan, *The Emergence of the Catholic Tradition*, 209–210.

4. Laurel Westbrook, "Becoming Knowably Gendered: The Production of Transgender Possibilities and Constraints in the Mass and Alternative Press from 1990–2005 in the United

that the journal *Transgender Studies Quarterly* leaves this key term in its title without definition.[5]

Trans* picks up on this trend, using the asterisk in part as a filler for a variety of forms of trans identity. In online searches the asterisk can often be used as a wildcard indicator, telling the search engine that the user wants to find a search term with a variety of endings. As such, the search for child* would return instances of "child," but also "children," "childlike," and so on. Trans* indicates that there are multiple different forms of trans existence that, while they are included, should not be collapsed into one another. The asterisk is also used to reject the idea, potentially implied in "transitioning," that what is at stake is necessarily imagined as moving back or forth over a binary division. The asterisk in this sense is a symbol pointing in many different directions.[6]

Trans* is a term that seems fit to achieve the desired goal in saying what needs to be said about Christ's sex/gender identity without saying too much. This is an extremely desirable quality in theological vocabulary. Specifically, what I want to suggest, following Gregory of Nazianzus' claim that "whatever is not assumed is not healed," is that we should claim that Christ is trans* in whatever way is sufficient to assume/incarnate gendered/sexed diversity to allow for the opening of salvation to all persons who accept Christ. How Christ does so must partially be a mystery. How many different gender/sexed identities must Christ incarnate? What is the mechanism by which Christ is transsexed? Such questions may well be of theological interest for further elaboration. But as with the mysteries of the virgin birth, the incarnation, and the resurrection, we need not have a scientific account to have an acceptable doctrine. The Christian church can take up such a doctrine as it has so many others, with a disposition of *fides quaerens intellectum* (faith seeking understanding).

States," in *Transgender Identities: Towards a Social Analysis of Gender Diversity*, ed. Sally Hines and Tam Sanger, Routledge Research in Gender and Society 24 (New York: Routledge, 2010), 44; Edward Schiappa, *The Transgender Exigency: Defining Sex and Gender in the 21st Century* (New York: Routledge, 2022), 3; Aaron H. Devor and Ardel Haefele-Thomas, *Transgender: A Reference Handbook*, Contemporary World Issues (Santa Barbara, CA: ABC-CLIO, 2019), 8; Sally Hines, "Introduction," in *Transgender Identities: Towards a Social Analysis of Gender Diversity*, ed. Sally Hines and Tam Sanger, Routledge Research in Gender and Society 24 (New York: Routledge, 2012), 1; Beemyn and Rankin, *The Lives of Transgender People*, 14; Virginia R. Mollenkott, *Omnigender*, 38–78.

5. Cáel Keegan, "Transgender Studies, or How to Do Things with Trans*," in *The Cambridge Companion to Queer Studies*, ed. Siobhan B. Somerville (New York: Cambridge University Press, 2020), 66.

6. Susan Stryker, *Transgender History: The Roots of Today's Revolution*, Revised edition (Berkeley, CA: Seal Press, 2017), 10–11; Keegan, "Transgender Studies, or How to Do Things with Trans*."

Christ Transcending Sex and Gender

As noted above, many theologians today are interested in articulating or rearticulating Christian understandings of Christ's sex and gender to address a variety of theological problems. Several theologians have embraced some version of the claim that Christ transcends sex and gender.[7] Exactly what this looks like depends on the proposal. Adrian Thatcher, drawing partially on a modified version of the "one sex" model from premodern society, suggests that Christ incarnates the one human sex and gender. He then relocates human (but not sexual) difference with reference to the interrelation and difference internal to the trinitarian persons in the Godhead.[8] Graham Ward emphasizes the constant activity and transformation of the body as a meaningful (and not simply physical) reality. Though he accepts Jesus was incarnated as a male, he locates moments in Jesus' life at which Christ's body was made to reveal its transcendence. He posits that the ascension is the climactic moment at which this happens, and this paves the way for a Christ who is ever afterwards seen as transcending sex and gender. Gregory of Nyssa is hardly a contemporary theologian, but he has been recovered by many contemporary theologians focused on sex and gender. Gregory looks back toward creation and forward to the eschaton to find bodies that are beyond sexual differentiation. Let us look at each in turn.

Adrian Thatcher

Thatcher's argument begins with creation. While Christians have often read binary sex and gender back into Genesis, Thatcher argues the text fits much better with a "one sex" reading. As many commentators have noted, it is not clear whether *adam*, when created in Genesis 2:7, was sexed. It is possible to read the story as suggesting that *adam* was androgynous, containing both male and female *in potentia*.[9] On this reading, it was only with the creation of Eve in 2:21–22 that humanity is sorted out into male and female. What moderns see to be two opposed sexes are not originally separated. There is one sex, the human sex.

This divine intention comes across even more clearly when we take Christ seriously as the paradigmatic manifestation of the image of God. Whatever is to

7. For earlier arguments that Jesus should be taken to transcend gender and sex, see Ruether, *Sexism and God-Talk*, 137; Elizabeth A. Johnson, *She Who Is: The Mystery of God in Feminist Theological Discourse* (New York: Crossroad, 2002), 151–167.

8. Adrian Thatcher, *Redeeming Gender*.

9. Thatcher, 144; Wayne Meeks, "The Image of the Androgyne: Some Uses of a Symbol in Earliest Christianity," *History of Religions* 13, no. 3 (February 1974): 165–208; Margaret A. Farley, *Just Love: A Framework for Christian Sexual Ethics* (New York: Continuum, 2012), 142–145; Dunning, *Specters of Paul*, 7.

be said of *adam*, it is Christ who is the ground of Christian anthropology. No doubt, Christ was incarnated as a male. But within a one-sex theory of humanity, this is an accident and not an essential quality of Christ. As Thatcher writes: "the nature that the creeds ascribe to him is a *human* one, which, like his divine nature, is neither male nor masculine."[10]

We can see this even more clearly if we consider the polyvalence that the phrase "body of Christ" takes on in scripture. Thatcher, following Paul Dinter, finds five different meanings of this phrase in Paul's writing: (1) the physical body that is crucified, (2) the mystical body into which Christians are incorporated, (3) the sacramental body found in the Eucharist, (4) the ecclesial body or church, and (5) the ethical body of Christians in action together.[11] Why, Thatcher asks, should we consider Christ's "body" as such to be masculine? "Of the five meanings of 'body of Christ' in Dinter's list, only one of these, the crucified body of Christ, is noticeably male."[12] We ought instead to accept Christ's body as polymorphic.

But even as Christian theology pushes us toward a "one sex" (or really one humanity) model, it also must undermine the classical version of this model. This is because the classical model assumed superiority on one end of the continuum and inferiority at the other. Here, we must see Christ's body as in some ways a radically new creation.

> The new creation is not the same thing as the liberal proposal to advocate the equality of the sexes, achieved (to some extent) in modernity, and dubiously read back into the Bible. It is nothing less than a new start for humanity where divisions of race, sex, and class are exposed as sinful structures of an older order. The proposal is theological and Christological, based on no particular text, but on faith in Christ as the bringer of New Being, the image of God, and instigator of a new model of humanness.[13]

Thatcher believes that this is driven home further by a consideration of Christ's divine nature.

> The question just raised 'Can a male Savior save women?', has, as one answer, that Christ is not male. The Word made flesh is the divine

10. Thatcher, *Redeeming Gender*, 154.

11. Paul Dinter, "Christ's Body as Male and Female," *Cross Currents* 44, no. 3 (2013): 390–399.

12. Thatcher, *Redeeming Gender*, 149.

13. Thatcher, 153.

> Word. The human nature of the incarnate Word belongs to all human nature; the maleness of Jesus belongs to that nature because that nature cannot exist merely abstractly.[14]

Or again: "What Christ shares with us in order to save us is our human nature without further distinction."[15]

Shall we then do away with all that fits under the categories of sex and gender difference? As concerns sex, Thatcher's rhetoric often suggests so. Thatcher suggests that "there are strong reasons for abandoning all talk of sexual difference, both in the church and in the academy, and speaking instead of sexual similarity (when we need to speak of 'sex' at all)."[16] Elsewhere he suggests that we should stop speaking even of a "one-sex continuum" in favor of speaking of the "human continuum."[17]

But Thatcher does want to recognize the realities of potential biological procreative differences between different persons, and he wants to acknowledge the importance of the vulnerability that women often experience in ways that men do not.[18] As such, he suggests at one point that we should distinguish men and women as "classes" within the broader human "essence."[19] His goal, he says, is "not to deny differences between men and women" but to deny their essential quality; to relativize such distinctions "without eliminating them."[20]

Eventually, Thatcher changes his category from sex to gender, which he focuses on "redeeming." This redemption, he suggests is found in achieving a balance of sameness and difference modeled on the trinitarian persons. This must be an analogical model, because the trinity is unified in a way that humanity cannot be. But in the equality, mutuality, and cooperativeness of the trinitarian relations, Thatcher finds a model that can be used to oppose gender violence and oppression.[21]

---

14. Thatcher, 157.

15. Thatcher, 158.

16. Thatcher, 162.

17. Thatcher, 169.

18. Thatcher, 173.

19. Thatcher, 174.

20. Thatcher, 178.

21. Thatcher, 187–204.

Graham Ward

Graham Ward begins his article "There is no sexual difference" with a provocative juxtaposition of post-resurrection narratives: the story of Jesus meeting with Mary in the garden outside the tomb and the story of doubting Thomas. He sees each of these stories as eroticized, as, he thinks, are all engagements of bodies in proximity. Thus, he claims, the figures in the stories are mythologized: "Mary as Eve, Jesus as Adam, Jesus as a hermaphrodite, and Thomas as opening up the womb of Christ."[22]

Ward rejects the reductive naturalism of what he calls "positivist" accounts of the body. Using the Pauline distinction between *sarx* (flesh) and *soma* (body), he identifies reductive naturalist accounts as fixated on *sarx*, and thus worldly and idolatrous. He contrasts this with phenomenological accounts of the body (*soma*) that see the body as always already caught up in a web of relational becoming and meaning that is not reducible to physiological appearance or stable self-subsistence. The shift from the inadequate conception of the embodied self as *sarx* to the robust account of the embodied self as *soma* should challenge our usual thinking about sex and gender.

> A body is always in transit, always exceeding its significance or transgressing the limits of what appears. The body is constantly in movement and in a movement. It is these complex movements in and upon the body that the economies of response attempt to sketch. Put differently, the body exists fluidly in a number of fluid operations between reception and response. . . . There is no sexuality or sexual difference as such, just as there is no difference as such, only distance and affinities occurring across networks of relation.[23]

This is certainly true of Jesus's body. "If Jesus the Christ can be understood as the second Adam, then incarnation does not just characterize his body but, in some sense, all bodies."

Ward does not wish to deny "the gendered body of that Jewish man, Jesus the Christ."[24] But even here we must qualify. Unlike the bodies of other humans

---

22. Graham Ward, "There Is No Sexual Difference," in *Queer Theology: Rethinking the Western Body*, ed. Gerard Loughlin (Malden, MA: Blackwell, 2007), 78.

23. Ward, 84.

24. Graham Ward, "The Displaced Body of Jesus Christ," in *Radical Orthodoxy: A New Theology*, ed. John Milbank, Catherine Pickstock, and Graham Ward (New York: Routledge, 1999), 163, 176, 177.

after the fall, Jesus' incarnate body participated in the "pre-lapsarian faculties" of human embodiment. This was a body that was not that of "other men (or women). This man can walk on water. This man can sweat blood."[25]

Jesus body was "displaced" at key moments in Jesus' life; moments that mark the instability of incarnated gender and point toward the iconic transcendence of gender in the Christ. The first of these moments is found at Christ's birth: "The XY chromosomal maleness of Jesus Christ issues from the XX chromosomal femaleness of his mother as miracle, and so this male body is unlike any other male body to date. Its materiality is, from its conception, unstable; though, with the circumcision, its specifically sexed nature is affirmed."[26] The circumcision, as bloodletting, also prefigures the crucifixion and thus stretches Jesus's body temporally and looks to the creation of the ecclesial body, which will finally transcend gender.

The transfiguration recalls the pre-lapsarian glorification of Adam. "The pre-lapsarian body of Adam (and Eve) is erotically charged—perfect in its form, its goodness and its beauty—and naked . . . In so far as in Christ human beings are restored to their pre-fallen splendor, the transfiguration scene on the Mount of Olives presents us with Jesus as the Second Adam."[27]

In the Eucharist, "transfiguration turns into transposition" as Christ's body becomes the bread to be eaten. "What had throughout the Gospel story been an unstable body is now to be understood as an extendable body. For it is not that Jesus, at this point, stops being a physical presence. It is more that his physical presence can extend itself to incorporate other bodies, like bread, and make them extensions of his own."[28]

The next setting for the displacement of Christ's body is in the crucifixion. Here Jesus's body is taken up as an object of "play" by Jesus's crucifiers. "Throughout the play of these erotic and political power games the actual maleness of the body of Jesus is forgotten. This is a man among men; no sexual differentiation is taken account of. It is no longer 'this' body or 'my' body, but 'that' undifferentiated body."[29]

Here also we find Christ transformed into icon. "Iconicity transcends physicality. It does not erase the physical but overwhelms it, drenching it with significance. The maleness of Christ is made complex and ambivalent, in the way

25. Ward, 164–65.

26. Ward, 164.

27. Ward, 166.

28. Ward, 167.

29. Ward, 169.

that all things are made ambivalent as their symbolic possibilities are opened up by their liminality."[30]

In the resurrection, Jesus body is no longer recognizable. It flits in and out of the narrative without accounts of its movements, just as it moves through walls with apparent ease.

The final and most definitive displacement of Christ's body occurs in the ascension. Here, the "body of the gendered Jew" becomes inaccessible. But the body of Christ remains in the body of believers united in the church. This body cannot be said to be male or female; it contains the full diversity of the Christian community. And yet, it is really Christ's body.[31]

In the light of this analysis, Ward concludes that "those theologians framing questions such as 'Can a male savior save women?' or engaged in investigating the sexuality of Jesus, fail to discern the nature of the body of Christ; fail to understand the nature of bodies and sex in Christ."[32]

Gregory of Nyssa

Gregory has become the focus of a considerable number of contemporary scholars interested in sex and gender because of the intersection of three factors in his thought. First is his understanding of the "double creation" and the correlative state of the eschatological body. Second is his theological understanding of the role of desire in the Christian life. And third is his embrace of erotic imagery in articulating the pursuit of glory in relation with God and Christ. Here I am not interested in Gregory so much as I am interested in contemporary interpretations and uses of his thought. As such, I shall draw from a range of different contemporary theologians in setting forth my picture of Gregory.

The potential significance of his embrace of the "double creation" theory was noted by Rosemary Radford Reuther.[33] Since then, it has been deployed by multiple theologians in discussions of gender and sexuality.[34] Reading

30. Ward, 170; Elizabeth Stuart, "Sacramental Flesh," in *Queer Theology: Rethinking the Western Body*, ed. Gerard Loughlin (Malden, MA: Blackwell, 2007), 66.

31. See also Tonstad, *Queer Theology*, 32.

32. Ward, "The Displaced Body of Jesus Christ," 177.

33. Rosemary Radford Reuther, "Misogynism and Virginal Feminism in the Fathers of the Church," in *Religion and Sexism: Images of Woman in the Jewish and Christian Traditions*, ed. Rosemary Radford Ruether (Eugene, OR: Wipf and Stock, 1998), 153–155.

34. Virginia Burrus, "Queer Father: Gregory of Nyssa and the Subversion of Identity," in *Queer Theology: Rethinking the Western Body*, ed. Gerard Loughlin (Malden, MA: Blackwell, 2007),

backward from Galatians 3:28 (in Christ "there is no longer male and female") Gregory embraces a reading of Genesis 1:27 as including two acts of creation. The first act of creation (So God created humankind in his image, in the image of God he created him) was a "non-physical, non-sexed angelic creation."[35] Like angels, humans had bodies, but they were spiritual in nature and had no genitalia. Here we find humanity in its pre-lapsarian state of goodness. Without sexed difference, the human was focused entirely upon the love of God. The creation of sexed difference was not original but was a step toward the fall.

Desire is key to understanding what went wrong. With the creation of sexed difference came desire oriented toward something other than God. Eventually, marriage "institutionalized heteroeroticism—a concession to the taint of difference that was introduced into love's economy."[36] While mutual human eroticism is not necessarily lustful or vicious, it still appears that this eroticism is "a barrier between humanity and Paradise."[37] The reorientation of *erōs* back toward God is central to the process of salvation in Gregory's thought. And this purification of *erōs* will one day outlive the sexed status of the body, as in the eschaton humans will again lose their sexed difference but find themselves in intimate, even symbolically sexual relation with God.

Exactly what upshot should be taken from Gregory's theology depends on which theologians we focus on. Verna Harison, for instance, sees the transcendence of all gendered differences as Gregory's ultimate contribution.[38] In contrast, Sarah Coakley sees Gregory as moving beyond sexed (genitalized) existence, but maintaining a kind of "gendered" difference in a process of ascetic ascent to God. For Coakley, this allows for gendered performativity that destabilizes established gender roles, at least within the broader life of *erōs* directed at the divine. We shall have to take up the differences between these proposals to understand Gregory's work below.

150, 158; Stuart, "Sacramental Flesh," 71; Sarah Coakley, *God, Sexuality and the Self: An Essay "on the Trinity"* (New York: Cambridge University Press, 2013), 281–288; Sarah Coakley, *Powers and Submissions: Spirituality, Philosophy, and Gender*, Challenges in Contemporary Theology (Malden, MA: Blackwell, 2002), 161–166; Kari Elisabeth Børresen, ed., "God's Image, Man's Image? Patristic Interpretation of Genesis 1:27 and I Cor. 11:7," in *The Image of God: Gender Models in Judaeo-Christian Tradition* (Minneapolis: Fortress Press, 1995), 187–209.

35. Coakley, *God, Sexuality and the Self*, 281.

36. Burrus, "Queer Father: Gregory of Nyssa and the Subversion of Identity," 150.

37. Burrus, 150; Coakley, *God, Sexuality and the Self*, 282.

38. Verna Harrison, "Male and Female in Cappadocian Theology," *The Journal of Theological Studies* 41.2 (1990): 470.

Is Transcendsexualism Enough?

How should we evaluate the above positions from the perspective of the current project? First, we should affirm some of the conclusions reached by these scholars. I take Ward's and Thatcher's treatments about the eucharistic and ecclesial body of Christ to be particularly helpful. In the communal and liturgical life of Christianity we are required to speak of Christ in ways that defy and destabilize binary images of sex and gender. In light of my argument for the trans* status of Christ, I would just push for a slightly different language from Ward and Thatcher. In the Eucharist, we could say that Christ body *trans*-substantiates (to borrow a bit of contested theological terminology). More generally, we could speak of Christ as in some senses *trans*cendsexual in the light of the above analyses. Such rhetorical/grammatical shifts need not indicate a disagreement about the qualities discussed, but they certainly mark a shift in emphasis, because my argument suggests that transcending sex and gender alone is insufficient. We should take seriously the ways in which Christ *trans*gresses sex and gender categories, and even *trans*itions between categories.

Take, for example, the case of Christ's ecclesial body. Here, we should all agree that it is not sexed or gendered in the sense that any other individual is. But what should we *say* about this? How should we name the difference? I would propose that it makes sense to say that Christ's ecclesial body is intersex. This is, of course, analogical language. Like so much about Christ's and God's existence we cannot approach it as directly with our language as we might other things in the world. But the analogy seems at least a reasonable one given the composition of the ecclesial body. And, if my argument for Christ's trans* status in the incarnation works, then it should be allowed to impact claims about Christ's body beyond the incarnation.

Of course, engaging in such terminological disputes at this point is putting the cart before the horse. This is because the above theologians have reasons that they might want to resist the conclusion of my broader argument. My argument that Christ must incarnate or assume sexed and gendered difference seems to reinscribe the importance of gendered difference that they have labored to eliminate, or at least marginalize.

Here we should be careful. At this point, neither I nor those I am engaging are arguing for an essentialist account of sex and gender, or a sex or gender binary. Thatcher suggests a sex continuum, which he later generalizes to a human continuum. Then he alternates between suggesting that we should abolish sexual distinctions or reduce their importance to "classes." Ward acknowledges that Christ was incarnated in a sexed, gendered body, but seeks to transcend that by focusing on the ways in which this body was displaced and ultimately transcended. Gregory of Nyssa, as constructed by contemporary theologians, destabilizes sex and gender by suggesting that sex is a temporary reality, which is further relativized by our proper desire that draws us away from binarity toward the one and triune God.

On the other side of the argument, in my account of sex and gender as contexts of responsibility I have no interest in essentializing these categories as they exist at any particular time. And, I have argued against the construction of this context so as to produce and require gender binarity.

My disagreement with these positions, then, focuses on questions of (1) whether and how we recognize the significance of sex and gender differences once we accept that their particular shapes are not immutable, (2) how central the status of the incarnate Christ is in our theologies. Finally, my difference from these scholars is related to (3) the particular Christian traditions on which we are drawing. Let us take each of these points.

Sex and Gender

As concerns sex and gender, I have provided an account in which these categories are both constitutive of our lived, embodied identities and culturally constructed. They are part of the contexts of responsibilities in which we live, and part of the callings to which we constantly respond. They are not the good, but they do allow us to organize and access human goods. Indeed, because they are tied to our forms of embodiment, they are much more intimately intertwined with our identities than many of the other contexts of responsibility. They provide part of the warp and woof of human existence. They did not have to be ordered as they are, but every form of human life has them somehow ordered.

In favor of my position, I will note that, though their rhetoric occasionally suggests the contrary, none of the above scholars wants to eliminate sex and gender categories, and all recognize that they do prove to be of some enduring use. Thatcher must admit that different forms of embodiment change how one relates to particular goods and potential evils. Ward and those who draw upon Gregory of Nyssa see sex and gender categories as destabilized by theology. But Ward must look for specific moments of displacement within the broader context of Christ's sexed and gendered existence. Nyssa places the de-sexing of the body as bookends around life as we currently know it. Notably, none of these scholars has suggested that Christ *in Christ's incarnation* simply transcends sex and gender. At most, they have suggested that his being sexed and gendered is not as significant as it often appears. Plato once argued that there can be no injustice without justice. Similarly, I might suggest that there can be no transcendence of sex and gender without sex and gender. This might explain why, much as they wish to transcend sex and gender, none of these theologians is able to escape it.

Take, for instance, Ward's moments of displacement. The transfiguration, he suggests, "presents us with Jesus as the Second Adam." With Paul, Ward has here erased Eve and thus reinscribed the importance of Jesus' gender precisely in a moment of apparent displacement. Trying to patch for the problem, as he approaches the claim that Jesus is the new Adam, Graham writes of the "prelapsarian body of Adam (and Eve) . . ." Eve's parenthetical inclusion here echoes the early church's efforts to find a second path to include her in the narrative of salvation. The problem is that the moment that Graham is trying to draw out as a displacement of Jesus' gender is layered with gendered baggage that has been placed upon it from the pre-Christian tradition glorifying Adam on to the present.

Another case is one in which, arguably, Ward is simply wrong in his interpretation. Ward posits that in the crucifixion, Christ's body ceases to be gendered because it becomes a thing; a plaything of the Roman empire. This is a creative interpretation of the body at the crucifixion, but it is one with little grounding in the context of the first century understanding of actual crucifixion. As Stephen Moor writes:

> Ward would seem to be suggesting that gender is erased during the course of Jesus' trial and execution, but it could more easily be argued, to the contrary, that gender receives intense accentuation precisely at these points in the narratives. Jesus' passivity, his submissiveness, his stripping and whipping, his role as a plaything in the rough hands of the soldiers, his 'strung-up nakedness' (as Ward himself puts it), penetration, and abject helplessness on the cross would all have conspired, in complicity with the hegemonic gender codes, to throw his masculinity into sharp relief—precisely as a problem.[39]

This moment, as I shall argue below, is better understood in terms of a moment of gender transgression than a moment of gender transcendence.

Returning to Gregory of Nyssa with the question of locating sex and gender brings us to significant differences in how different scholars interpret his thought. Verna Harrison emphasizes the distinction between the higher, rational part of the human, which reflects the image of God, and the lower, irrational part in which we find gender differentiation. Intermixing quotes from Gregory with her own interpretation, she writes "The distinction between male and female 'is alien to our conceptions of God', and it 'has no reference to the divine archetype,

39. Stephen D. Moore, "'O Man, Who Art Thou. . .?': Masculinity Studies and New Testament Studies," in *New Testament Masculinities*, ed. Stephen D. Moore and Janice Capel Anderson, Society of Biblical Literature Semeia Studies 45 (Atlanta, GA: Society of Biblical Literature, 2003), 11.

but . . . is an approximation to the less rational nature', i.e., an image of the sub-human animals."[40] In this context, according to Harrison, "gender plays a temporary and instrumental role" in human life and the search for God. Eventually, "moral beauty will displace other kinds of human division, including gender, but even it will be resolved into unity in the final ἀποκατάστασις, when everyone will possess all the virtues in their fullness, as all are raised to the same godlike level in Christ."[41] Harrison does not wish to suggest that this will entirely dissolve individual identities. But individuals will all exist with the same qualities.

To many, perhaps especially "Western" theologians, this will seem an insufficiently differentiated form of eschatological existence, not only with reference to gender but with reference to other personal and embodied markers. Summarizing Tertullian's view, Caroline Walker Bynum writes: "Christians believe they receive back 'the self-same bodies in which they died' (*corpora eadem. . . in quibus discesserunt*), for it is these details (i.e., of age, size, manner, etc.) that make bodies who they are."[42] Contemporary theologian Patricia Beattie Jung writes that:

> Our embodiment differentiates and distinguishes us as individually unique, while it simultaneously unites us together in the human family and with the rest of creation. For these reasons, a truly personal notion of salvation must include the redemption and sanctification of our bodies *in all their particularity*.[43]

Sarah Coakley shifts Harrison's reading of Gregory subtly but significantly in her works. Interpreting Gregory as seeing the process of attaining perfection as an ongoing, perhaps never-ending process, she emphasizes the potential for continuity in bodily existence across this process. "We are on a continuum, then, from this 'body' to our 'angelic' future 'bodies', and death need not be a *dramatic* shift in the case of a holy ascetical body."[44] Coakley does admit that Gregory sees the original creation and the eschatological body as "non-sexed (that is non-genitalized)." But she wants to make a distinction between being "sexed" in the above sense and being able to participate in forms of gendered performativity. "It is a mistake . . . as Harrison helps illuminate, to read Gregory here as

40. Harrison, "Male and Female in Cappadocian Theology," 467.

41. Harrison, 470.

42. Caroline Walker Bynum, *The Resurrection of the Body in Western Christianity, 200–1336*, American Lectures on the History of Religion (New York: Columbia University Press, 2017), 37.

43. Patricia Beattie Jung, *Sex on Earth as It Is in Heaven: A Christian Eschatology of Desire* (Albany, NY: State University of New York, 2017), 5. Italics mine.

44. Coakley, *Powers and Submissions*, 163.

divorcing our development from the exigencies of *gender*; even if our genitalia are finally irrelevant to our 'bodily' conditions before God."[45]

The reference to Harrison here is interesting given that Coakley and Harrison come to what could appear to be contradictory conclusions. What Harrison writes is that "although gender distinction itself is secondary and temporary, it becomes a *symbol* pointing beyond itself to something truly fundamental and eternal, the human person's relationship with God."[46] For Harrison, *gender* will be eschatologically transcended but will function as a symbol in illuminating the ongoing relationship with God. Coakley reinterprets this claim from the perspective of her distinction between being sexed (genitalized) and gendered. What for Harrison were "symbols" of ongoing relationship become "gender performativity" for Coakley.

The shift here is justified. As Harrison does point out, Gregory thought that the distinction between male and female must have some purpose beyond procreation. He posits that "it probably has some purpose related to regaining the blessing of good things promised by God. . . . The generative power of nature will be transferred" to the eternal project of "bringing forth the spirit of salvation."[47] In Harrison's scheme, this transference moves generation beyond gender difference. For Coakley, who is emphasizing the continuity in the process of perfection, it carries gender across the continuum, even as sex is left behind.

The upshot is that Coakley can continue to talk about the play of gendered existence into the eschaton. This serves even more to destabilize established gender roles. In the process of ascension to perfection, even eschatologically we continue "questing, longing, desiring," experiencing both "'male' *erōs*" and "giving birth" to goodness. Thus, via continuance of ascetic performativity, the eschatological body eternally moves between gendered categories in relation to God.[48]

What should be said about Coakley's interpretation of Gregory on sex and gender? First, one should note the strangeness of Gregory's treatment of the role of genitalia in this picture. It represents a odd fixation on genitalia. Coakley repeatedly identifies the desexing of the human in the eschaton with degenitalization. This is, at best, a seriously reductive account of sex. The location of a person in terms of sex concerns many facets of the self, including physical facets that extend to influence the whole of the body. Further, as I and many others have concluded, there is no clean distinction between sex and gender. As Judith Butler rightly concludes, gender performativity is not separable from sexed embodiment.

---

45. Coakley, 163.

46. Harrison, "Male and Female in Cappadocian Theology," 470.

47. Quoted in Harrison, 469.

48. Coakley, *God, Sexuality and the Self*, 283.

Approached from another angle, Gregory's picture of the self radically underestimates the importance of sex to personal identity. For many individuals, the presence or absence of sexual embodiment, including genitalia, is crucially important to their identities—so much so that the experience of not having the right genitalia, or having ambiguous genitalia, is reason enough for invasive surgical correction. Perhaps the Gregorian theologian would want to retort that this kind of attachment to sexed identity is indicative of an underlying pathology. But with the non-Gregorian arguing that being sexed is a part of the goodness of creation, the Gregorian is going to need a defeating reason to break the claim. Gregory's reading of Genesis 1:26–27 is not going to suffice.

Here, however, we are already moving into arguments about the importance of embodiment, and thus transitioning to issues that fit better under the discussion of the incarnation. To this topic we now go.

Incarnation

The above discussion of sex and gender has already raised the issue of the importance of the incarnation. Certainly, from the position I have staked out, the incarnation is central to the process of salvation. But in many of the arguments for Christ's trandscendsexualism, there is danger of marginalizing the incarnation.

Take, for instance, Thatcher's treatment of the multiple bodies of Christ. In favor of his de-emphasis on sex and gender, he notes that of all the different conceptions of Christ's body (physical, mystical, sacramental, ecclesial, ethical) "only one of these, the crucified body of Christ, is noticeably male." This is true, but this is the body of the Logos become flesh. Is this not a rather significant form of Christ's body? Thatcher comes quite close to a kind of Nestorianism in his discussion of the human and divine nature in Christ. The thrust of his discussion suggests that though Christ's human nature was sexed and gendered, Christ's divine nature was not. If carried all the way through, this would appear to suggest that Christ's divine nature was not fully incarnated. It is here, at his rhetorical extreme, that he claims that "Christ is not male." In the next sentence, he draws back from this position, writing that "the maleness of Jesus belongs to [the divine] nature because that nature cannot exist merely abstractly." This qualification draws him back from Nestorianism. But, at least within my argument, this seems a more significant point than Thatcher is willing to grant. To be incarnate is to become particular. This particularity is essential to the process of salvation. One cannot be the new Adam without incarnating the particulars that allow the kind of typological formula found in Romans. The problem is not the particularity of Christ's incarnation, but that to recapitulate the whole of the drama of sinful humanity, Christ must also transition across the particularities of human existence; to become not only the new Adam, but also the new Eve, thus recapitulating the reality of gendered difference within the incarnation. Better to allow this transition than to withdraw the depth of the incarnation.

Ward is aware of the danger here. Near the beginning of one of his articles he anticipates the criticism: "In what follows, then, I am not denying the credal statement that Christ is both fully God and fully man."[49] He then proceeds to articulate how Jesus's body is displaced during his life and transformed during and after his life. His holding onto the "body of the gendered Jew" as a background for these displacements is a way of acknowledging the importance of the incarnation, but this returns him to part of the bind that he is trying to escape by focusing on the transcendsexualism of Christ. Christ's incarnation requires Christ's physical, gendered body and cannot be seen primarily in the displacement of that body.

As in Thatcher's arguments, there is a danger here of marginalizing the incarnation. At one point, Ward suggests that (apparently in contrast to the other forms of the body of Christ), "We have no access to the body of the gendered Jew."[50] The immediate conclusion that Ward draws from this claim is that critical historical arguments about Jesus's sexuality are fruitless. Here, he and I have some agreement. I am not grounding my own conclusions in speculative historical arguments about Jesus's sex or gender. But we should not allow the limitations of this route to knowledge about Jesus to be the only route we have. Theologically, we certainly do have access to the body of the gendered Jew. The church came to its articulation of the doctrine of the full, embodied incarnation long after eyewitnesses had passed from the scene. What was key here was that theologically, Christ had to be fully God and fully human to secure salvation. Via theological arguments, we certainly do have access to justifications of claims about the body of the gendered Jew, and we should be careful not to let that truth fall away simply because the ecclesial body is more immanently available to our senses. Below we shall have the opportunity to revisit this question and make even more robust claims about our potential access to the incarnate body of Christ, but for present it is enough to have gone this far.

The reading of Gregory presented above does not focus primarily upon Christ's body. Rather, we can take up the issue in terms of more general embodiment. To rejoin the argument where I broke it off above, let us reframe the last point. I had suggested that Gregory was too fixated on genitalia. But perhaps reading Gregory as so focused on these organs is too wooden a reading. Genitalia are, as we now recognize, only one potential marker of sex, and are related to a set of other markers, such as chromosomes, hormones, and the development of

49. Ward, "The Displaced Body of Jesus Christ," 164.

50. Ward, 177.

secondary sexual traits. Shall we take the loss of genitalia as shorthand for the loss of all these markers? If this is right, it leads us back to something that appears much closer to Harrison's picture of Gregory, which aims at a transcending of gendered embodiment more completely. It seems that what we are heading for is really a loss of bodily differentiation. We may still have some form of angeloid, spiritual body, but these bodies seem so different from the things we currently call bodies that it should be wondered whether we can maintain the kind of continuity of body that Coakley envisions across death. As Beth Felker Jones writes, in Coakley's use of Gregory

> she nuances this gender fluidity, but there is still a danger lurking: the erasure of difference, the denial of its importance. A disconcerting shadow of flight from the messiness of physicality hangs over both Gregory and such appropriation of him. Must redemption of the sinful ways we experience gendered bodies necessarily mean that those bodies themselves are outside of God's redemptive intention?[51]

To be fair, in the end, Coakley may share at least some of these concerns. After treating both Gregory and Augustine in her book *God, Sexuality, and the Self*, Coakley goes on to suggest that the comparison "exposed two major traditional alternatives for women in the thought of (the 'Eastern') Gregory and (the 'Western') Augustine, highlighting the supposed double bind of either desexed equality, on the one hand, or of sexual subordination, on the other."[52] She hopes that her treatment of the two has taken her reader beyond this simple contrast, but she also suggests that overcoming the problem fully requires drawing on yet further theological resources.

In her own treatment of "gender," Coakley seems to endorse a more robust picture of bodily difference than Gregory's scheme may allow, even on Coakley's interpretation. Gender, she writes "'matters' primarily because it is about *differentiated, embodied relationship*—first and foremost to God, but also to others; and its meaning is therefore fundamentally given in relation to the human's role as made in the 'image of God' (Genesis 1:26–27)"[53] To whatever extent we should interpret Gregory's theory of the eschatological body as insufficient in providing for robust bodily differentiation, the most generous reading of Coakley would suggest that she too dissents from Gregory's conclusions.

51. Beth Felker Jones, *Marks of His Wounds: Gender Politics and Bodily Resurrection* (New York: Oxford University Press, 2007), 91.

52. Coakley, *God, Sexuality and the Self*, 54.

53. Coakley, 53.

If this is a fair reading, then Coakley should also be read as going beyond the option of transcendsexuality. If our eschatological bodies are in some sense sexed (avoiding both Gregory's strange fixation on genitalia and the danger of undifferentiated angeloid bodies), then Coakley envisions ascetic gender bending as occurring in, or transforming, these bodies in the process of rising toward perfection. As she writes: "(I am always, even after death . . . a particular sort of 'differentiated, relational being'); but gender is not unchangeable: it too is in via."[54] If the pursuit of perfection requires in some sense being transsexed and transgendered, we should surely also see Christ, at least in the resurrected body, as similarly being transformed, constantly and in multiple directions. Virginia Burris writes: "If Christ can be all things to all people, any gendering of the object of desire will also do: the beloved is equally divine whether figured as the queenly Sophia or the incorruptible Bridegroom . . ."[55] To the extent that embodiment is significant, we should be able to talk of this as even more than being "figured." Perhaps Christ is so embodied. And, since Coakley believes that this ascetic gender bending precedes death for those on the journey to perfection, we may be able to expand these claims even to the incarnation itself.

Traditions

In tilting against some of the conclusions of these scholars, I am offering reasons that are hopefully accessible from the perspective of their own positions. But part of the difference between their approaches and my own also concern the Christian traditions on which we are drawing. Christianity does not deliver us one coherent picture of the world. Rather, it bequeaths us multiple strands of history, intersecting, diverging, and living together relatively well or relatively poorly depending on the age. In preceding chapters I argued that Paul's formula in Romans 5 *de facto* presumes the significance of gendered difference inasmuch as the choice of Adam as the type of Christ presupposed one or another form of culturally embedded, gendered reasoning. I then traced the problem of locating Eve through the work of early Christian narrative and theology, where gendered distinctions continued to shape theological conclusions. Both Irenaeus and Tertullian, for instance, take gendered difference to have marked humanity from the creation, and both see it as continuing past the eschaton. Coakley recognizes this tradition and represents it in her own work via the figure of Augustine.[56]

54. Coakley, 54.

55. Burrus, "Queer Father: Gregory of Nyssa and the Subversion of Identity," 152.

56. Coakley, *God, Sexuality and the Self*, 288–296; For an overview of early Christian views on resurrection and sexed bodies, see Taylor G. Petrey, "The Resurrection Body," in *The Oxford*

If Coakley's development of the Cappadocian tradition faces the hurdle of securing the significance of bodily differentiation, the tradition from Irenaeus, through Tertullian, to Augustine faces an alternative hurdle: overcoming a binary image of sex and gender that subordinates the female/feminine to the male/masculine. As Daniel Boyarin writes: "the insistence on embodiment and sexuality as the foundational primitives of human essence almost ineluctably produces gender and sexuality-role differentiations as dominant characteristics of the social formation."[57]

In what has preceded, in accord with the conclusions of my theological argument, I have worked to temper the tradition on which I am drawing by denying that any particular sex and gender construction is essential or natural to humanity while at the same time insisting that sex and gender constitute one of the contexts of responsibility in which we find our embodied, differentiated identities by following our calling within and beyond that context. I have also insisted that any adequate construction of sex and gender today includes diversity that not only denies that sex and gender exist only in binary alternatives but recognizes that sex and gender exist in multiple dimensions. Sex and gender identities should take into account a full range of issues beyond simply genitalia and morphology.

In this, like the above scholars, I am both drawing on and only critically appropriating the theological tradition in which I am locating myself. If viewed from this perspective, I suspect that rather than disagreeing, these theologians and I should be viewed as moving in the direction of agreement from different starting points.

Christ Transgressing Sex and Gender

To move beyond the transcendsexual Christ, we can start further back in Christian history. We need to return to Jesus's life and teachings to look at how he challenged and transgressed sex and gender norms in his own culture.

While we can find resemblances between the alternative constructions of sex and gender, sex and gender in the first century CE was quite different from contemporary sex and gender. As covered in the last chapter, ancient medicine and culture admitted multiple models of sex/gender with overlapping features. To summarize with minimal oversimplification, sex and gender could be located in relation to the ideal, to man, and to the failure to manifest the ideal in woman.

Handbook of New Testament, Gender, and Sexuality, ed. Benjamin H. Dunning (New York: Oxford University Press, 2019), 666–669.

57. Daniel Boyarin, *Carnal Israel: Reading Sex in Talmudic Culture*, The New Historicism 25 (Berkeley: University of California Press, 2011), 10.

According to the dominant construction of masculinity, to be male was to be able to maintain one's personal bodily integrity against violation. To be a man was to be active and dominant. To be feminine was to be passive and dominated. It was the place of the man to be the head of the household; the *paterfamilias*. This required providing for the members of one's house. But it also meant that the lives of those members were lived largely at the discretion of the *paterfamilias*. One's freedom to coerce and abuse was related to one's status in the house. As their status descended, the power of the *paterfamilias* over them grew. The *paterfamilias* oversaw the house, but it could also be said that he dominated the house.[58] It is not too much of an oversimplification to identify this gender construction with what Plato considered a timocratic mindset; the thought world of the warrior, the Spartan.

Of course, this was not the only conception of masculinity in the first century. This view was partially tempered by, partially challenged by, and partially overlapped with a conception of masculinity that had its roots in Plato's own alternative to this kind of sex and gender construction.[59] By the first century, this more philosophical conception of masculinity was represented especially by the Stoics.[60] Here masculinity was identified primarily with self-control. To be manly was to be rational and to be virtuous. Moderation, or even abstemiousness, could be lauded. Eloquence was a sign of manly education. One might suffer pain, but one should never express undue emotional distress.[61] Service to others and to the common good was constitutive of manliness. Even the sacrifice of the self could make sense if it were for the public good.

These two conceptions of masculinity could come to loggerheads. One area of tension, for instance, concerned the appropriateness of expressions of anger.[62] On the one hand, rage could seem an act of righteous assertion: an active disposition fitting the man. On the other, it could appear to be an instance in which one allowed oneself to be overwhelmed by passions, and thus unfitting for the true man. But in most cases, these two models of masculinity did not so much clash as they gelled together, agreeing at least on the superiority of manliness, self-sufficiency, control over oneself and others, and public spiritedness and public life.

---

58. Susanna Asikainen, *Jesus and Other Men: Ideal Masculinities in the Synoptic Gospels*, Biblical Interpretation Series 159 (Boston, MA: Brill, 2018), 27.

59. Angela Hobbs, *Plato and the Hero: Courage, Manliness, and the Impersonal Good* (New York: Cambridge University Press, 2006).

60. Asikainen, *Jesus and Other Men*, 20.

61. Conway, *Behold the Man*, 29.

62. Conway, 26–28.

These two then composed the dominant gender constructs, at least for the Roman social, political, and military elites. As we have seen, underclasses in society often had to construct their own alternative accounts of masculinity and femininity given cultural differences from the Roman elites and the impossibilities of living up to Roman standards of masculinity if one was not a Roman citizen. In the last chapter I highlighted how the Rabbis constructed their own alternative masculinity to the Romans, valorizing studiousness. I also looked at how early Christians challenged the structures of masculinity by raising up the symbol of the eunuch and then lauding actual eunuchs within the church. While each of these constructions could find some overlap with the dominant models of sex and gender in the Roman context, especially the more philosophical version, they also pushed against these dominant constructs. From one perspective they were proposing alternative models of masculinity, but from another they were challenging masculinity and subverting it.

In this section, we need to carry the conversation beyond this to explore the ways in which Jesus' embodied ministry, life, and death transgressed the gender boundaries of Roman society. Within the plurality of sex and gender constructions available, Jesus's actions had an historical context, and we should see Jesus's actions as fitting into that context. At times Jesus's recorded actions reflect the patriarchy of the first century, and those who recorded Jesus's actions at times tried to bolster Jesus's status as a masculine character.[63] But at times, Jesus and his movement must be seen as constructing alternative pictures of masculinity. First century cultures were uniformly, deeply patriarchal. What was masculine was synonymous with what was good and virtuous. As such, the only way to challenge one picture of masculinity was with an alternate picture of masculinity. But we can and should go further than this. At some points Jesus's actions were so transgressive that even the early Christians who reported them appear to have been embarrassed by them. And those who reported them saw Jesus as challenging what it was to be masculine across Jewish and Roman cultures. Charting out some of these transgressions provides an opening for developing a doctrine of Jesus' incarnate, trans* status.

A Theological Caveat

Before we get into the details of Christ's teaching and actions, however, a bit of theological work needs to be done to sort out (or rather to refuse to sort out) a set of background problems. Christ, "emptied himself, taking the form of a slave, being born in human likeness. And being found in human form, he humbled himself and became obedient to the point of death—even death on a cross"

63. Conway, 6.

(Phil 2:7–8). Kenosis (self-emptying) is a fundamentally paradoxical act. Christ lowers himself even into death. Through death comes life. "Therefore God also highly exalted him and gave him the name that is above every name" (Phil 2:9).

Immediately the paradoxical nature of such claims about Christ throws us onto a set of tensions that we should not too quickly straighten out. Does Christ choose the crucifixion, or does he suffer the crucifixion? Is the crucifixion the site of defeat or victory? Is Jesus a servant or a leader? Was Jesus a vulnerable human or self-sufficient God? Answering such questions is important to assessing Jesus' masculinity and femininity because the different sides of each tension move in opposite directions on the Roman gender continuum. If we resolve these tensions in one or the other direction, we could produce opposing conclusions about Christ's gender in first century Roman terms. If Christ is eternal God and leader of humanity, who chooses the cross as a site of victory, then Jesus can be conceived of as a manly man. If Christ is a vulnerable human servant, who suffered defeat in the crucifixion, then Jesus has been entirely effeminated.

Traditionally Christianity has refused to abandon either side of these tensions. It has insisted that Christ is both servant and leader, both vulnerable human and self-sufficient God, and both chooses and suffers the crucifixion. It also has insisted that the cross is the site of both defeat and victory. Further, it has insisted on holding these claims without making one side subordinate to the other. Here already we find a sense in which the incarnate Jesus is theologically trans*. Jesus's life and activity manifest both masculinity and femininity in terms of the dominant constructs in his own time. Jesus is paradoxically trans*, both male and female at once, without reducing or subordinating the one to the other.

The problem of this paradox makes assessment of particular teachings and activities in Jesus's life fraught. If read in line with the more masculine side of the above tensions, Jesus's teaching to his disciples that they should become servants can easily be assimilated to a more philosophical reading of masculinity. Jesus was providing a teaching about civic-oriented leadership and thus was saying something quite similar to the Stoics. The problem is that by reading Jesus' teaching through one side of the tension, such an interpretation underestimates the radicalness of what Jesus was doing. Drawing on Jewish tradition, Jesus is suggesting that, for instance, one should be of service to the poor of the society. This teaching does not even make sense in Roman categories. Early Christianity through a mix of politics and charitable orientation had to create the category of "the poor" in Roman society.[64] Care for and service to the poor were not concepts that were covered under civil service in the first century Stoic mind. To get to this, we must take seriously the other side of the tension of service and

64. Peter Brown, *Poverty and Leadership in the Later Roman Empire*, The Menahem Stern Jerusalem Lectures (Hanover, NH: Published by University Press of New England, 2002).

leadership. Jesus was calling his disciples not just to embrace servant leadership. He was also calling them genuinely to become servants.

Many of Jesus's particular teachings and activities are open to such Janus-faced interpretations, and there is no doubt that they overlap more with the philosophical/Stoic conception of masculinity than with the more timocratic construction noted above. But many of his teachings and actions clearly transgress against both. In what follows, I am focused on transgression. As such, I will take it that when Jesus' teachings and actions appear on their face to be transgressive in relation to dominant Roman conceptions of masculinity, that they are in fact transgressive. In doing so I am not abandoning the tensions internal to the Christian perception of Jesus teaching and mission. But I am focusing on the ways in which Jesus's activities and teachings should not too easily be assimilated to the dominant patterns in the ancient world.

Jesus and Roman Gender

Jesus did not have a choice about being something less than fully manly according to Roman standards. As a peasant, Hebrew laborer, he was *homo* (man), but could not be true *vir* (a truly manly man).[65] He was not a Roman citizen. He was not trained in rhetoric. And he was not in a position to secure his own bodily integrity or to dominate others. This, of course, did not make Jesus transgressive. It just meant that he necessarily occupied a location in society from which the attainment of full "manliness" was impossible. He was, necessarily, partially effeminate.

Within this social location there were options and apparent dangers from the Roman perspective. One could critique the dominant gender construction in the society, and one was always liable to "gender slippage, particularly from male to female."[66] Gender slippage could be due to action a person took, as when one accepted penetrative sex acts from another. But slippage could also be imposed. One could be forced to slide down the gender continuum. Indeed, being coerced was itself a sign of one's sliding down. In each of these ways, Jesus would challenge and slide on the Roman gender continuum. He would critique. He would transgress. And he would accept or suffer the imposition of effemination.

Jesus's teaching at times challenges established gender roles. This can be seen in his teaching on public piety and family relations. Roman society in the imperial period was conceived as a macrocosm of the family, with the emperor as the *paterfamilias* of the entire citizen body. Thus, the family was held up as the model institution for society. And the *paterfamilias* was the linchpin of society.

65. Asikainen, *Jesus and Other Men*, 26.

66. Conway, *Behold the Man*, 18.

On the one hand, the *paterfamilias* oversaw and ordered the household. Within the house everyone else had a duty to obey the father. On the other hand, the *paterfamilias* was the public-facing embodiment of the family. His public activities were required to secure the honor of the family and to contribute to the common good through civic and religious ritual.

Jesus's teaching against the publicity of piety (Matt 6:1–6, 17–18) "runs counter to what would be expected of the ideal man in the Roman Empire."[67] The Roman *paterfamilias* according to this teaching would be a hypocrite who could expect no heavenly reward. Jesus's rejection of his own family (Mark 3:35, Matt 12:49) raises significant questions about his fulfillment of duty as a son.[68] His teaching that "I have come to set a man against his father" and that "Whoever loves father or mother more than me is not worthy of me" (Matt 10:35, 37; Luke 12:53) would have been seen as clear indictments of Roman family values. Such "antifamily language signals a renunciation of the dominant social order represented by the household."[69] Jesus' refusal to allow one of his disciples to bury his father (Matt 8:21) would be seen as corrosive to the family even more in the first century than it would be today.

Jesus's own singleness, and the encouraged singleness of his followers, itself had gendered implications. This ran contrary to standards both within Jewish and Roman cultures. "By eschewing marriage and family, Jesus cedes the masculine roles of father and husband."[70] Jesus himself rejects the context in which he or his followers could be the *paterfamilias* at all.

Of course, Jesus was calling his followers away not only from the family, but from established institutions of home, work . . . indeed, "everything" (Matt 19:27).[71] He was calling them to a life of roving homelessness (Matt 8:20). None of this fit within the expectations for a male, either as son or as householder. The closest parallel in Roman society is the ethic of the Cynics, a philosophical sect that purposely lived on the extreme margins of Roman civilization.[72] This was, at the very least, a radical minority/alternative vision of masculinity.

While Jesus's teachings on family deconstructed Roman images of masculinity, his teachings on social roles in the kingdom of God often inverted the Roman picture of reality. Jesus's teaching that he came "not to be served, but to

67. Conway, 122; Asikainen, *Jesus and Other Men*, 88.

68. Asikainen, *Jesus and Other Men*, 90.

69. Conway, *Behold the Man*, 122.

70. Amy-Jill Levine, "The Gospels and Acts," in *The Oxford Handbook of New Testament, Gender, and Sexuality*, ed. Benjamin H. Dunning (Oxford University Press, 2019), 301.

71. Conway, *Behold the Man*, 122.

72. Conway, 122.

serve" evokes the image of a menial, and thus unmanly, position in society. He also taught his disciples to follow suit: "whoever wishes to become great among you must be your servant, and whoever wishes to be first among you must be slave of all" (Mark 10:43–44). The language of service and even slavery here "was commonly associated with being effeminate."[73] As Colleen Conway writes: "From the perspective of masculine identity in the ancient world, the implication of such teaching is that to be a disciple of Jesus means to give up any claim to masculine status."[74]

We do not have to rely on contemporary experts to reach such a conclusion. The contrast with Roman conceptions of masculinity is explicit. Jesus is encouraging his disciples not to be like the Romans. "You know that among the Gentiles those whom they recognize as their rulers lord it over them, and their great ones are tyrants over them" (Mark 10:42). This picture of the "gentile" stereotypes what Jesus sees as a Roman construction of masculinity. Christ is not simply calling out bad apples. He is critiquing the culture that can come to consider such men "great ones."

Nor, according to the Gospels, was Jesus only challenging Roman conceptions of masculinity. The image of messianism that the Gospels suggest he defended looked definitively emasculated in comparison with the images assumed by many other Jews.[75] After Peter confesses his belief that Jesus is the Messiah, Jesus chooses his next teaching to immediately head off misunderstanding. Peter assumes that being the Messiah entails being the dominating leader of a powerful rebellion. But Jesus teaches that "the Son of Man must undergo great suffering, and be rejected by the elders, the chief priests, and the scribes, and be killed." (Mark 8:31). This describes a process of emasculation from Peter's perspective, which contributes to Peter's immediate attempt to rebuke Jesus for the teaching.[76] But Jesus instead rebukes Peter: "Get behind me, Satan! For you are setting your mind not on divine things but on human things" (Mark 8:33).

Jesus then continues to teach: "If any want to become my followers, let them deny themselves and take up their cross and follow me. For those who want to save their life will lose it, and those who lose their life for my sake, and for the

---

73. Asikainen, *Jesus and Other Men*, 94; Levine, "The Gospels and Acts," 301.

74. Conway, *Behold the Man*, 98.

75. In *The Jewish Gospels*, Daniel Boyarin reminds us that thought about the Messiah in Judaism was (and is) quite diverse. Peter's response to Jesus is representative of some, but clearly not all Jewish tradition. More research is needed on how Jesus fit into various Jewish constructions of masculinity from the first century. His embrace of emotion clearly fits better with the Jewish tradition of lament than it does with Stoicism. And his passion is most similar to the martyrdoms collected in the books of the Maccabees than to Roman models.

76. Asikainen, *Jesus and Other Men*, 79–81.

sake of the gospel, will save it" (Mark 8:34–35). Here we find the paradoxical teaching of glorious life through emasculating crucifixion. As I have suggested above, in such cases we should take a moment to take seriously the call to crucifixion. Jesus, it is suggested, knew that his teaching would be seen as subversive, and not subversive in a way that could be associated with manly virtue. He was worried that his audience would be "ashamed" of him and his teaching (Mark 8:38).

The above examples mostly focus on the extent to which Jesus's teachings required gender bending of his followers in relation to Roman norms. But, as noted in his comments on service and foreshadowing the crucifixion, this was not simply something he commanded of others. Jesus' own "gender performativity" often challenged masculine standards. This can be seen in the depictions of Jesus emotions, his "crying and lamenting," which were seen as feminine in Roman society.[77] In the Gospels Jesus "is perturbed, he is anxious. Jesus cries over Jerusalem (Luke 19:41–44); he cries at the grave of Lazarus (John 11:35). Luke goes as far as to describe Jesus's lament with a word that implies a loud expression of pain and sorrow."[78]

The feminizing of Jesus builds as the narratives of the Gospels move toward the crucifixion. There is a sense in which this is necessary. In the crucifixion, Jesus will have feminization forced upon him. But the Gospels do not want to clearly separate what is suffered from what is chosen. And the entire narrative from the Garden of Gethsemane to the Cross highlights the crossing of gendered borders that are occurring.

The ancient world did know of relatively "manly" deaths, even deaths at the hands of persecutors. The trick to avoiding feminization was found in self-control. One should resist to the end, then go forward to death without regret, without emotion, and ideally while providing an eloquent martyr's speech.[79] Jesus does none of these things.

In Gethsemane Jesus tells his disciples that he is "deeply grieved, even to death" (Mark 14:34). He asks only that his followers stay awake, something that they fail to do. He then prays "Abba, Father, for you all things are possible; remove this cup from me; yet, not what I want, but what you want." He is willing to accept death, but "he decidedly does not want to die."[80] Colleen Conway concludes: "If there is a masculine aspect to this scene, it would be found in the 'heroic overcoming of passions and the display of Jesus' supreme self-mastery.

77. Asikainen, 135–38.

78. Asikainen, 146.

79. Asikainen, 41.

80. Asikainen, 162.

But it is questionable whether such a submissive posture, even if it involves self-restraining, would be understood by a man in the Greco-Roman world as masculine deportment."[81] Susanna Asikainen writes that "The emotions that Jesus expresses in Gethsemane are not in accordance with either the self-assertive or the self-controlled ideals of masculine behavior."[82]

Nor does Jesus resist his captors. According to the Gospel of Luke, when his disciples attempt to fight the approaching guards, Jesus tells them to stop and hands himself over (Luke 22:49–51).[83] In the Gospel of Mark, Jesus's followers desert Jesus, fleeing full of fear. One even runs away in the nude (Mark 14:50–52).[84] The picture of Jesus is the opposite of a valiant, resistant leader of men. His followers have left him, and he has accepted the loss of control over himself that is to come.

The Greek πάσχω (páskhō) and the Latin passionem are forever associated with what comes next. These terms point toward deep feeling. But they are also tied to the concept of passions and to passivity. In the passion of Christ, they denote suffering, both in the sense of experiencing the violation of one's body and being outside of one's own control. This is the nature of the punishment Jesus was to undergo. It was not just to harm and kill him. It was to embarrass, emasculate, and demean him. As the female was, in the Roman system, a failed man, this was a process to make Jesus into a female.

This is all to say, again, that Graham Ward is wrong in his evaluation of the significance of the passion. It did not make Jesus body into a non-gendered thing. It was the drawn-out process of Jesus' transition across gendered barriers. Both forced and chosen, Jesus is violated by the power of the empire, moving beyond what any Roman man would (or even could under the law) suffer.

Approaching the moment of his death one "can trace the increasing passivity and hence 'feminizing' of Jesus."[85] Jesus is repeatedly "handed" from one Roman leader to another, highlighting his lack of self-control.[86] On the via dolorosa,

81. Conway, *Behold the Man*, 101.

82. Asikainen, *Jesus and Other Men*, 161.

83. Asikainen, 79–83.

84. Tat-siong Benny Liew, "Re-Mark-Able Masculinities: Jesus, the Son of Man, and the (Sad) Sum of Manhood?," in *New Testament Masculinities*, ed. Stephen D. Moore and Janice Capel Anderson, Society of Biblical Literature Semeia Studies 45 (Atlanta, GA: Society of Biblical Literature, 2003), 116.

85. Eric Thurman, "Looking for a Few Good Men: Mark and Masculinity," in *New Testament Masculinities*, ed. Stephen D. Moore and Janice Capel Anderson, Society of Biblical Literature Semeia Studies 45 (Atlanta, GA: Society of Biblical Literature, 2003), 151.

86. Asikainen, *Jesus and Other Men*, 167.

he drops the cross, showing his own weakness and inability to withstand his punishment.[87] He is repeatedly mocked, with his persecutors contrasting the claim to be the Messiah (a manly conquering hero) with his present reality.

All of this, however, pales in comparison to the feminization that comes on the cross. "In the ancient context, a crucified body was a violated or penetrated body. It was a body subjected to the power of others, and thus an emasculated body."[88] One can hardly slide further down the continuum of masculinity than a cross. In the crucifixion "any earlier ambivalence regarding the manly or unmanly death of Jesus is resolved in favor of the latter."[89] This reality is capped off with Jesus' cries from the cross in the synoptic Gospels. He delivers no martyr's speech. Rather he laments God's abandonment of him, and finally lets forth a tortured sob before dying. This was not the actions of one under his own control. It was the cry of a man who has lost the ability to withhold his own agony.[90]

The Romans had stripped Jesus of his manhood. He was, in the end, "unmanned" to borrow a term from Colleen Conway.[91] Yet, at this point, having plumbed the depths of the feminizing crucifixion, we must bring back the paradox of the cross.

> Jesus' suffering on the cross exposes his ultimate lack of divinity, and hence masculinity, expressed in his cry of abandonment (15:34). Yet, paradoxically, the cross is also the crowning moment of his kingship and his obedience as a son, and Jesus' broken male body is taken up (especially through the resurrection), into the divine employment of history. Jesus approximates the masculine identity of the Messiah and Son of God precisely and paradoxically by enduring feminizing shame and humiliation on the cross.[92]

If the cross is located at the heart of salvation history, so also is the transgender nature of Christ. In the martyrdom of Perpetua, noted in the last chapter, Perpetua believed herself to be transformed from a woman into a man. Reflecting on Christ's death in the context of Perpetua's "gender shift," Colleen Conway

---

87. Asikainen, 174.

88. Conway, *Behold the Man*, 67.

89. Conway, 102.

90. Asikainen, *Jesus and Other Men*, 176; Levine, "The Gospels and Acts," 301.

91. Conway, *Behold the Man*, 70.

92. Thurman, "Looking for a Few Good Men: Mark and Masculinity," 152.

writes: "In some sense, language of the crucifixion signals the reverse for Jesus."[93] As Conway suggests, despite Jesus's command not to be ashamed, many of the New Testament authors worked to emphasize the manliness of Christ in the face of such clear emasculation. But there was no way to entirely efface this reality. It was at the center of the story of salvation. Christ could not have saved the world as a man in the Roman sense. He could only do so by transgressing gender norms. That is part of the scandal of the cross: Christ the new Adam and the new Eve.

Jesus Transitioning Gender and Sexuality

We have arrived at more than one sense in which we can affirm Christ as trans* within Christian theology. Christ's body in the Eucharist and in the ecclesia at the very least transcends binary sex and gender categorization. And in his own historical context, Christ deconstructs, and transgresses, and even slides across sex and gender boundaries. But we should not stop here for two reasons.

First, while we can accept that Christ purposely transgresses against Roman sex and gender constructions, we do not live under these constructions and should not accept them. To do so would leave women identified as failed men and suggest that femininity should be associated with violation and abuse. Whatever is to be said for the gendered context of responsibility in Roman times, it certainly cannot and should not be our own.

The identification of Christ as trans* can help in interpreting God's activity in the gender-bending activity of Christ in the Roman context. If simply a male, Christ is effeminized by the crucifixion in his own context. His maleness is degraded. But, understood as trans*, we can see that Christ moves beyond this effemination. Christ becomes female, not in the sense of accepting that femininity is the negation of male goodness, but in solidarity with the female as crucified by the ancient Roman gender regime. Christ's crucifixion is not an acceptance or approval of the Roman signification of the cross as a machine of death. It is a rejection of the power of the order represented by the Roman cross, and the replacement of that sign with a sign that the divine stands with the oppressed. Seeing Christ as trans* allows us to take more seriously the extent to which the divine, in the incarnation, stands with women and other sex/gender minorities against the forms of oppression in every particular context. However, to deliver fully on the promise of this concept will require going beyond Jesus in his Roman context. It will require a further elaboration of Christ's nature as trans*.

Second, one cannot help feeling that we have not gone far enough to make the case that Christ is robustly trans* in a contemporary sense. There is too

93. Conway, *Behold the Man*, 72.

strong a sense in which we may still see Christ as incarnated in a male body, and thus failing to fully incarnate sexed and gendered difference. Here we should be careful. Being trans* does not require undergoing body modification, and those who do undertake bodily modification have a wide variety of options concerning what modifications to make.[94] Further, in the passion Jesus did undergo body modifications that represent the furthest possible extent of even a special ascetic calling. None of these realities should be minimized or written off. But we can go further in exploring the ways in which Christ's incarnate body transitions across gender and sex boundaries, and we should pursue this.

To make the case here, two moves are required. First is to make a point about the endurance of the incarnate body of Christ. While it is possible to see the incarnation ending at the resurrection, when Jesus gains a spiritual body, this fails to grasp the continuity of the body across death and resurrection. It is better to hold that Christ's resurrected body is still Christ's incarnate body. Second, we should explore the experiences that Christians have had of the resurrected body. Contradicting the suggestion that the resurrected body is beyond sex and gender, those who have had these experiences have often encountered a sexed and gendered Christ, and a Christ who is sexed and gendered as a woman.

The Resurrected, Incarnate Body

In July of 2018, only a few months after the two scholars had taken swings at each other over Hart's new translation of the New Testament, David Bentley Hart launched an attack on N. T. Wright's understanding of the resurrection.[95] The fulcrum of the argument was 1 Corinthians 15. Write had contended that a nuanced reading of the passage allowed it to be compatible with the doctrine of the resurrection of the flesh. Hart saw no reason to read the passage in this way in part because he saw no reason to accept the doctrine of resurrection of the flesh. According to Hart, the fleshly body is something to be left behind in the resurrection. While, in the Gospel of John, the Logos became flesh, "this involves no particular affirmation of the goodness of fleshly life; the Logos descends to us that we might ascend with him, and in so doing, presumably, shed the flesh." Hart wanted to make the case that the resurrection in a "spiritual body" could be robust enough to achieve everything that Wright was attempting to secure with the "fleshly body" and to condemn Wright's reading as reflective of

94. Lori B. Girshick, *Transgender Voices: Beyond Women and Men* (Hanover, NH: Univ. Press of New England, 2008), 75–83.

95. David Bentley Hart, "The Spiritual Was More Substantial than the Material for Ancients," *Church Life Journal*, July 26, 2018, https://churchlifejournal.nd.edu/articles/the-spiritual-was-more-substantial-than-the-material-for-the-ancients/.

post-Cartesian, Protestant concerns that would not have made sense to early Christians.

For those keeping points in the ongoing match between these two theologians, Hart loses this round, not so much because Wright was correct (exegesis of 1 Corinthians 15 is extremely contentious), but because Hart scored so many own goals in his article. As we have seen in our treatment of Justin Martyr, arguments about whether the flesh was resurrected were very much live issues in the early church. And most of the Christian tradition (perhaps contradicting Paul) ended up concluding that flesh was a category that should be used to talk about the resurrected body.

In an article pointing out several of Hart's errors, James Ware also notes that Hart's understanding of the "spiritual" body is off as well. In the ancient world "all were in agreement that spirit (πνεῦμα; Latin, *spiritus*), in contrast with the coarse, dense, tangible human body, is as a fine air or breath, incapable of being touched or handled, entirely intangible and impalpable."[96] Thus, a body of spirit could not function in the way that Jesus resurrected body is said to have in cases where the Gospels record Jesus being touched and even eating.

Ware goes on to stress the theological importance of the fleshly resurrection.

> Simply put, apart from the resurrection of Jesus's crucified body from the dead, there is no good news. If the hope of resurrection in the New Testament involves nothing more than entry into a "spiritual existence" apart from the earthly body, as Hart claims, then the apostolic gospel offered merely one more expectation of spiritual afterlife among many in the ancient pagan world. On Hart's view that Jesus rose as a disincarnate "spiritual being," the Incarnation was only a temporary episode.

But the incarnation was not a temporary episode. The resurrected body of Jesus *is still* the incarnate body of Jesus. In contrast to Hart's claims that the flesh is not affirmed by the incarnation, Ware sees the incarnation as echoing Genesis claim that the creation is "very good." The "same body that was cruelly tortured and murdered by the rulers and authorities of this world is now enthroned at the right hand of God in universal power and dominion, and the one who possesses that body is coming again in glory to judge the living and the dead." Rather than signaling a release from the fleshly body of the incarnation, "Jesus's bodily resurrection and ascension *continued* the story of the Incarnation."

We see here repeated the intra-Christian argument about whether the faith should emphasize continuity or difference between the present body and the

96. James Ware, "The Incarnation Doesn't End with the Resurrection," *Church Life Journal*, June 21, 2019, https://churchlifejournal.nd.edu/articles/the-incarnation-doesnt-end-with-the-resurrection/.

eschatological body. To be fair to Hart, it is not clear that he would disagree with Ware's conclusion that the resurrection continues the incarnation. Hart was trying to claim that the spiritual body was more robust than is often conceived, so perhaps in his own system he would also be able to make the claim that the incarnation continues beyond death. Regardless, the claim that the incarnation continues in the resurrected body of Jesus is certainly representative of the tradition that I have been arguing from.

This does have a significant upshot for the argument we have been pursuing. Graham Ward had claimed that "We have no access to the body of the gendered Jew."[97] The incarnate body of the gendered Jew had been finally displaced in the ascension. But, if the incarnation continues beyond death, and even beyond the ascension, there is no reason to accept that the incarnate body is necessarily inaccessible to us. It is our eschatological hope to see the incarnate Christ return in the Parousia, and there is no reason to think that Christ might not pop by before that. Indeed, many mystics believe they have had experiences of what at times appears to be a very tangible Christ. To these we must turn now.

The Trans-sexual Christ

Early Christianity had no problem with symbolic depictions of Christ that crossed gender lines. In Matthew 23:37, Jesus laments: "Jerusalem . . . How often have I desired to gather your children together as a hen gathers her brood under her wings." Christ was often pictured as the manifestation of divine wisdom, which was usually personified as a woman. Within this context, Jesus uses a female pronoun for self-reference in Matthew 11:19. Jesus will be "vindicated by her deeds."[98]

The early church expanded on such symbolism, drawing together images that we might think strange. In ancient medical theory it was thought that milk was a form of blood that mothers discharged to sustain their children.[99] In another bit of ancient wisdom, it was thought (probably based on a confused observation of molting) that the mother pelican pecked at her own body, causing wounds to let loose blood for her young to feed upon. In the Eucharist, of course, Christians drank of Jesus's blood and partook of his broken body. As such, the

97. Ward, "The Displaced Body of Jesus Christ," 177.

98. For a full analysis, see Conway, *Behold the Man*, 116–77.

99. Clement of Alexandria, *Pedagogus*, n.d., 1.6.39; Caroline Walker Bynum, *Jesus as Mother: Studies in the Spirituality of the High Middle Ages*, Publications of the Center for Medieval and Renaissance Studies, UCLA 16 (Berkeley, CA: University of California Press, 1984), 132; Bynum, *Holy Feast and Holy Fast*, 179.

pelican became an early Christian symbol for Christ.[100] Placing these different bits of belief together it was possible to identify Jesus wounds (especially the wound on his side) with the mother's breast, and to conceive of Jesus as the "lactating Christ."[101] Eventually the links between these concepts became so secure that references to drinking from Christ's breast and to Christ as mother proliferated. In this context "the writings of Clement, Origen, Irenaeus, John Chrysostom, Ambrose, and Augustine all describe Christ as mother."[102]

The use of this symbolism ebbed and flowed over time, but as Caroline Walker Bynum has exhaustively documented, the twelfth through the fourteenth centuries saw it become a dominant framework for understanding the work of Christ, especially in the context of the Eucharist. This was one part of a complex of shifts during this period that included emphasis on the humanity of Christ, Christ's suffering in the flesh, and the need for intimate relationship with Christ. The image of Christ as suckling mother fit this framework perfectly. As the earlier church saw the glorification of Adam taken over by Christ in his triumph, the medieval church could see Christ in the humanity of the woman, sharing her vital fluids in close contact with her child. To extend the metaphor in a direction that they did not, one might say that Eve, the mother of all, could be seen as a type (τύπος) of Christ who gave birth to and nourished the new creation.

What is important for our own inquiry here is the extent to which this framework for thinking about Christ overflowed its location as a symbol. Theologians, both male and female, regularly wrote of Jesus as mother, and of suckling upon Jesus's wound or Jesus's breast. But more than this, Bynum writes, men and women "drank from the breast of Christ, in vision and in image."[103] To many mystics, the lactating Christ was more than an allegory. As Bynum does here, it is common to speak of mystical visions, but even this is inadequate to capture the realities that medieval mystics experienced.

For many the only language adequate to their experiences is the language of physical encounter. Alice of Schaerbeke was said to have been "restored by liquid from the breasts of Christ." She experienced Christ who took her in his arms with an embrace and said: 'Welcome daughter! I have long desired this tabernacle. As long as you are in this body, I will remain with you and I will be your cellarer

100. Bynum, *Holy Feast and Holy Fast*, 270.

101. Bynum, 122.

102. Bynum, *Jesus as Mother*, 126; Verna Harrison, "The Breast of the Father," in *Feminism and Theology*, ed. Janet Martin Soskice and Diana Lipton, Oxford Readings in Feminism (New York: Oxford University Press, 2003).

103. Bynum, *Holy Feast and Holy Fast*, 270.

[the monastic official in charge of food] to provide you with what you need.'"[104] Lutgard of Aywières "saw Christ in the doorway of the Church, and she nursed from his side."[105] Agnes Blannbekin spoke of drinking from Jesus's side.[106] To Angela of Foligno "Christ appeared . . . all bleeding and gave her his wound to suck."[107] Raymond of Captua records one of Catherine of Sienna's experiences as follows:

> [Christ] tenderly placed his right hand on her neck, and drew her toward the wound in his side. 'Drink, daughter, from my side,' he said, 'and by that draught your soul shall become enraptured with such delight that your very body, which for my sake you have denied, shall be inundated with its overflowing goodness.' Draw close . . . to the outlet of the Fountain of Life, she fastened her lips upon that sacred wound, and still more eagerly the mouth of her soul, and there she slaked her thirst.[108]

Advising others, Catherine wrote: "Do as the child does who, wanting to take milk, takes the mother's breast and places it in his mouth and draws to himself the milk by means of the flesh. So . . . we must attach ourselves to the breast of the crucified Christ, in whom we find the mother of charity, and draw from there by means of his flesh (that is, the humanity) the milk that nourishes our soul."[109]

Several points are important here. These saints of the church report these as embodied experiences of Christ, often in terms of experiences of Christ in the flesh. They also often report what we would consider physiological effects of these encounters. Having been nourished by the liquid from Christ's breast, they are invigorated or even inebriated. Such encounters with Christ are far more robust than what is recorded in any of the reports of Paul's postascension encounter with the resurrected Christ (Acts 9:1–19; 22:6–16; 26:12–23; Gal 1:11–16; 1 Cor 15:8). As such, there is good reason to consider these to be not merely visions, but rather encounters with the resurrected Christ. And, if Christ's incarnation includes his incarnation in the resurrected body, then these can be taken as reports about the state of Christ's resurrected, incarnate body: reports that indicate that this body is at least at times incarnated as female in a significant sense.

---

104. Bynum, 116.

105. Bynum, 122.

106. Bynum, 355 n. 103.

107. Bynum, 142.

108. Bynum, 172.

109. Bynum, 176.

In the context of the broader argument of this book, such reports do not stand alone as evidence for the conclusion that Christ is incarnate as both male and female. My argument throughout has held that we should conclude on theological grounds that Christ is trans* in a way that incarnates both male and female. Such experiences of Christ being so incarnated stand as independent support not only that such a claim makes sense internal to Christianity, but that it has the benefit of a kind of confirmation found in saintly witness. But it is, if my argument is correct, exactly what we should have expected to find, and what we might have been obligated to posit even if we did not find it. Christ as the new Adam *and the new Eve* recapitulates the entirety of the story of sin to gather up the whole history of humanity to Christself, and in this way we find a story of sin and salvation in which Eve not only finds her place, but is the very type (τύπος) of Christ with Adam.

Conclusion

This chapter has argued that there are significant senses in which Christ is trans* both in Christ's life prior to death and in the eternal incarnation that goes beyond death and the ascension. Do we need to go yet further, to argue that Christ incarnated female and male sexual morphology prior to death? To cover the full range of sex and gender diversity do we need to show the ways in which Christ incarnates a greater range of sex and gender identities? My doctrinal proposal is that we should claim that Christ is trans* in whatever way is sufficient to assume/incarnate gendered/sexed diversity to allow for the opening of salvation to all persons who accept Christ. Perhaps there are good theological arguments for going further than I have in this text. And in a tradition that affirms the virgin conception and the ability of Christ to walk on water there is no reason to think that Christ could not have incarnated sex and gender diversity prior to death, or that there is a limit to the sex and gender diversity that Christ can and does incarnate, aside from the limits of the divine nature itself. If others wish to make such arguments, I am open to them. But I take it at least that I have secured the core of my own argument here and have shown that it is not something either entirely new or unsupported by Christian witness across the tradition. We may not have had the language of trans* prior to the present moment, but as far as my argument has been successful, Christ has always been trans* and we have simply had to wait for adequate ways to talk about this in theology.

There is only one last bit that needs to be said on the subject. As we saw in the last chapter on sex and gender theology, sex and gender calling is not something that an individual can fulfill on their own. Calling, by nature, is a repeated process of antiphonal call and response. The individual needs recognition and affirmation. Ultimately, and especially in cases of special calling that lie on the margins of established contexts of responsibility, this recognition and affirmation must come from the God, who is both intimate with and transcendent of creation. There can be no doubt that Christ's identity as trans* is affirmed internal to the Godhead. But human society, and especially Christ's body as the church, properly find themselves caught up in this process as well. In short, it is important that the church recognize and affirm Christ's identity as trans* in recognition of its participation in Christ's being called.

No doubt, how to do this is a sensitive issue. As with discussions of God the Father, the situation is complicated by traditional and creedal language and iconography. But, as noted above, when considering "herself" in relation to lady wisdom, even Jesus in the Gospel had no problem using female pronouns for self-reference. I can see no reason to place strictures on ourselves that Jesus did not place on themselves. And, again as Caroline Walker Bynum has documented, the church of the twelfth through the fourteenth century explored ways to explore Christ's femaleness (what we are calling Christ's trans*ness) in its iconography. More recently, feminists have experimented with icons of the female Christ, such as Edwina Sandys' "Christa," a crucifix featuring a bare-breasted female Christ hung on an acrylic cross.[110]

Sensitivity should be used in exploring such images, not so much to avoid giving offense as to be aware of the polyvalence of gendered imagery around issues of violence. As I noted above, there are dangers in taking over too much of Christ's trans* status as it existed in the first century lest one bring that construction of gender along unintentionally. But even as sensitivity must be deployed in developing new images and new language, the church must also expand, not only exploring Christ's femininity but the full range of Christ's trans* identity in its iconography and language.

No doubt, there is much more that could be said on these matters, and much more that should be said. Having laid out my argument, and taken it to its conclusion, I look forward to engaging others as we develop these areas of theology more fully.

110. James Barron, "An 'Evolving' Episcopal Church Invites Back a Controversial Sculpture," October 4, 2016, https://www.nytimes.com/2016/10/05/nyregion/an-evolving-episcopal-church-invites-back-a-controversial-sculpture.html?

POSTSCRIPT

Fortuitous Convergence

> After all these years I see that I was mistaken about Eve in the beginning; it is better to live outside the Garden with her than inside it without her.
>
> —Mark Twain

IN MATTHEW 25, Jesus suggests a scheme for the final judgment which seems out of place in most post-Lutheran, Protestant theology. God will judge the nations, dividing them according to how they treated the hungry, the thirsty, the stranger, the naked, the sick, and the incarcerated. Those who are saved are marked not primarily by belief but by the virtue of caring. From a post-Lutheran standpoint, one might be tempted to conclude that this is a passage lacking in theology. But that would not be right. The passage does not remove relation to God from soteriology, it just refuses to accept that the relationship to God necessary to salvation is constituted by belief. Solidarity with the poor, needy, and oppressed is service to God whether one realizes it or not, and this solidarity is salvific: "just as you did it to one of the least of these who are members of my family, you did it to me" (v. 40).

This is a significantly different soteriology than the ones we have been working with in previous chapters. This book has argued that Christians should claim that Christ is trans*. It made this argument based on a critical analysis of scriptural and patristic sources. I have avoided making arguments from the claim that the identification of Christ as trans* would be liberative. I have done so to show that the argument in previous chapters stands on its own, independent from the forms of argument in liberation or queer theology. The argument thus cannot be dismissed by dismissing liberation or queer starting points or modes of argument.

But this is not to deny the power of liberative theological arguments. As Matthew 25 suggests, theologies of solidarity are no less ancient than the traditions of theology on which I have been drawing for my argument. Indeed, in the traditions of Israel the preferential option for the poor and oppressed extends as far back as the formulations of the stories of creation themselves.

If conceived in relation to liberation theology, the argument of this book can be seen as setting the stage for a liberation theological argument. Liberation theology aims to liberate human beings to ever greater levels of fulfillment of human life that can be gained through relatively more just social organization. To fight for such liberation, we need accounts of what human fulfillment looks like. The argument of this book is not a piece of liberation theology, but it does suggest that there are good reasons for Christians to revise their views of what fulfilling human lives might look like in terms of sex and gender. It argues that there are good theological reasons to conceive of some versions of trans* and queer life as fulfilling a calling from God internal to or on the margins of the contexts of responsibility in which we live. To the extent that the contexts as they exist inhibit people from living out the fulness of their callings, there is a need for liberative action to reform the contexts.

Liberation Theology

Starting from this point, we can produce a supporting argument for conceiving of Christ as trans* from within liberation theology. In the 1970s, James Cone famously argued that Christians must worship the *Black Christ.*[1] No less a theological argument than my own, Cone's argument followed the logic of Matthew 25. God is identified with the poor and oppressed. America, indeed, *white America,* was (and still is) in the business of oppressing and killing Black men. It was up to Black theology to identify "revelation as a manifestation of the Black Christ," claiming that Christ "is those very black men whom white society shoots and kills."[2]

This identification reveals the partisanship of God within present-day society. It shapes Christian praxis on behalf of those with whom Christ is identified. It opens our ears to hearing the message of Christ from those with whom Christ is identified. And it stands as a symbol of God's recognition of the identity of those who are oppressed in the current society.

Having followed the current study, we can note an unsurprising problem in Cone's identification of Christ. Christ as Cone conceived him in the 1970s was the new Black Adam. Again, we must ask where Eve has gone. In following decades Cone himself, with the help of feminist, womanist, and mujerista critics and compatriots, would work to expand the Black Christ into an intersectional Christ, living at the crossroads of categories of oppression.

There can be no doubt that today, under such an argument, the trans* Christ must also be the subject of theology. Straining against the modernist dual sex/gender model, trans* persons often lack social support and recognition necessary to well-being, much less flourishing. They are frequently the target of bullying

1. James H. Cone, *A Black Theology of Liberation* (New York: Lippincott, 1970), 80.

2. Cone, 80.

and ostracization. Recent studies have found that such treatment has led trans* persons to attempt suicide at rates two to four times those of their non-trans* peers.[3] Nor is the abuse heaped onto trans* persons limited to popular social pressures. Trans* identity has been taken up in the whirlwind of the culture wars and made into a political issue. In public statements by politicians, trans* identities are belittled and negated. Increasingly today this denial of identity is being codified in law. According to an analysis of the Williams Institute at the UCLA School of Law, at the time of this writing, fifteen states in the US have restricted or eliminated access to gender affirming medical care for young trans* persons.[4] This is so even though such care has been shown to reduce the incidence of suicide and increase well-being in this population.

If trans* persons are oppressed today, and Christ is identified with the oppressed, then there is another clear theological argument for considering Christ as trans*. As Marcella Althaus-Reid writes, "we can envision a transgendered Christ, taking on Christself the oppression and injustice that a person suffers when gender and sexuality are dislocated."[5]

This is clearly a different argument from that which I have been pursuing in the rest of this volume, and the sense in which it requires us to think of Christ as trans* is not exactly the same in this argument as in my own. This said, the coincidence of the two different arguments provides mutual strength for each. And both point toward a set of important next steps in theology. As with the identification of Christ as Black, the identification of Christ as trans* should help us locate God's preference in our cultural conflicts, shape Christian praxis, and open our ears to the Word of God from the trans* community. The location of Christ as trans* might also be a liberative symbol for those trans* persons who find themselves in need of recognition in the search for their own callings.

Queer Theology

But, queer theologians remind us, our job cannot simply be expanding the present order to include more people. It must also include the perpetual deconstruction of the present order. Opening the eighth chapter of her book *God and Difference*, Linn Marie Tonstad recalls a commercial she once saw in which a lesbian couple

---

3. R. B. Toomey, A. K. Syvertsen, and M. Shramko., "Transgender Adolescent Suicide Behavior," *Pediatrics* 142, no. 4 (2018): 1–9; J. L. Herman, T. N. T. Brown, and A. P. Haas, *Suicide Thoughts and Attempts among Transgender Adults: Findings from the 2015 U.S. Transgender Survey* (Los Angeles, CA: Williams Institute, UCLA School of Law, 2019).

4. K. Conron, K. O'Neill, L. Vasquez, and C. Mallory. *Prohibiting Gender-Affirming Medical Care for Youth* (Los Angeles, CA: Williams Institute, UCLA School of Law, 2022).

5. Althaus-Reid, *Indecent Theology,* 116.

enter squeamishly into a new church.[6] The tension in the scene builds as they move toward the front of the sanctuary, unsure how they will be treated. But at the end of their walk up the aisle they are greeted by a pastor who proclaims "Welcome, *everyone*." Instantly the room lightens, the family finds a place on a pew, and the scene ends with everyone smiling. Tonstad spends the rest of the chapter registering her unease with this image and the ecclesiology it suggests.

The problem, she thinks, is that in this image the church stands as the center of order, a home of righteousness and grace, which needs only to be expanded to those outside its usual circle. The outsiders need to be brought into the order that exists. The whole picture gets things backwards, she suggests. It is the present order that needs to give way to the inbreaking kingdom of God. It is the church that is in need of deconstruction and reconstruction. And without that, expanding the present order to new people will constitute expanding an order that God has placed under judgment.

We live in a strange time, when male celebrities can become fashion icons by crossdressing at galas at the same time that trans* persons are fighting for the right to use a restroom that aligns with their identities. It is worth asking, when Harry Styles wears a Gucci dress on the cover of *Vogue*, whether he is challenging the unjust structures of the world or whether he is domesticating and commodifying queerness. Are such instances to be celebrated as progress, or lamented as a glitz-capitalist usurpation of a once radical movement? The answer can be, and in a sinful world often is, both.

The body of Christ plays an important role in Tonstad's response to the dangers of a church that "reproduces" and expands the present order rather than deconstructing that order in the face of the transcendent God. The resurrection is an ambiguous symbol for Tonstad. If one emphasizes the continuity between the pre-crucified and resurrected body, the ecclesial upshot is that the church as the body of Christ is seen as the present manifestation of the ideal of the kingdom. The members of the church are to conform ever more and more to the order it now represents.

Tonstad sees another option for conceiving of the resurrection, however. This option sees the resurrected body as a radical, new, unforeseen possibility brought about by God. The resurrected body is ascended and thus absent from the present. The church awaits in expectation of Christ's return. "Expectation cannot be wholly indexed to the world as it is. The form of *this* world is passing away, resurrection time is not the continuance of the self or the social integration of whole-healed subjects."[7]

---

6. Tonstad, *God and Difference*, 254.

7. Tonstad, 264.

This conception of the resurrection locates Christ outside of, and in judgment over, the church and its order at any given time. Tonstad draws this together with the theology represented in Matthew 25. Jesus is not identified with the church, or even with the Christian. Christ is identified with those falling outside of the order of the church. And the church must be a place where Christians are called to move beyond the current order of the church. This ecclesiology "figures forth the abortion of the current order of continuity and repetition, and ultimately the abortion of the Church."[8]

As part of the discontinuity represented in resurrection, Tonstad foresees the overcoming of gender in the resurrected body. Jesus, she accepts, was male. But the resurrected body requires "the end of both wound-womb and phallic logic."[9] Of all of the symbols of sex, it is only the clitoris that remains viable as "the nonbounded self that resurrection promises to transform without destroying."[10] This is because of its liminality, being neither womb nor phallus. The clitoris is not implicated in the "reproduction" of present order. It represents the promise of intimacy without the need for penetration and violation.

The theology of sex and gender that I have offered in this work is clearly quite different from Tonstad's. My treatment of the order of the world in terms of contexts of responsibility is not as consistently focused on deconstruction as Tonstad's. This is, I think, to be expected. Like Butler's queer philosophy, Tonstad's queer theology emphasizes one side of the dialectic that is highlighted in the contexts. The difference emerges also in my picture of a gendered eschaton in comparison to Tonstad's gender-transcending apocalypse. But also as with Butler's philosophy, there is significant overlap between my own position and Tonstad's.

Indeed, in some ways, my proposal is more radical than Tonstad's. Tonstad accepts the maleness of the pre-crucifixion Jesus in ways that my account seeks to problematize. As I have argued, there are good theological reasons to emphasize the liminality of Christ's sex/gender at all points in Christ's life. As we have seen, at least in terms of the sex/gender regime of Rome, Christ's sex/gender was more liminal than the simple identification "male" suggests. And, on my account, Christ's trans* identity is part of his special calling. Just as celibates and ascetics stand at the boundaries of the worldly order, reminding us of its impermanence, those whose trans* identities go beyond sex/gender binaries remind us of the evanescence of any particular ordering of the context of sex and gender. Christ, on my account, transcends, transgresses against, and transitions across sex/gender

8. Tonstad, 273.

9. Tonstad, 275.

10. Tonstad, 275.

identities. As such, quite similarly to Tonstad's resurrected Christ, who is absent from and expected by the church, my picture of Christ locates Christ as "other" in relation to the order of the world, even the order found in the church at any particular time.

With Tonstad, and with the author of Matthew, I locate Christ with those who stand outside. This does not lead to a call for the collapse of the order in which we live. But it does require constant reformation of that order and a perpetual sense of unease and dissatisfaction with the order as it exists. The context of sex/gender is a gift of God. But it is always a gift received and corrupted by our sin. Thus, the gift of God is found not only in the context, but in the judgment of the context. Accepting that perpetual judgment against the context is part of accepting that Christ is trans*.

This will be a difficult step for many Christians, especially as Christianity's ties to modern patterns of thought have been one of the driving forces in anti-trans* rhetoric and activism. But if the move to embracing trans* persons is a significant shift for many modern Christians, it would be even more of a shock for the trans* community. Having been abused, can trans* people open themselves to these shifts that are only beginning in Christianity? In some ways, this is an even more important question than the ones that we have been pursuing thus far. To the extent that Christ is trans*, it is the church that needs acceptance from the trans* community far more than the trans* community needs acceptance from the church.

BIBLIOGRAPHY

Agnew, Lois. "The Classical Period." In *The Present State of Scholarship in the History of Rhetoric: A Twenty-First Century Guide*, edited by Lynée Lewis Gaillet and Winifred Bryan Horner. Columbia: University of Missouri Press, 2010.

Allen, Troy D. *The Ancient Egyptian Family: Kinship and Social Structure*. New York: Routledge, 2012.

Althaus-Reid, Marcella. *Indecent Theology: Theological Perversions in Sex, Gender and Politics*. New York: Routledge, 2010.

Amir, Yehoshua. "The Figure of Death in the 'Book of Wisdom.'" *Journal of Jewish Studies* 30 (1979): 154–178.

Anderson, Gary A. "The Exaltation of Adam and the Fall of Satan." In *Literature on Adam and Eve: Collected Essays*, edited by Gary A. Anderson, Michael E. Stone, and Johannes Tromp. Studia in Veteris Testamenti Pseudepigrapha 15. Boston: Brill, 2000.

———, Gary A. *The Genesis of Perfection: Adam and Eve in Jewish and Christian Imagination*. Louisville, KY: Westminster John Knox Press, 2001.

Anderson, Gary A, Michael E Stone, and Johannes Tromp. *Literature on Adam and Eve Collected Essays*. Studia in Veteris Testamenti Pseudepigrapha 15. Boston: Brill, 2000.

Asikainen, Susanna. *Jesus and Other Men: Ideal Masculinities in the Synoptic Gospels*. Biblical Interpretation Series 159. Boston: Brill, 2018.

Augustine. *The City of God: 11–22*. Translated by William Babcock. Works of Saint Augustine 7. Hyde Park, NY: New City Press, 2013.

Bader-Saye, Scott. "Gender Identity, Redemption, and Sanctification." In *Routledge Companion to Christian Ethics*, edited by Rebekah Miles and D. Stephen Long. New York: Routledge, Forthcoming.

———. "The Transgender Body's Grace." *Journal of the Society of Christian Ethics* 39, no.1 (2019): 75–92.

Balthasar, Hans Urs von. *Theo-Drama: Theological Dramatic Theory: Volume 2: The Dramatis Personae: Man in God*. Translated by Graham Henderson. San Francisco: Ignatius, 1992.

Barr, James. *Biblical Faith and Natural Theology: Gifford Lectures for 1991*. Oxford: Clarendon Press, 1993.

———. *The Garden of Eden and the Hope of Immortality*. Minneapolis, MN: Fortress Press, 1993.

Barrett, C. K. *A Commentary on the First Epistle to the Corinthians*. New York: Charles Scribner's Sons, 1962.

———. *From First Adam to Last: A Study in Pauline Theology*. New York: Scribner, 1961.

Barron, James. "An 'Evolving' Episcopal Church Invites Back a Controversial Sculpture," October 4, 2016. https://www.nytimes.com/2016/10/05/nyregion/an-evolving-episcopal-church-invites-back-a-controversial-sculpture.html?

Barton, Stephen C., ed. *Where Shall Wisdom Be Found? Wisdom in the Bible, the Church, and the Contemporary World*. Edinburgh: T&T Clark, 1999.

Bassler, Jouette. "1 Corinthians." In *Women's Bible Commentary*, edited by Carol A. Newsom and Sharon H. Ringe, expanded ed. Louisville, KY: Westminster John Knox Press, 1998.

———. *1 Timothy, 2 Timothy, Titus*. Abingdon New Testament Commentaries. Nashville, TN: Abingdon Press, 1996.

Baudry, Gérard-Henry. "La Responsabilité d'Eve Dans La Chute. Analyse d'une Tradition." *Mélanges de Science Religieuse* 53, no. 3 (1996): 293–320.

Beardsley, Christina. "Taking Issue: The Transsexual Hiatus in 'Some Issues in Human Sexuality.'" In *This Is My Body: Hearing the Theology of Transgender Christians*, edited by Christina Beardsley and Michelle O'Brien. London: Darton, Longman and Todd, 2016.

Beardsley, Christina, and Michelle O'Brien, eds. *This Is My Body: Hearing the Theology of Transgender Christians*. London: Darton, Longman and Todd, 2016.

Beattie, Tina. *God's Mother, Eve's Advocate: A Marian Narrative of Women's Salvation*. New York: Continuum, 2002.

Beeley, Christopher A. *Gregory of Nazianzus on the Trinity and the Knowledge of God: In Your Light We Shall See Light*. Oxford Studies in Historical Theology. New York: Oxford University Press, 2008.

Beeley, Christopher A., and Andrew Hofer, eds. "The Stoning of Christ and Gregory Nazianzus." In *Re-Reading Gregory of Nazianzus: Essays on History, Theology, and Culture*, 143–158. CUA Studies in Early Christianity. Washington, DC: Catholic University of America Press, 2012.

Beemyn, Genny, and Susan Rankin. *The Lives of Transgender People*. New York: Columbia University Press, 2011.

Behr, John. *Asceticism and Anthropology in Irenaeus and Clement*. Oxford Early Christian Studies. New York: Oxford University Press, 2000.

Benko, Stephen. *The Virgin Goddess: Studies in the Pagan and Christian Roots of Mariology*. Studies in the History of Religions 59. New York: Brill, 1993.

Bennett, Judith M. *History Matters: Patriarchy and the Challenge of Feminism*. Gender in History. Philadelphia: University of Pennsylvania Press, 2006.

Benny Liew, Tat-siong. "Re-Mark-Able Masculinities: Jesus, the Son of Man, and the (Sad) Sum of Manhood?" In *New Testament Masculinities*, edited by Stephen D. Moore and Janice Capel Anderson, 93–136. Society of Biblical Literature Semeia Studies 45. Atlanta, GA: Society of Biblical Literature, 2003.

Bentley Hart, David. "The Spiritual Was More Substantial than the Material for Ancients." *Church Life Journal*, July 26, 2018. https://churchlifejournal.nd.edu/articles/the-spiritual-was-more-substantial-than-the-material-for-the-ancients/.

Berg, Shane. "Ben Sira, the Genesis Creation Accounts, and the Knowledge of God's Will." *Journal of Biblical Literature* 132, no. 1 (2013): 139–157.

Bingham, D. Jeffery. "Irenaeus and Hebrews." In *Irenaeus: Life, Scripture, Legacy*, edited by Sara Parvis and Paul Foster, 65–80. Minneapolis: Fortress Press, 2012.

Black, Matthew. *Romans*. New Century Bible Commentary. London: Oliphants, 1973.

Bolz-Weber, Nadia. *Pastrix: The Cranky, Beautiful Faith of a Sinner & Saint*. New York: Jericho Books, 2013.

Bonhoeffer, Dietrich. *Ethics*. Edited by Clifford J. Green. Translated by Reinhard Krauss, Charles C. West, and Douglas W. Stott. Dietrich Bonhoeffer Works 6. Minneapolis, MN: Fortress Press, 2005.

Børresen, Kari Elisabeth, ed. "God's Image, Man's Image? Patristic Interpretation of Genesis 1:27 and I Cor. 11:7." In *The Image of God: Gender Models in Judaeo-Christian Tradition*, 187–209. Minneapolis, MN: Fortress Press, 1995.

Boyarin, Daniel. *A Radical Jew: Paul and the Politics of Identity*. Contraversions 1. Berkeley, CA: University of California Press, 1997.

———. "Against Rabbinic Sexuality: Textual Reasoning and the Jewish Theology of Sex." In *Queer Theology: Rethinking the Western Body*, edited by Gerard Loughlin, 131–146. Malden, MA: Blackwell, 2007.

———. *Carnal Israel: Reading Sex in Talmudic Culture*. The New Historicism 25. Berkeley, CA: University of California Press, 2011.

———. "Homotopia: The Feminized Jewish Man and the Lives of Women in Late Antiquity." *Differences* 7, no. 2 (July 1, 1995): 41–81.

———. "Justin Martyr Invents Judaism." *Church History* 70, no. 3 (September 2001): 427–461.

———. *The Jewish Gospels: The Story of the Jewish Christ*. New York: The New Press, 2012.

———. *Unheroic Conduct: The Rise of Heterosexuality and the Invention of the Jewish Man*. Contraversions 8. Berkeley, CA: University of California Press, 1997.

Brayford, Susan Ann. *Genesis*. Septuagint Commentary Series. Boston: Brill, 2007.

Brown, Cheryl Anne. *No Longer Be Silent: First Century Jewish Portraits of Biblical Women*. Gender and the Biblical Tradition. Louisville, KY: Westminster/John Knox Press, 1992.

Brown, Peter. *Poverty and Leadership in the Later Roman Empire*. The Menahem Stern Jerusalem Lectures. Hanover, NH: University Press of New England, 2002.

———. *The Body and Society: Men, Women and Sexual Renunciation in Early Christianity*. London: Faber and Faber, 1989.

Brunner, Emil. *The Divine Imperative: A Study in Christian Ethics*. Translated by Olive Wyon. Cambridge, UK: Lutterworth, 2003.

Burrus, Virginia. "Queer Father: Gregory of Nyssa and the Subversion of Identity." In *Queer Theology: Rethinking the Western Body*, edited by Gerard Loughlin, 147–162. Malden, MA: Blackwell, 2007.

———. *Saving Shame: Martyrs, Saints, and Other Abject Subjects*. Divinations. Philadelphia, PA: University of Pennsylvania Press, 2008.

Busch, Austin. "The Figure of Eve in Romans 7:5–25." *Biblical Interpretation* 12, no. 1 (2004): 1–36.

Butler, Judith. *Bodies That Matter: On the Discursive Limits of "Sex."* Routledge Classics. New York: Routledge, 2011.

———. *Gender Trouble: Feminism and the Subversion of Identity*. Thinking Gender. New York: Routledge, 1990.

Bynum, Caroline Walker. *Holy Feast and Holy Fast: The Religious Significance of Food to Medieval Women*. The New Historicism. Berkeley, CA: University of California Press, 2000.

———. *Jesus as Mother: Studies in the Spirituality of the High Middle Ages*. Publications of the Center for Medieval and Renaissance Studies, UCLA 16. Berkeley, CA: University of California Press, 1984.

———. *The Resurrection of the Body in Western Christianity, 200–1336*. American Lectures on the History of Religion. New York: Columbia University Press, 2017.

Byrne, Brendan. *Romans*. Sacra Pagina Series 6. Collegeville, MN: Liturgical Press, 2007.

Cahill, Lisa Sowle. *Sex, Gender, and Christian Ethics*. New Studies in Christian Ethics. New York: Cambridge University Press, 1996.

Cameron, Lynne. *Metaphor in Educational Discourse*. Advances in Applied Linguistics. London and New York: Continuum, 2003.

Carnahan, Kevin. "Moral Realism." In *The Oxford Handbook of Reinhold Niebuhr*, edited by Robin Lovin and Joshua Mauldin, 328–346. New York: Oxford University Press, 2021.

Carr, Anne E. *Transforming Grace: Christian Tradition and Women's Experience*. San Francisco: Harper & Row, 1988.

Charles, R. H. *The Greek Version of the Testament of the Twelve Patriarchs*. Oxford: Clarendon Press, 1908.

Charlesworth, James H. "A History of Pseudepigrapha Research: The Re-Emerging Importance of the Pseudepigrapha." In *Aufstieg und Niedergang der Römischen Welt*, Part II, Volume 19, Half Volume 1, edited by Wolfgang Haase and Hildegard Temporini, 54–88. Boston: De Gruyter, 1979.

———, ed. *The Old Testament Pseudepigrapha. Vol. 1*. Garden City, NY: Doubleday, 1983.

———, ed. *The Old Testament Pseudepigrapha, Vol. 2*. Garden City, NY: Doubleday, 1985.

Childes, Brevard. "Adam." In *Interpreter's Dictionary of the Bible*, 1:42–44. Nashville, KY: Abingdon Press, 1962.

Church, F. Forrester. "Sex and Salvation in Tertullian." *Harvard Theological Review* 68, no. 2 (April 1975): 83–101.

Clark, Elizabeth. "Status Feminae: Tertullian and the Uses of Paul." In *Tertullian and Paul*, edited by Todd D Still and David E Wilhite, 127–155. New York: Bloomsbury, 2019.

Cloutier, David, and Luke Timothy Johnson. "The Church & Transgender Identity." *Commonweal*, February 27, 2017. https://www.commonwealmagazine.org/church-transgender-identity.

Coakley, Sarah. *God, Sexuality and the Self: An Essay "on the Trinity."* New York: Cambridge University Press, 2013.

———. *Powers and Submissions: Spirituality, Philosophy, and Gender*. Challenges in Contemporary Theology. Malden, MA: Blackwell, 2002.

Collins, John J. "Before the Fall: The Earliest Interpretations of Adam and Eve." In *The Idea of Biblical Interpretation: Essays in Honor of James L. Kugel*, edited by Hindy Najman and Judith Newman, 83:293–308. Supplements to the Journal for the Study of Judaism. Leiden: Brill, 2004.

———. *Jewish Wisdom in the Hellenistic Age*. The Old Testament Library. Louisville, KY: Westminster John Knox Press, 1997.

Cone, James H. *A Black Theology of Liberation*. New York: Lippincott, 1970.

Congar, Yves. "Marie et l'Église dans la Pensée Patristique." *Revue des Sciences Philosophiques et Théologiques* 38, no. 1 (1954): 3–38.

———. "Marie et l'Église: Perspective Médiévale." *Revue des Sciences Philosophiques et Théologiques* 39, no. 3 (1955): 408–412.

Congregation for the Doctrine of the Faith. "Instruction on the Ecclesial Vocation of Theologian." Accessed October 5, 2022. https://www.vatican.va/roman_curia/congregations/cfaith/documents/rc_con_cfaith_doc_19900524_theologian-vocation_en.html.

Conron, K., K. O'Neill, L. Vasquez, and C. Mallory. *Prohibiting Gender-Affirming Medical Care for Youth*. Los Angeles, CA: Williams Institute, UCLA School of Law, 2022.

Conway, Colleen M. *Behold the Man: Jesus and Greco-Roman Masculinity*. New York: Oxford University Press, 2008.

Conzelmann, Hans. *1 Corinthians: A Commentary on the First Epistle to the Corinthians*. Edited by George MacRae. Translated by James Weitch. Hermeneia. Philadelphia: Fortress Press, 1975.

Daley, Brian E. *God Visible: Patristic Christology Reconsidered*. Changing Paradigms in Historical and Systematic Theology. Oxford, UK: Oxford University Press, 2018.

Daniel-Huges, Carly. "'We Are Called to Monogamy': Marriage, Virginity, and the Resurrection of the Fleshly Body in Tertullian of Carthage." In *Coming Back to Life: The Permeability of Past and Present, Mortality and Immortality, Death and Life in the Ancient Mediterranean*, edited by Carly Daniel-Hughes and Frederick S. Tappenden. Montréal, QC: McGill University Library and Archives, 2017.

Daniels, Brandy. "Queer Theory." In *Religion: Embodied Religion*, edited by Kent Brintnall, 289–308. Macmillan Interdisciplinary Handbooks. Farmington Hills, MI: Macmillan Reference USA, a part of Gale, Cengage Learning, 2016.

Daston, Lorraine, and Katharine Park. "The Hermaphrodite and the Orders of Nature: Sexual Ambiguity in Early Modern France." In *Premodern Sexualities*, edited by Louise Fradenburg and Carla Freccero, 117–136. New York: Routledge, 1996.

Davidmann, Sara. "Beyond Borders: Lived Experiences of Atypically Gendered Transsexual People." In *Transgender Identities: Towards a Social Analysis of Gender Diversity*, edited by Sally Hines and Tam Sanger, 186–203. Routledge Research in Gender and Society 24. New York: Routledge, 2012.

Davidson, Richard M. *Typology in Scripture: A Study of Hermeneutical Typos Structures*. Berrien Springs, MI: Andrews University Press, 1981.

Davila, J. R. "The Similitudes of Enoch." Lecture, University of St. Andrews, March 2, 2007. https://otp.wp.st-andrews.ac.uk/abstracts-lectures/the-similitudes-of-enoch/.

De Lauretis, Teresa. *Technologies of Gender: Essays on Theory, Film, and Fiction*. Theories of Representation and Difference. Bloomington, IN: Indiana University Press, 1987.

DeFranza, Megan K. *Sex Difference in Christian Theology: Male, Female, and Intersex in the Image of God*. Grand Rapids, MI: Eerdmans, 2015.

Deignan, Alice. *Metaphor and Corpus Linguistics*. Converging Evidence in Language and Communication Research 6. Amsterdam and Philadelphia: J. Benjamins Publishing, 2005.

DesCamp, Mary Therese. *Metaphor and Ideology: Liber Antiquitatum Biblicarum and Literary Methods through a Cognitive Lens*. Biblical Interpretation Series 87. Boston: Brill, 2007.

———. "Why Are These Women Here? An Examination of the Sociological Setting of Pseudo-Philo through Comparative Reading." *Journal for the Study of the Pseudepigrapha* 8, no. 16 (July 1997): 53–80.

DeSilva, David A. *Introducing the Apocrypha: Message, Context, and Significance*. Grand Rapids, MI: Baker Academic, 2018.

Devor, Aaron H., and Ardel Haefele-Thomas. *Transgender: A Reference Handbook*. Contemporary World Issues. Santa Barbara, CA: ABC-CLIO, 2019.

DeVun, Leah. *The Shape of Sex: Nonbinary Gender from Genesis to the Renaissance*. New York: Columbia University Press, 2021.

Dinter, Paul. "Christ's Body as Male and Female." *Cross Currents* 44, no. 3 (2013): 390–399.

Dodson, Joseph. *The "Powers" of Personification: Rhetorical Purpose in the "Book of Wisdom" and the Letter to the Romans*. Beihefte zur Zeitschrift für die Neutestamentliche Wissenschaft 161. New York: De Gruyter, 2008.

Donovan, Mary Ann. *One Right Reading? A Guide to Irenaeus*. Collegeville, MN: Liturgical Press, 1997.

Dulk, Matthijs den. *Between Jews and Heretics: Refiguring Justin Martyr's Dialogue with Trypho*. New York: Routledge, 2020.

Dunn, Geoffrey. "Mary's Virginity 'in Partu' and Tertullian's Anti-Docetism in 'De Carne Christi' Reconsidered." *The Journal of Theological Studies* 58, no. 2 (October 2007): 467–484.

Dunn, James D. G. *Christology in the Making: A New Testament Inquiry into the Origins of the Doctrine of the Incarnation*. 2nd ed. Grand Rapids, MI: Eerdmans, 1996.

———. *Romans 1–8*. Word Biblical Commentary 38. Dallas, TX: Word Books, 1988.

———. *The New Perspective on Paul*. Rev. ed. Wissenschaftliche Untersuchungen Zum Neuen Testament 185. Grand Rapids, MI: Eerdmans, 2008.

———. *The Theology of Paul the Apostle*. Grand Rapids, MI: Eerdmans, 2008.

Dunning, Benjamin H. *Christ without Adam: Subjectivity and Sexual Difference in the Philosophers' Paul*. Gender, Theory, and Religion. New York: Columbia University Press, 2014.

———. *Specters of Paul: Sexual Difference in Early Christian Thought*. Divinations. Philadelphia: University of Pennsylvania Press, 2011.

Ehrman, Bart D., and Zlatko Pleše, eds. *The Apocryphal Gospels: Texts and Translations*. New York: Oxford University Press, 2011.

Elder, Nicholas. "'Wretch I Am!' Eve's Tragic Speech-in-Character in Romans 7:7–25." *Journal of Biblical Literature* 137, no. 3 (2018): 743–763.

Ellis, Theresa Ann. "Is Eve the 'Woman' in Sirach 25:24?" *The Catholic Biblical Quarterly* 73, no. 4 (October 2011): 723–742.

Elm, Susanna. *Sons of Hellenism, Fathers of the Church: Emperor Julian, Gregory of Nazianzus, and the Vision of Rome*. Transformation of the Classical Heritage 49. Berkeley, CA: University of California Press, 2014.

Farley, Margaret A. *Just Love: A Framework for Christian Sexual Ethics*. New York: Continuum, 2012.

Fastiggi, Robert. "Mary in the Work of Redemption." In *The Oxford Handbook of Mary*, edited by Chris Maunder, 303–319. Oxford Handbooks. New York: Oxford University Press, 2019.

Fausto-Sterling, Anne. *Sexing the Body: Gender Politics and the Construction of Sexuality*. New York: Basic Books, 2000.

———. "The Five Sexes." *The Sciences* 33, no. 2 (March 4, 1993): 20–24.

———. "The Five Sexes Revisited." *The Sciences* 40, no. 4 (July 8, 2000): 18–23.

Fee, Gordon D. *Pauline Christology: An Exegetical-Theological Study*. Peabody, MA: Hendrickson Publishers, 2007.

———. *The First Epistle to the Corinthians*. Rev. ed. The New International Commentary on the New Testament. Grand Rapids, Michigan: William B. Eerdmans Publishing Company, 2014.

Finlay, Barbara. "Was Tertullian a Misogynist? A Reconsideration." *Journal of The Historical Society* 3, no. 3–4 (June 2003): 503–525.

Fitzmyer, Joseph A. *First Corinthians: A New Translation with Introduction and Commentary*. The Anchor Yale Bible 32. New Haven, CT: Yale University Press, 2008.

———. *Paul and His Theology: A Brief Sketch*. 2nd ed. Englewood Cliffs, NJ: Prentice Hall, 1989.

———. "The Consecutive Meaning of ΕΦ' Ω in Romans 5.12." *New Testament Studies* 39 (July 1993): 321–339.

Flannery, Austin, ed. "Dogmatic Constitution on the Church, Lumen Gentium, 21 November, 1964." In *Vatican Council II: The Conciliar and Post Conciliar Documents*, 350–426. Vatican Collection. Collegeville, MN: Liturgical Press, 1974.

Flemming, Rebecca. *Medicine and the Making of Roman Women: Gender, Nature, and Authority from Celsus to Galen*. New York: Oxford University Press, 2000.

Forbs, Christopher. "Paul and Rhetorical Comparison." In *Paul in the Greco-Roman World: A Handbook Volume I*, edited by J. Paul Sampley. London: Bloomsbury T&T Clark, 2016.

Ford, Craig. "Born That Way? The Challenge of Trans/Gender Identity for Catholic Theology." In *Sex, Love, and Families: Catholic Perspectives*, edited by Julie Hanlon Rubio and Jason E. King, 91–102. Collegeville, MN: Liturgical Press Academic, 2020.

Foster, Paul. "Justin and Paul." In *Paul and the Second Century*, edited by Michael F. Bird and Joseph R. Dodson. Library of New Testament Studies 412. New York: T&T Clark, 2011.

Fredriksen, Paula. *Paul: The Pagans' Apostle*. New Haven: Yale University Press, 2017.

———. *When Christians Were Jews: The First Generation*. New Haven, PA: Yale University Press, 2018.

Fretheim, Terrence. "Genesis," in *New Interpreter's Bible*, Vol. 1, edited by Leander Keck, 367. Nashville, TN: Abingdon Press, 1994.

Fulford, Ben. "Gregory of Nazianzus and Biblical Interpretation." In *Re-Reading Gregory of Nazianzus: Essays on History, Theology, and Culture*, edited by Christopher A. Beeley, 31–48. CUA Studies in Early Christianity. Washington, D.C: Catholic University of America Press, 2012.

Gambero, Luigi, and Thomas Buffer. *Mary and the Fathers of the Church: The Blessed Virgin Mary in Patristic Thought*. San Francisco: Ignatius Press, 1999.

Gaventa, Beverly Roberts. *Mary. Glimpses of the Mother of Jesus*. Personalities of the New Testament. Edinburgh: T&T Clark, 1999.

Gilligan, Carol. *In a Different Voice: Psychological Theory and Women's Development*. Cambridge, MA: Harvard University Press, 2003.

Girshick, Lori B. *Transgender Voices: Beyond Women and Men*. Hanover, NH: University Press of New England, 2008.

Glicksman, Andrew T. *Wisdom of Solomon 10: A Jewish Hellenistic Reinterpretation of Early Israelite History through Sapiential Lenses*. Deuterocanonical and Cognate Literature Studies 9. Berlin: De Gruyter, 2011.

Goppelt, Leonhard. *Typos: The Typological Interpretation of the Old Testament in the New*. Grand Rapids, MI: Eerdmans, 1982.

Goss, Robert, ed. *Queering Christ: Beyond Jesus Acted Up*. Cleveland, OH: Pilgrim Press, 2002.

Grant, Robert M. *Irenaeus of Lyons*. The Early Church Fathers. New York: Routledge, 1997.

Gregory of Nazianzus. *On God and Christ: The Five Theological Orations and Two Letters to Cledonius*. Edited by Frederick Williams. Translated by Lionel R. Wickham. Crestwood, NY: St. Vladimir's Seminary Press, 2002.

———. *On God and Man: The Theological Poetry of St. Gregory of Nazianzus*. Translated by Peter Gilbert. Popular Patristics Series. Crestwood, NY: St. Vladimir's Seminary Press, 2001.

———. *Select Orations*. Translated by Martha Vinson. Fathers of the Church 107. Washington, DC: Catholic University of America Press, 2017.

Gregory of Nazianzus, and Cyril of Jerusalem. *Cyril of Jerusalem and Gregory Nazianzen*. Edited by Philip Schaff and Henry Wace. Translated by Charles Browne and Swallow. Nicene and Post-Nicene Fathers: Second Series 7. Buffalo, NY: Christian Literature Publishing, 1894.

Gudorf, Christine. "The Erosion of Sexual Dimorphism: Challenges to Religion and Religious Ethics." *Journal of the American Academy of Religion* 69, no. 4 (December 1, 2001): 863–892.

Hadas-Lebel, Mireille. *Philo of Alexandria: A Thinker in the Jewish Diaspora*. Studies in Philo of Alexandria 7. Boston: Brill, 2012.

Halperin, David M., and Michel Foucault. *Saint Foucault: Towards a Gay Hagiography*. New York: Oxford University Press, 1997.

Hampson, Margaret Daphne. *Theology and Feminism*. Signposts in Theology. Cambridge, MA: Blackwell, 1990.

Hanneken, Todd Russell. *The Subversion of the Apocalypses in the Book of Jubilees*. Early Judaism and Its Literature 34. Atlanta, GA: Society of Biblical Literature, 2012.

Harrison, Verna. "Eve, the Mother of God, and Other Women." *The Ecumenical Review* 60, no. 1–2 (January 4, 2008): 71–81.

———. "Gender, Generation, and Virginity in Cappadocian Theology." *The Journal of Theological Studies* 47 (April 1, 1996): 38–68.

———. "Male and Female in Cappadocian Theology." *The Journal of Theological Studies* 41, no. 2 (1990): 441–471.

———. "The Breast of the Father." In *Feminism and Theology*. Edited by Janet Martin Soskice and Diana Lipton. Oxford Readings in Feminism. New York: Oxford University Press, 2003.

Hays, Richard B. *First Corinthians*. Interpretation. Louisville, KY: John Knox Press, 1997.

———. *The Moral Vision of the New Testament: Community, Cross, New Creation: A Contemporary Introduction to New Testament Ethics*. San Francisco: HarperSanFrancisco, 1996.

Hayward, C. T. R. "The Figure of Adam in Pseudo-Philo's Biblical Antiquities." *Journal for the Study of Judaism in the Person, Hellenistic, and Roman Period* 23, no. 1 (June 1992): 1–20.

Heffernan, Thomas J., ed. *The Passion of Perpetua and Felicity*. New York: Oxford University Press, 2012.

Herdt, Gilbert H., ed. *Third Sex, Third Gender: Beyond Sexual Dimorphism in Culture and History*. New York: Zone Books, 1996.

Herman, J. L., T. N. T. Brown, and A. P. Haas. *Suicide Thoughts and Attempts among Transgender Adults: Findings from the 2015 U.S. Transgender Survey*. Los Angeles, CA: Williams Institute, UCLA School of Law, 2019.

Higgins, Jean. "Anastasius Sinaita and the Superiority of the Woman." *Journal of Biblical Literature* 97, no. 2 (1978): 253–256.

Hines, Sally. "Introduction." In *Transgender Identities: Towards a Social Analysis of Gender Diversity*. Edited by Sally Hines and Tam Sanger. Routledge Research in Gender and Society 24. New York: Routledge, 2012.

Hitchcock, Francis. *The Treatise of Irenaeus of Lugdunum against the Heresies*. London: Society for Promoting Christian Knowledge, 1916.

Hobbs, Angela. *Plato and the Hero: Courage, Manliness, and the Impersonal Good*. New York: Cambridge University Press, 2006.

Hock, Ronald. "Paul and Greco-Roman Education." In *Paul in the Greco-Roman World: A Handbook Volume I*, edited by J. Paul Sampley, 230–253. London: Bloomsbury T&T Clark, 2016.

———. *The Infancy Gospels of James and Thomas*. The Scholars Bible 2. Santa Rosa, CA: Polebridge Press, 1995.

Hofer, Andrew. *Christ in the Life and Teaching of Gregory of Nazianzus*. Oxford Early Christian Studies. New York: Oxford University Press, 2013.

Holmes, Mary. *What Is Gender? Sociological Approaches*. Los Angeles: Sage, 2007.

Holsinger-Friesen, Thomas. *Irenaeus and Genesis: A Study of Competition in Early Christian Hermeneutics*. Journal of Theological Interpretation Supplements 1. Winona Lake, IN: Eisenbrauns, 2009.

Horst, Pieter Willem van der. "Portraits of Biblical Women in Pseudo-Philo's Liber Antiquitatum Biblicarum*." *Journal for the Study of the Pseudepigrapha* 3, no. 5 (October 1989): 29–46.

Hultgren, Stephen. "The Origin of Paul's Doctrine of the Two Adams in 1 Corinthians 15:45–49." *Journal for the Study of the New Testament* 25, no. 3 (2003): 343–370.

Irenaeus. *On the Apostolic Preaching*. Translated by John Behr. Crestwood, NY: St. Vladimir's Seminary Press, 1997.

Isherwood, Lisa, and Marcella Althaus-Reid, eds. *Trans/Formations*. London: SCM Press, 2009.

Jacobs, Sue-Ellen, Wesley Thomas, and Sabine Lang, eds. *Two-Spirit People: Native American Gender Identity, Sexuality, and Spirituality*. Urbana, IL: University of Illinois Press, 1997.

Jensen, Anne. *God's Self-Confident Daughters: Early Christianity and the Liberation of Women*. Louisville, KY: Westminster John Knox Press, 1996.

Jewett, Robert. *Romans: A Commentary*. Hermeneia. Minneapolis, MN: Fortress Press, 2007.

Johnson, Elizabeth A. *She Who Is: The Mystery of God in Feminist Theological Discourse*. New York: Crossroad, 2002.

———. *Truly Our Sister: A Theology of Mary in the Communion of Saints*. New York: Continuum, 2006.

Jones, Beth Felker. *Marks of His Wounds: Gender Politics and Bodily Resurrection*. New York: Oxford University Press, 2007.

Jonge, Marinus de, and Johannes Tromp. *The Life of Adam and Eve and Related Literature*. Guides to Apocrypha and Pseudepigrapha. Sheffield, England: Academic Press, 1997.

Jung, Patricia Beattie. *Sex on Earth as It Is in Heaven: A Christian Eschatology of Desire*. Albany, NY: State University of New York, 2017.

Jung, Patricia Beattie, and Joan Roughgarden. "Gender in Heaven: The Story of the Ethiopian Eunuch in Light of Evolutionary Biology." In *God, Science, Sex, Gender: An Interdisciplinary Approach to Christian Ethics*, edited by Patricia Beattie Jung and Aana Marie Vigen, 225–240. Urbana, IL: University of Illinois Press, 2010.

Karkazis, Katrina. "The Misuses of 'Biological Sex.'" *The Lancet* 394, no. 10212 (November 2019): 1898–1899.

Käsemann, Ernst. *Commentary on Romans*. Translated by Geoffrey William Bromiley. Grand Rapids, MI: William B. Eerdmans, 1980.

———. *New Testament Questions of Today*. Philadelphia: Fortress Press, 1969.

Katajala-Peltomaa, Sari, and Raisa Maria Toivo. *Lived Religion and Gender in Late Medieval and Early Modern Europe*. Themes in Medieval and Early Modern History. New York: Routledge, 2021.

Keck, Leander E. *Romans*. Abingdon New Testament Commentaries. Nashville, TN: Abingdon Press, 2005.

Keegan, Cáel. "Transgender Studies, or How to Do Things with Trans*." In *The Cambridge Companion to Queer Studies*, edited by Siobhan B. Somerville, 66–78. New York: Cambridge University Press, 2020.

Kelly, Henry Ansgar. "Adam Citings before the Intrusion of Satan: Recontextualizing Paul's Theology of Sin and Death." *Biblical Theology Bulletin* 44, no. 1 (February 2014): 13–28.

Kertelge, Karl. "Adam und Christus: Die Sünde Adams im Lichte der Erlösungstat Christi nach Röm 5,12–21." In *Anfänge der Christologie: Festschrift für Ferdinand Hahn zum 65. Geburtstag*, edited by Cilliers Breytenbach, Henning Paulsen, and Christine Gerber, 141–145. Göttingen: Vandenhoeck & Ruprecht, 1991.

Kierkegaard, Søren. *Journalen JJ:167 (1843)*. Søren Kierkegaards Skrifter 18. Søren Kierkegaard Research Center, 1997.

King, Helen. "The Body beyond Laqueur: Hippocratic Sex and Its Rediscovery." In *Natur—Geschlecht—Politik*, edited by Andreas Höfele and Beate Kellner, 199–216. Leiden: Brill | Fink, 2020.

———. *The One-Sex Body on Trial: The Classical and Early Modern Evidence*. The History of Medicine in Context. Burlington, VT: Ashgate, 2013.

King, Karen L. "Jesus." In *The Oxford Handbook of New Testament, Gender, and Sexuality*, edited by Benjamin H. Dunning, 405–427. New York: Oxford University Press, 2019.

———. *The Secret Revelation of John*. Cambridge, MA: Harvard University Press, 2006.

Kretschmar, Georg. "'Natus ex Maria Virgine': Zur Konzeption und Theologie des Protevangelium Jacobi." In *Anfänge der Christologie: Festschrift für Ferdinand Hahn zum 65. Geburtstag*, edited by Cilliers Breytenbach, Ferdinand Hahn, and Henning Paulsen, 417–428. Göttingen: Vandenhoeck und Ruprecht, 1991.

Kuefler, Mathew. *The Manly Eunuch: Masculinity, Gender Ambiguity, and Christian Ideology in Late Antiquity*. The Chicago Series on Sexuality, History, and Society. Chicago: University of Chicago Press, 2001.

Kugel, James L. *A Walk through Jubilees: Studies in the Book of Jubilees and the World of Its Creation*. Supplements to the Journal for the Study of Judaism 156. Boston: Brill, 2012.

———. *How to Read the Bible: A Guide to Scripture, Then and Now*. New York: Free Press, 2008.

———. *Traditions of the Bible: A Guide to the Bible as It Was at the Start of the Common Era*. Cambridge, MA: Harvard University Press, 1998.

Kugler, Robert A. *The Testaments of the Twelve Patriarchs*. Guides to Apocrypha and Pseudepigrapha. Sheffield, UK: Sheffield Academic Press, 2001.

Lachs, S. T. "Some Textual Observations on the Apocalypsis Mosis and the Vita Adae et Evae." *Journal for the Study of Judaism in the Person, Hellenistic, and Roman Period* 13, no. 1/2 (December 1982): 172–176.

Lang, Sabine. *Men as Women, Women as Men: Changing Gender in Native American Cultures*. Austin, TX: University of Texas Press, 1998.

Lanne, Emmanuel. "Marian Doctrine and Piety up to the Council of Chalcedon: The Fathers and the Liturgy." Edited by Anglican/Roman Catholic International

Commission, Nicholas Sagovsky, and Adelbert Denaux, 36–59. New York: T&T Clark, 2007.

Laqueur, Thomas. *Making Sex: Body and Gender from the Greeks to Freud*. Cambridge, MA: Harvard University Press, 2003.

Lawson, John. *The Biblical Theology of Saint Irenaeus*. Eugene, OR: Wipf & Stock, 2006.

Lee, Chris W. *Death Warning in the Garden of Eden: The Early Reception History of Genesis 2:17*. Forschungen Zum Alten Testament. 2. Reihe 115. Tübingen: Mohr Siebeck, 2020.

Levine, Amy-Jill. "The Gospels and Acts." In *The Oxford Handbook of New Testament, Gender, and Sexuality*, edited by Benjamin H. Dunning, 293–314. Oxford University Press, 2019.

Levison, John R. "Is Eve to Blame? A Contextual Analysis of Sirach 25:24." *The Catholic Biblical Quarterly* 47, no. 4 (October 1985): 617–623.

———. *Portraits of Adam in Early Judaism: From Sirach to 2 Baruch*. Journal for the Study of the Pseudepigrapha, Supplement Series 1. Sheffield: Sheffield Academic Press, 1988.

———. "The Exoneration of Eve in the Apocalypse of Moses." *Journal for the Study of Judaism in the Person, Hellenistic, and Roman Period* 20, no. 2 (December 1989): 135–150.

Li, Xi. "Ben Sira on the Free Will Problem: A Comparison with Chrysippus." *Harvard Theological Review* 114, no. 3 (July 2021): 328–345.

Lightfoot, J. L., ed. *The Sibylline Oracles: With Introduction, Translation, and Commentary on the First and Second Books*. New York: Oxford University Press, 2007.

Lightsey, Pamela R. *Our Lives Matter: A Womanist Queer Theology*. Eugene, OR: Pickwick Publications, 2015.

Littlemore, Jeannette. *Metonymy: Hidden Shortcuts in Language, Thought and Communication*. New York: Cambridge University Press, 2015.

Loughlin, Gerard. "Omphalos." In *Queer Theology: Rethinking the Western Body*, edited by Gerard Loughlin, 115–127. Malden, MA: Blackwell, 2007.

Loughlin, Gerard, and Gerard Loughlin, eds. "Introduction: The End of Sex." In *Queer Theology: Rethinking the Western Body*. Malden, MA: Blackwell Pub, 2007.

Louth, Andrew. "Mary in Patristics." In *The Oxford Handbook of Mary*. Edited by Chris Maunder. Oxford Handbooks. New York: Oxford University Press, 2019.

Lovin, Robin W. *Christian Faith and Public Choices: The Social Ethics of Barth, Brunner, and Bonhoeffer*. Philadelphia, PA: Fortress Press, 1984.

———. *Christian Realism and the New Realities*. New York: Cambridge University Press, 2008.

———. *Reinhold Niebuhr and Christian Realism*. New York: Cambridge University Press, 1995.

MacDonald, Dennis Ronald. *The Legend and the Apostle: The Battle for Paul in Story and Canon*. Philadelphia: Westminster, 1983.

MacDonald, Margaret Y. *Early Christian Women and Pagan Opinion: The Power of the Hysterical Woman*. New York: Cambridge University Press, 1996.

Markert, Katja, and Udo Hahn. "Understanding Metonymies in Discourse." *Artificial Intelligence* 135, no. 1–2 (February 2002): 145–198.

Martin, Dale B. *New Testament History & Literature*. New Haven, CT: Yale University Press, 2012.

Matthews, Shelly. "A Feminist Analysis of the Veiling Passage (1 Corinthians 11:2–16): Who Really Cares That Paul Was Not a Gender Egalitarian After All?" *Lectio Difficilior* 2 (2015): 1–20.

McGlynn, Moyna. *Divine Judgement and Divine Benevolence in the Book of Wisdom*, 127–130. Tübingen: Mohr Siebeck, 2001.

Meeks, Wayne. "The Image of the Androgyne: Some Uses of a Symbol in Earliest Christianity." *History of Religions* 13, no. 3 (February 1974): 165–208.

Migne, Jacques Paul, ed. *Patrologiae Cursus Completus*. Series Graeca 35–36. Paris: Imprimerie Catholique, 1857.

Milbank, John. "What Liberal Intellectuals Get Wrong about Transgenderism." *Catholic Herald*, January 13, 2017. https://catholicherald.co.uk/long-read-what-liberal-intellectuals-get-wrong-about-transgenderism/.

Miravalle, Mark I. *"With Jesus": The Story of Mary Co-Redemptrix*. Goleta, CA: Queenship, 2003.

Mollenkott, Virginia R. *Omnigender: A Trans-Religious Approach*. Revised and Expanded edition. Cleveland, OH: Pilgrim Press, 2007.

Moltmann, Jürgen. *The Trinity and the Kingdom: The Doctrine of God*. Minneapolis, MN: Fortress Press, 1993.

Moo, Douglas J. *The Letter to the Romans*, 2nd ed. The New International Commentary on the New Testament. Grand Rapids: Eerdmans, 2018.

Moore, Stephen D. "'O Man, Who Art Thou. . .?': Masculinity Studies and New Testament Studies." In *New Testament Masculinities*, edited by Stephen D. Moore and Janice Capel Anderson, 1–22. Society of Biblical Literature Semeia Studies 45. Atlanta, GA: Society of Biblical Literature, 2003.

Moss, Candida. "Heavenly Healing: Eschatological Cleansing and the Resurrection of the Dead in the Early Church." *Journal of the American Academy of Religion* 79, no. 4 (December 1, 2011): 991–1017.

Mosse, George L. *The Image of Man: The Creation of Modern Masculinity*. New York: Oxford University Press, 2010.

Murphy, Frederick J. *Pseudo-Philo: Rewriting the Bible*. New York: Oxford University Press, 1993.

Nasr, Seyyed Hossein, ed. *The Study Quran: A New Translation and Commentary*. New York: HarperOne, 2015.

Newsom, Carol A., and Sharon H. Ringe, eds. *Women's Bible Commentary*. Expanded ed. Louisville, KY: Westminster John Knox Press, 1998.

Niebuhr, Reinhold. *The Nature and Destiny of Man*. 2 vols. London, UK: Nisbet & Co., 1941.

Niehoff, Maren. *Philo of Alexandria: An Intellectual Biography*. The Anchor Yale Bible Reference Library. New Haven, CT: Yale University Press, 2018.

Norden, Christopher G. "Paul's Use of the Psalms in Romans: A Critical Analysis." *Evangelical Quarterly* 88, no. 1 (April 26, 2016): 71–88.

Nussbaum, Martha. "Constructing Love, Desire, and Care." In *Sex, Preference, and Family: Essays on Law and Nature*. Edited by Martha Nussbaum and David Estlund. New York: Oxford University Press, 1997.

———. "The Professor of Parody." *The New Republic*, February 22, 1999.

Nyström, David E. *The Apology of Justin Martyr: Literary Strategies and the Defence of Christianity*. Wissenschaftliche Untersuchungen Zum Neuen Testament. 2. Reihe 462. Tübingen: Mohr Siebeck, 2018.

O'Brien, Michelle. "Intersex, Medicine, Diversity, Identity and Spirituality." In *This Is My Body: Hearing the Theology of Transgender Christians*. Edited by Christina Beardsley and Michelle O'Brien. London: Darton, Longman and Todd, 2016.

O'Donovan, Oliver. "Transsexualism and Christian Marriage." *The Journal of Religious Ethics* 11, no. 1 (1983): 135–162.

Ong, Walter J. *The Presence of the Word: Some Prolegomena for Cultural and Religious History*. New Haven, CT: Yale University Press, 1967.

Ong, Walter J., and John Hartley. *Orality and Literacy: The Technologizing of the Word*. New York: Routledge, 2002.

Orlov, A., Gabriele Boccaccini, and Jason Zurawski, eds. *New Perspectives on 2 Enoch: No Longer Slavonic Only*. Studia Judaeoslavica 4. Boston: Brill, 2012.

Osborn, Eric. *Irenaeus of Lyons*. New York: Cambridge University Press, 2001.

———. *Tertullian, First Theologian of the West*. New York: Cambridge University Press, 2003.

Otten, Willemien. "Christ's Birth of a Virgin Who Became a Wife: Flesh and Speech in Tertullian's De Carne Christi." *Vigiliae Christanae* 51, no. 3 (1997): 247–260.

Ovidius Naso, Publius. *Ovid. 3: Metamorphoses Books I–VIII*. Translated by Frank Justus Miller. The Loeb Classical Library 42. New York: G.P. Putnam's Son's, 1916.

Pagels, Elaine. *Adam, Eve, and the Serpent*. Penguin Book. New York: Penguin Books, 1990.

Park, Katharine. "Rethinking the 'One-Sex' Body." Lecture presented at the The Lionel Trilling Seminar, Columbia University, November 24, 2014. https://www.youtube.com/watch?v=AyC5J9riUWM.

Parker, Holt. "The Teratogenic Grid." In *Roman Sexualities*, edited by Judith P. Hallett and Marilyn B. Skinner, 47–65. Princeton, NJ: Princeton University Press, 1997.

Parvis, Sara. "Irenaeus, Women, and Tradition." In *Irenaeus: Life, Scripture, Legacy*. Edited by Sara Parvis and Paul Foster. Minneapolis, MN: Fortress Press, 2012.

Parvis, Sarah, and Paul Foster. "Introduction: Irenaeus and His Traditions." In *Irenaeus: Life, Scripture, Legacy*. Edited by Sarah Parvis and Paul Foster. Minneapolis, MN: Fortress Press, 2012.

Pasternack, Carol Braun. "Negotiating Gender in Anglo-Saxon England." In *Gender and Difference in the Middle Ages*, edited by Sharon A. Farmer and Carol Braun Pasternack, 107–142. Medieval Cultures 32. Minneapolis, MN: University of Minnesota Press, 2003.

Pate, C. Marvin. *The Reverse of the Curse: Paul, Wisdom, and the Law*. Wissenschaftliche Untersuchungen zum Neuen Testament 114. Tübingen: Mohr Siebeck, 2000.

Peletz, Michael G. *Gender Pluralism: Southeast Asia since Early Modern Times*. New York: Routledge, 2009.

Pelikan, Jaroslav. *Mary through the Centuries: Her Place in the History of Culture*. New Haven, CT: Yale University Press, 1996.

———. *The Emergence of the Catholic Tradition: 100–600*. The Christian Tradition: A History of the Development of Doctrine 1. Chicago, IL: University of Chicago Press, 2007.

Petrey, Taylor G. "The Resurrection Body." In *The Oxford Handbook of New Testament, Gender, and Sexuality*, edited by Benjamin H. Dunning, 660–674. New York: Oxford University Press, 2019.

Philo of Alexandria. *Philo: Questions and Answers on Genesis*. Translated by Ralph Marcus. The Loeb Classical Library 380. Cambridge, MA: Harvard University Press, 2007.

———. *Philo, Volume 1*. Translated by F. H. Colson and G. H. Witaker. The Loeb Classical Library 226. Cambridge, MA: Harvard University Press, 2004.

Philo of Alexandria, Albert C. Geljon, and David T. Runia. *Philo of Alexandria, On Cultivation: Introduction, Translation, and Commentary*. Philo of Alexandria Commentary Series 4. Boston: Brill, 2013.

Philo of Alexandria, and David T. Runia. *On the Creation of the Cosmos According to Moses: Introduction, Translation and Commentary*. Philo of Alexandria Commentary Series 1. Boston: Brill, 2001.

Porter, Stanley, and Bryan Dyer. "Oral Texts? A Reassessment of the Oral and Rhetorical Nature of Paul's Letters in Light of Recent Studies." *Journal of the Evangelical Theological Society* 55, no. 2 (2012): 323–341.

Porter, Stanley E. "Paul of Tarsus and His Letters." In *Handbook of Classical Rhetoric in the Hellenistic Period (330 B.C.–A.D. 400)*. Edited by Stanley E. Porter. New York: Brill, 1997.

Presley, Stephen O. *The Intertextual Reception of Genesis 1–3 in Irenaeus of Lyons*. The Bible in Ancient Christianity 8. Boston: Brill, 2015.

Prosser, Jay. "Judith Butler: Queer Feminism, Transgender, and the Transubstantiation of Sex." In *The Transgender Studies Reader*, edited by Susan Stryker, 257–280. New York: Routledge, 2006.

Quasten, Johannes. *Patrology. 1: The Beginnings of Patristic Literature*. Westminster, MD: Newman Press, 1962.

Radden, Günter, and Zoltán Kövecses. "Towards a Theory of Metonymy." In *Human Cognitive Processing*, edited by Klaus-Uwe Panther and Günter Radden, 17–59. Amsterdam: John Benjamins Publishing Company, 1999.

Raymond, Janice G. *The Transsexual Empire: The Making of the She-Male*. Boston: Beacon Press, 1979.

Reuther, Rosemary Radford. "Misogynism and Virginal Feminism in the Fathers of the Church." In *Religion and Sexism: Images of Woman in the Jewish and Christian Traditions*, edited by Rosemary Radford Ruether, 150–183. Eugene, OR: Wipf and Stock, 1998.

Reynolds, Brian. "Marian Typological and Symbolic Imagery in Patristic Christianity." In *The Oxford Handbook of Mary*. Edited by Chris Maunder. Oxford Handbooks. New York: Oxford University Press, 2019.

Rhee, Helen. "Irenaeus and Paul: Sexuality, Virginity, and Women." In *Irenaeus and Paul*, edited by Todd D. Still and David E. Wilhite, 203–218. London: T&T Clark, 2020.

Ringrose, Kathryn. "Reconfiguring the Prophet Daniel: Gender, Sanctity, and Castration in Byzantium." In *Gender and Difference in the Middle Ages*. Edited by Sharon A. Farmer and Carol Braun Pasternack. Medieval Cultures 32. Minneapolis, MN: University of Minnesota Press, 2003.

Roetzel, Calvin J. *Paul, a Jew on the Margins*. Louisville, KY: Westminster John Knox Press, 2003.

Rogers, Eugene F. *Sexuality and the Christian Body: Their Way into the Triune God*. Challenges in Contemporary Theology. Malden, MA: Blackwell, 1999.

Roller, Duane W. *Cleopatra: A Biography*. First issued as an Oxford University paperback. Women in Antiquity. Oxford, UK: Oxford University Press, 2011.

Ruether, Rosemary Radford. *Mary, the Feminine Face of the Church*. Philadelphia: Westminster Press, 1977.

———. *Sexism and God-Talk: Toward a Feminist Theology: With a New Introduction*. 10th anniversary ed. Boston: Beacon Press, 1993.

Salih, Sara. "Introduction to 'The Lesbian Phallus and the Morphological Imaginary.'" In *The Judith Butler Reader*. Edited by Judith Butler and Sara Salih. Malden, MA: Blackwell, 2003.

Sax, Leonard. "How Common Is Intersex? A Response to Anne Fausto-Sterling." *The Journal of Sex Research* 39, no. 3 (August 1, 2002): 174–178.

Schellenberg, Ryan S. *Rethinking Paul's Rhetorical Education: Comparative Rhetoric and 2 Corinthians 10–13*. Early Christianity and Its Literature 10. Atlanta: Society of Biblical Literature, 2013.

Schiappa, Edward. *The Transgender Exigency: Defining Sex and Gender in the 21st Century*. New York: Routledge, 2022.

Schneemelcher, Wilhelm, and R. McL Wilson, eds. *New Testament Apocrypha. Vol. 1*. Revised ed. Louisville, KY: Westminster John Knox, 2003.

Schottroff, Louise. "The Seduction of Eve and Adam's Sin: Social Historical Feminist Interpretation of Paul's Understanding of Sin and Freedom." In *Text and Logos: The Humanistic Interpretation of the New Testament*, edited by Theodore W. Jennings and Hendrikus Boers, 165–174. Atlanta, GA: Scholars Press, 1990.

Schüssler Fiorenza, Elisabeth. *Jesus: Miriam's Child, Sophia's Prophet: Critical Issues in Feminist Christology*. Second ed. Cornerstones. New York: T&T Clark, 2015.

Scroggs, Robin. *The Last Adam: A Study in Pauline Anthropology*. Philadelphia: Fortress Press, 1966.

Segal, Michael. *The Book of Jubilees: Rewritten Bible, Redaction, Ideology and Theology*. Supplements to the Journal for the Study of Judaism 117. Boston: Brill, 2007.

Setzer, Claudia. *Resurrection of the Body in Early Judaism and Early Christianity: Doctrine, Community, and Self-Definition*. Boston: Brill, 2004.

Sharpe, John. "The Second Adam in the Apocalypse of Moses." *The Catholic Biblical Quarterly* 35, no. 1 (January 1973): 35–46.

Shoemaker, Stephen J. *Mary in Early Christian Faith and Devotion*. New Haven, CT: Yale University Press, 2016.

Simons, Patricia. *The Sex of Men in Premodern Europe: A Cultural History*. Cambridge Social and Cultural Histories. New York: Cambridge University Press, 2011.

Skarsaune, Oskar. *The Proof from Prophecy: A Study in Justin Martyr's Proof-Text Tradition: Text-Type, Provenance, Theological Profile*. Supplements to Novum Testamentum 56. Leiden: E.J. Brill, 1987.

Skehan, Patrick William, and Alexander A. Di Lella, eds. *The Wisdom of Ben Sira: A New Translation with Notes*. The Anchor Bible 39. New Haven, CT: Yale University Press, 2007.

Sly, Dorothy. *Philo's Perception of Women*. Providence, RI: Brown Jewdaic Studies, 2020.

Stables, Daniel. "Asia's Isle of Five Separate Genders." BBC, April 12, 2021. https://www.bbc.com/travel/article/20210411-asias-isle-of-five-separate-genders.

Stanton, Elizabeth Cady. *The Woman's Bible: A Classic Feminist Perspective*. Mineola, NY: Dover Publications, 2002.

Steenberg, M.C. "The Role of Mary as Co-Recapitulator in St Irenaeus of Lyons." *Vigiliae Christianae* 58, no. 2 (2004): 117–137.

Still, Todd D. "Shadow and Light: Marcion's (Mis)Construal of the Apostle Paul." In *Paul and the Second Century*, edited by Michael F. Bird and Joseph R. Dodson, 91–107. Library of New Testament Studies 412. New York: T&T Clark, 2011.

Stone, Michael. *A History of the Literature of Adam and Eve*. SBL Early Judaism and Its Literature 3. Atlanta, GA: Scholars Press, 1992.

———. "The Axis of History at Qumran." In *Pseudepigraphic Perspectives: The Apocrypha and Pseudepigrapha in Light of the Dead Sea Scrolls*, edited by Esther G. Chazon, Michael Stone, and Avital Pinnick, 133–149. Studies on the Texts of the Desert of Judah 31. Leiden: Brill, 1999.

———. *The Penitence of Adam*. Corpus Scriptorum Christianorum Orientalium 430. Lovanii: Peeters, 1981.

Stone, Michael E., and Matthias Henze, eds. *4 Ezra and 2 Baruch*. Minneapolis, MN: Fortress Press, 2013.

Stone, Sandy. "The Empire Strikes Back: A Posttransexual Manifesto." In *The Transgender Studies Reader*, edited by Susan Stryker and Stephen Whittle, 221–235. New York: Routledge, 2006.

Strawbridge, Jennifer R. *The Pauline Effect: The Use of the Pauline Epistles by Early Christian Writers*. Studies of the Bible and Its Reception 5. Boston: De Gruyter, 2015.

Stryker, Susan. *Transgender History: The Roots of Today's Revolution*. Revised ed. Berkeley, CA: Seal Press, 2017.

Stuart, Elizabeth. "Sacramental Flesh." In *Queer Theology: Rethinking the Western Body*, edited by Gerard Loughlin, 65–75. Malden, MA: Blackwell, 2007.

Sweeny Block, Elizabeth. "Christian Moral Freedom and the Transgender Person." *Journal of the Society of Christian Ethics* 41, no. 2 (2021): 331–347.

Tanis, Justin Edward. *Trans-Gendered: Theology, Ministry, and Communities of Faith*. Cleveland, OH: Pilgrim Press, 2003.

Tanner, Kathryn. "Experiments in Early Christian Theology, Lecture 1." Costan Lectures, Virginia Theological Seminary, March 1, 2022. https://www.youtube.com/watch?v=GZPkDxYFtSg.

———. *Jesus, Humanity and the Trinity: A Brief Systematic Theology*. Minneapolis, MN: Fortress Press, 2001.

Tavard, George H. *Woman in Christian Tradition*. Notre Dame and London: University of Notre Dame Press, 1975.

Taylor, Charles. *A Secular Age*. Cambridge, MA: Belknap Press, 2018.

———. *Sources of the Self: The Making of the Modern Identity*. Cambridge, MA: Harvard University Press, 1989.

———. *The Ethics of Authenticity*. Cambridge, MA: Harvard University Press, 2018.

———. "The Politics of Recognition." In *Multiculturalism: Examining the Politics of Recognition*, edited by Amy Gutmann, 25–73. Princeton, NJ: Princeton University Press, 1994.

Tertullian. *Tertullian's Treatise on the Incarnation*. Translated by Ernest Evans. London: S.P.C.K., 1956.

Thatcher, Adrian. *Redeeming Gender*. New York: Oxford University Press, 2016.

Thomas, Gabrielle. *The Image of God in the Theology of Gregory of Nazianzus*. New York: Cambridge University Press, 2019.

Thurman, Eric. "Looking for a Few Good Men: Mark and Masculinity." In *New Testament Masculinities*, edited by Stephen D. Moore and Janice Capel Anderson, 137–162. Society of Biblical Literature Semeia Studies 45. Atlanta, GA: Society of Biblical Literature, 2003.

Tonstad, Linn Marie. *God and Difference: The Trinity, Sexuality, and the Transformation of Finitude*. Gender, Theology and Spirituality 17. New York: Routledge, 2017.

———. *Queer Theology: Beyond Apologetics*. Cascade Companions 40. Eugene, OR: Cascade Books, 2018.

Toomey, R. B., A. K. Syvertsen, and M. Shramko. "Transgender Adolescent Suicide Behavior." *Pediatrics* 142, no. 4 (2018): 1–9.

Truth, Sojourner. "Ain't I a Woman?" National Park Service. Accessed August 11, 2022. https://www.nps.gov/articles/sojourner-truth.htm.

Vanderkam, James C, trans. *Book of Jubilees: A Critical Text.* Corpus Scriptorum Christianorum Orientalium 511. Lovanii: Peeters, 2001.

Vatican Council. "Schema of the Dogmatic Constitution on the Blessed Virgin Mary, Mother of God and Mother of Men." Translated by James T. O'Connor. *Marian Studies* 37, no. 1 (1986): 198–211.

Vogt, Kari. "'Becoming Male': One Aspect of an Early Christian Anthropology." In *Feminism and Theology*, edited by Janet Martin Soskice and Diana Lipton, 49–71. Oxford Readings in Feminism. New York: Oxford University Press, 2003.

Walters, Jonathan. "Invading the Roman Body: Manliness and Impenetrability in Roman Thought." In *Roman Sexualities*, edited by Judith P. Hallett and Marilyn B. Skinner, 29–43. Princeton, NJ: Princeton University Press, 1997.

Ward, Graham. "The Displaced Body of Jesus Christ." In *Radical Orthodoxy: A New Theology*, edited by John Milbank, Catherine Pickstock, and Graham Ward, 163–181. New York: Routledge, 1999.

———. "There Is No Sexual Difference." In *Queer Theology: Rethinking the Western Body*, edited by Gerard Loughlin, 76–85. Malden, MA: Blackwell, 2007.

Ware, James. "The Incarnation Doesn't End with the Resurrection." *Church Life Journal*, June 21, 2019. https://churchlifejournal.nd.edu/articles/the-incarnation-doesnt-end-with-the-resurrection/.

Ware, Kallistos. "The Way of the Ascetics: Negative or Affirmative?" In *Asceticism*, edited by Vincent L. Wimbush and Gay L. Byron, 3–15. Oxford, UK: Oxford University Press, 2002.

Warner, Marina. *Alone of All Her Sex: The Myth and the Cult of the Virgin Mary*. New York: Vintage Books, 1983.

Watson, Francis. *Paul and the Hermeneutics of Faith*. T&T Clark Cornerstones. London, UK: Bloomsbury T&T Clark, 2016.

Watson, Wilfred G. E. *Classical Hebrew Poetry: A Guide to Its Techniques*. Journal for the Study of the Old Testament 26. Sheffield, England: JSOT Press, 1984.

Weinandy, Thomas. "The Annunciation and Nativity: Undoing the Sinful Act of Eve: The Annunciation." *International Journal of Systematic Theology* 14, no. 2 (April 2012): 217–232.

Wendel, Susan J. *Scriptural Interpretation and Community Self-Definition in Luke-Acts and the Writings of Justin Martyr*. Supplements to Novum Testamentum 139. Boston: Brill, 2011.

Werline, Rodney. "The Transformation of Pauline Arguments in Justin Martyr's 'Dialogue with Trypho.'" *The Harvard Theological Review* 92, no. 1 (1999): 79–93.

West, Candace, and Don Zimmerman. "Doing Gender." *Gender and Society* 1, no. 2 (1987): 125–151.

Westbrook, Laurel. "Becoming Knowably Gendered: The Production of Transgender Possibilities and Constraints in the Mass and Alternative Press from 1990–2005 in the United States." In *Transgender Identities: Towards a Social Analysis of Gender Diversity*. Edited by Sally Hines and Tam Sanger. Routledge Research in Gender and Society 24. New York: Routledge, 2010.

Westermann, Claus. *Genesis 1–11: A Continental Commentary*. Minneapolis, MN: Fortress Press, 1994.

Wevers, John William. *Notes on the Greek Text of Genesis*. Septuagint and Cognate Studies Series 35. Atlanta, GA: Scholars Press, 1993.

Williams, Rowan. "The Body's Grace." In *Theology and Sexuality: Classic and Contemporary Readings*, edited by Eugene F. Rogers, 309–321. Blackwell Readings in Modern Theology. Malden, MA: Blackwell Publishers, 2002.

Witchel, Selma Feldman. "Disorders of Sex Development." *Best Practice & Research Clinical Obstetrics & Gynaecology* 48 (April 2018): 90–102.

Witherington, Ben. *What's in the Word: Rethinking the Socio-Rhetorical Character of the New Testament*. Waco, TX: Baylor University Press, 2009.

Wollstonecraft, Mary. *A Vindication of the Rights of Woman: An Authoritative Text, Backgrounds, the Wollstonecraft Debate, Criticism*. Edited by Carol Poston. 2nd ed. A Norton Critical Edition. New York: Norton, 1988.

Wolterstorff, Nicholas. *Divine Discourse: Philosophical Reflections on the Claim That God Speaks*. New York: Cambridge University Press, 1995.

Wright, N. T. "Romans." In *The New Interpreter's Bible Commentary, Volume X*. Nashville, KY: Abingdon Press, 2015.

Zervos, George. *The Protevangelium of James: Greek Text, English Translation, Critical Introduction*. Vol. 1. New York: Bloomsbury Publishing, 2019.

Zulu, Edwin. "Sin, Gender, and Responsibility: A Contextual Interpretation of Genesis 3." In *Genesis*. Edited by Athalya Brenner-Idan, Archie Chi Chung Lee, and Gale A. Yee. Texts@contexts. Minneapolis, MN: Fortress Press, 2010.

SCRIPTURE INDEX

Genesis
1 xii, xxiii, xxiv, xxv, 1, 128, 137, 170
1:1 127
1:4 127
1:5 127
1:8 127
1:10 127
1:13 127
1:14 127
1:19 127
1:20 xxv, 127
1:23 127
1:24 127
1:26 xxiv, 34
1:26–27 154, 156
1:27–28 xxiv, 44–47, 52, 55, 126, 148
1:31 127
2 xii, xxiii, xxiv, xxv, 1, 127, 137
2:1 127
2:6 62
2:7 49, 127, 142
2:17 5
2:16–17 xxv, 6, 37
2:18 1, 37, 52
2:20 128
2:22 52
2:24 129
3 xii, xxiii, xxviii, 1, 29
3:1 62
3:3 xxv
3:5 34
3:6 xxv–xxvi,
3:8 6,10, 64
3:10 64
3:13 63
3:15 69, 73
3:16 12, 65
3:17 xxix
3:19 xxvi, 49
3:20 xxvi
3:22 xxvi

Exodus
16:10 65
18:4 1
19:9 65
24:15–16 65

Judges
1:13 19

Psalms
1:3 62
8 46
8:4–8 44
23 vii
90:4 6
110 46
146:5 1

Proverbs
11:30 63

Isaiah
2–3 xii
7:14 68
27:9 30

Matthew
6:1–6 162
6:17–18 162
8:20 163
8:21 163
10:35 163
10:37 163
11:19 171
12:49 163
19:10 123
19:12 117, 123
19:27 163
23:37 171
25 177–178

Mark
3:35 163
8:31 164
8:33 164
8:34–35 165
8:38 165
9:35 55
10:42 164
10:43–44 1
14:34 165
14:50–52 166
15:34 167

Luke
1:35 65
12:53 163
19:41–44 165
22:49–51 166

John
1:14 169
11:35 165

Acts
1:8 123
8:26–40 123
9:1–19 173
16:3 133
22:6–16 173
26:12–23 173

Romans
1:5 37
1:13–14 37
5 x, xii, xv, xxix, 91, 154, 157
5:12–21 vii, ix, x, xiii, xxix, 2, 23–56, 57, 72, 73
11:26 30, 32
16 51

1 Corinthians
7:1–24 42
11 55
11:2–16 42
11:7–9 52
11:11–12 52
14:33–36 51
15 47–50, 57, 73, 169–170
15:3 48
15:8 173
15:17 48
15:21–22 40, 48
15:34 48
15:38–39 49
15:46 49
15:49 46
15:50 71
15:56 48

2 Corinthians
11:2–3 24, 31, 51, 54–55
11:3 24, 31, 51

Galatians
1:11–16 173
2:16 xiii
3:28 1, 42, 51, 148
5:3 35

Ephesians
1:8–10 74
14:12–13 122

Philippians
2:6–11 34
2:7–8 161
2:8 72
2:9 161

1 Timothy
2:14–15 x, 23, 24, 66

GENERAL INDEX

Adam, ix–xi, xiii, xiv, xxiii–xxix, 1–21, 23–40, 42–56, 57–60, 62–64, 69, 72, 73, 77, 78, 79, 81, 86, 87–88, 89, 91–92, 93, 96, 98, 125, 127–29, 139, 142–43
  Black, 178
  Corporate Identity of, 39–40, 80
  Glorification of, 42, 43–47, 90–92, 146, 151, 172
  In Greek, 36–37
  In Hebrew xxiv–xxv, 36–37
Adam/Christ typology, ix, xi, xii, xiv, xv, xxi, 58, 66, 67, 69, 70, 72, 73–74, 77, 78, 79, 82, 83, 85–86, 90, 98, 125, 145, 146, 151, 154, 157, 168, 174, 178
Alice of Schaerbeke, xviii, 172
Althaus-Reid, Marcella, 179
Anderson, Gary, 11, 23–24, 32
Anthropos, 26–27, 30, 35–36, 43, 47
Apocalypse of Moses, 8–11, 12–13, 18, 54, 62; *See also Vita Adae et Evae*
Aristotelian medical theory, 103–104, 106, 107, 116
asceticism, 66, 121, 133–34, 148, 153, 157, 169
Asikainen, Susanna, 166
Augustine, xiii, xvii, xviii, 23–24, 32, 51, 117–18, 128, 130, 131, 137, 156, 157, 158, 172

Bader-Saye, Scott, 99n2, 113, 130n103
Balthasar, Hans Urs von, 109
Barrett, C. K., 36
2 Baruch, 25
Beardsley, Christina, 115
Beattie, Tina, 58, 67, 96
Behr, John, 76, 81
Blannbekin, Agnes, 173
Boyarin, Daniel, 24, 120–21, 158
Brown, Peter, 83–84, 120, 123
Butler, Judith, 110, 112–13, 135–36, 153, 181
Bynum, Caroline Walker, 152, 172, 175
Byrne, Brendan 39–40

Cain/Jesus typology, 85
calling, 99, 100, 115, 129–39, 158, 174–75, 178, 181
  embodiment, and 132–34, 169
  special, 133–34, 136–37, 138, 139, 169, 174–75, 178, 181
  sex and gender as, 115, 134–37, 158, 174–75
Catherine of Sienna, 173
Chalcedonian Definition, 89, 97
Charlesworth, James, x
circumcision, xiii, 35, 133, 146
Cloutier, David, 111
Coakley, Sarah, 148, 152–53, 155–58
Collins, John J., 7
Cone, James, 178–79
Congar, Yves, 95
contexts of Responsibility, xi, xvii, xx, xxi–xxii, 99–102, 113–15, 119–25, 126, 129–32, 133–34, 136–38, 139, 150, 158, 160, 168, 174–75, 178, 181–82
Conway, Colleen, 123, 164, 165, 167–68
Conzelmann, Hans, 49
crucifixion, 139, 146, 151, 161, 165, 167–68

Daniel-Huges, Carly, 84
Daston, Lorraine, 107
Davidson, Richard, 38
Davidson, Wendy, 135
Davila, James, 7
Devil. *See* Satan
Dinter, Paul, 143
Donovan, Mary Ann, 76
Dunn, James D. G., 3, 31, 34, 37–38, 40, 43, 46
Dunning, Benjamin, 59, 78, 81, 82, 84

ecclesial body of Crist, 143, 146, 149, 154–55
Elm, Susanna, 88
embodiment, 116, 129, 131, 132–34, 140, 145, 146, 150–57, 158, 160, 173
1 Enoch: *See* Similitudes, Book of; Watchers, Book of
2 Enoch 13–14, 44, 46
ethics of authenticity, 130–31
ethics of recognition, 109–10, 130–32, 135, 140, 174–75, 178–79
Eucharist, 143, 146, 149, 168, 171, 172
eunuchs, 117, 123–24, 127, 160
Eusebius, 123
Eve
  blaming, xxiii, xxviii, xxix, 1–22
  disappearance of, 23–56
  punishment of, x–xi, xxxvi, 1, 6, 12, 54, 63, 65–67
  the new, xi, xii, xxi, 59, 98, 125, 139, 154–55, 168, 174
Eve/Jesus typology, 172, 174
Eve/Mary typology, xii, xv, 58, 60, 65–66, 69–70, 72–74, 79–82, 83–86, 92–94, 96, 98
4 Ezra 25

Fausto-Sterling, Anne, 108, 117
feminism, 109–110, 125
Fitzmyer, Joseph, 49
Foster, Paul, 71–72
Foucault, Michel, xviii
Fredricksen, Paula, 24, 37
Freud, Sigmund, xviii, 108

Galenic medical theory, 104–105, 106, 108, 116, 142–44
Gaventa, Beverly, 24, 32, 35–36
Geddes, Patrick, 109
Gnosticism, 111
Goppelt, Leonhard, 39
Goss, Robert, 110
Gregory of Naziansus, 59, 87–95, 98, 122, 141
Gregroy of Nyssa, 89, 142, 147–48, 149–50, 151–54, 155–57, 158

Harrison, Verna, 91, 92, 93, 151–53
Hart, David Bentley, 169–71
Hays, Richard B., 38, 52
Hayward, C. T. R., 20
Hippocratic medical theory, 103–104, 106, 108
Hitchcock, Francis, 81
Hultgren, Stephen, 46–47, 53

incarnation, 29, 75–76, 80–82, 86, 87–95, 131, 141, 145, 149, 150, 154–57, 168, 169–71, 173, 174
Irenaeus 58–59, 73–83, 87–88, 91, 93, 95–96, 98, 130, 157–58, 172

Jesus
  breast of, 140, 172–73
  female pronouns for, 171, 175
  new Eve, xi, xii, xxi, 59, 98, 125, 139, 154–55, 168, 174
  Roman gender, xi, 162–68
  transcending sex/gender, xii, 141–58
  transgressing sex/gender, xii, 158–68
  transitioning across sex/gender, xii, 168–74
  wound of, 172–73
  See also, Adam/Jesus typology; Cain/Jesus typology; ecclesial body of Christ; eucharist; Eve/Jesus typology; incarnation

Johnson, Luke Timothy, 111
Jones, Beth Felker, 156
Jubilees, Book of, 5–6, 63
Jung, Patricia Beattie, 102, 152
Justin Martyr 58, 67–73, 74, 76, 170

Keck, Leander 24, 32
Kierkegaard, Søren, xvii, 130
King, Helen, 106
Kretchmar, George, 24, 32, 63, 65, 66
Kovecses, Zoltan, 34

Levison, John, 16
Liber Antiquitatum Biblicarum, 3, 19–21, 44–46
liberation theology, 177–79
Life of Adam and Eve. *See Vita Adae et Evae*
Lightfoot, J. B., 7
Lovin, Robin, xvii, 100–102, 132
Lutgard of Aywières, 173

Marcion, 68, 71, 73
Mariology, xi, 58, 60, 65, 67, 86, 95–96
Mary
- cult of, 60
- masculinity of, 122
- second savior, xi, 56, 57–96, 98
- virginity, 61, 63–65, 67, 68, 74, 77, 79, 83–86, 89, 92, 93, 95, 141, 174
- *See also* mariology; Eve/Mary typology

masculinity, xx, 53, 73, 105, 108–109, 116, 119–23, 143, 151, 158, 159–68
merism, 126–27
metonymy, 30–35, 40
Milbank, John, 110
Miravalle, Mark, 96
Moo, Douglas, 24, 32
Moore, Stephen, 151
Moss, Candida, 122
Mosse, George, 108
mystical experiences, xxi, 140, 172–74

naturalism
- nonreductive, 103
- reductive, 102, 103, 111, 113–15, 118, 134, 145, 153

Nestorianism, 154
Niebuhr, Reinhold, xvii

O'Brien, Michelle, 137
Odes of Solomon, 65, 122
one-sex model. *See* Galenic medical theory
Ong, Walter J., 42
oral tradition, 42–43
order of creation, xiv, xxiii, 32, 34, 47–51, 53, 57, 59, 78, 82, 88
order of salvation, xi
order of sin, x, xi, xiv, xxiii, xxviii, 34, 50, 57–8, 59, 78, 82, 86, 90, 92
Origen, 124
Orlov, Andrei, 13
Osborn, Eric, 76, 80–81

Park, Katharine, 107
Paul
- erasing Eve, xxix, 2, 17, 21, 22, 23–56, 151
- influence of, xv, 26, 59, 66–67, 70–74, 78, 82, 86, 91
- and sexism, ix, xxiv, 22, 24, 26, 33–35, 36, 42, 43, 47, 50–56, 66–67
- rhetoric, use of, 41–43
- Hebrew, 36–37
- Greek, 36–38
- soteriology, xiv, xv, xvii, 28–29
- *See also* Adam/Christ typology

perichoresis, 114, 137
Perpetua, 122, 167
Philo of Alexandria, 14–16, 19, 53–54
Platonism, 114
Protoevangelium of James, 58, 60–67, 70, 73, 85, 112–13, 115
Pseudo-Philo's Biblical Antiquities. *See Liber Antiquitatum Biblicarum*

queer theory/theology, xvii–xix, 99, 110, 177, 179–82

Radden, Gunter, 34
recapitulation, xvii, 29, 74–82, 87–95, 97, 139
Reuther, Rosemary Radford, 57–58, 147
Ringrose, Kathryn, 124
Rhee, Helen, 79
Roughgarden, Joan, 102

Satan, xxiv, xxv, 9–10, 11, 12–13, 18, 21, 23, 44–45, 50, 69, 70, 72, 84–85, 90, 91, 122
Schottroff, Louise, 31
sex/gender
  in Byzantium, 124
  definitions of, xix–xxi, 115–16
  diversity of, 96–99, 113, 116–29, 137, 139, 140, 141, 158, 174
  in Judaism, 121–22
  in the Roman empire, xi, xii, xxi, 66, 119–23, 158–68
  See also Aristotelian medical theory; calling; contexts of responsibility; Galenic medical theory; Hippocratic medical theory; naturalism; trans*
Sibylline Oracles, 6–7, 44
Similitudes, Book of, 7–8
Skarsaune, Oscar, 71
Steenberg, M. C., 80, 81–82
synecdoche, 30–35
synkrisis, 41–42, 43

Tanner, Kathryn, xiv, xvi, xvii
Taylor, Charles, 130–31
Tertullian, xvii, 59, 74, 78, 82–86, 87, 93, 157–58
Thatcher, Adrian, 142–44, 149, 150, 154–55
Thecla, 66, 122
theology, xii–xix, xxi–xxii. *See also* queer theory/theology; liberation theology
Theotokos, xi, 95
Thomas, Gabrielle, 89, 90
Tonstad, Linn Marie, xviii, 179–82
trans*, xix–xxi, 140–41
trinity, xxi, 114, 131, 140, 142, 144
typology, 38–39. *See also* Adam/Jesus typology; Eve/Mary typology; Eve/Jesus typology; Cain/Jesus typology

Ultichs, Karl Heinrich, 111

virgin conception/birth, 63–65, 67–68, 74, 77, 79, 83, 84, 85–86, 89, 92, 93, 95, 141, 174
Vita Adae et Evae, 11–13, 44–45, 53–54
vocation. *See* calling
volunteerism, 110, 112–13, 114, 130, 132, 136

Ward, Graham, 142, 145–47, 149, 150–51, 155, 166, 171
Ware, James, 170
Ware, Kallistos, 133–34
Watchers, Book of, 8
Williams, Rowan, 131–32
Wisdom of Jesus son of Sirach, 3–5, 31
Wisdom of Solomon, 3, 16–19, 50
Write, N. T., 30–31, 169
Wyant, Nicholas A. M., 37

Zajkowski, Robert, 37
Zulu, Edwin, 51